MW01289256

PRACTICE

# PRACTICE

*Becoming a Better Doctor, Patient, and Person*

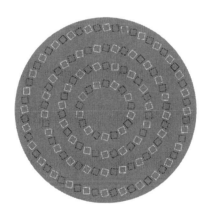

MICHAEL ROTBERG, MD

Soak Up The Sun
Words and Music by Jeff Trott and Sheryl Crow
Copyright © 2001 by Trottsky Music,
ole Red Cape Songs, | Warner-Tamerlane Publishing Corp.
and Old Crow Music
All Rights for Trottsky Music and ole Red Cape Songs Administered by ole
International Copyright Secured All Rights Reserved
Reprinted by Permission of Hal Leonard LLC

Image on title page created by Jochen Burghardt:
https://commons.wikimedia.org/wiki/File:Pinna%27s_
illusory_intertwining_effect.gif
Book design by Phillip Gessert
Cover design by Shimon Gorkin

©2018 Michael Rotberg—All Rights Reserved

*For Heidi, the main character in my story*

# CONTENTS

# AUTHOR'S NOTE

'PRACTICE' CONTAINS STORIES from my years as a student, doctor, and patient. I never recorded or tran-
scribed conversations, so you might wonder if they happened
exactly as written. They did not. While all spring from real en-
counters with patients and colleagues, I either recreated the
dialogue from memory or expanded it as needed for clarity. I
attempted to faithfully portray the substance of these conversations, but none should be considered entirely factual. Also,
for privacy and confidentiality, I altered name, age, gender,
and identifying characteristics, and combined actual inci-
dents.

*"We learn by practice. Whether it means to learn to dance by practicing dancing or to learn to live by practicing living, the principles are the same."*

MARTHA GRAHAM

*"The practice of medicine is... a calling in which your heart will be exercised equally with your head."*

WILLIAM OSLER

*"Who is wise? One who learns from every person."*

PIRKE AVOT (ETHICS OF OUR FATHERS) 4:1

PART ONE

# INTRODUCTION

# CHAPTER 1

I AM AN eye surgeon who suddenly became a seriously ill patient. After thirty years in practice I thought I knew my way around the health care system, but when I got cancer, I found myself as bewildered and adrift as anyone facing the unknown. Turns out I knew how to pitch, but not how to catch. I was unprepared for the new role that illness dumped on me and had hundreds of questions. What's about to happen? Will I suffer? Will I die? How should I live in the time I have left? Will I be a good patient? What does that question even mean?

This book is about how I found answers to these questions and what I learned, not only about my illness, but about how to get the most out of life—and what you can learn as well.

At the start of my illness, one thing going for me was that I have known many others in the same boat. My patients were experts in what I was about to face. This is a collection of their, and my, stories. Teasing out the lessons they hold has guided me through my illness.

Whether you are healthy or ill, these stories have lessons for you too. Maybe you are a patient who wonders what you can do to give yourself a better chance. Maybe you want to know what to look for in a doctor. Or how to grow through illness. Even if you're lucky enough to be healthy and would like to become a better boss, a better colleague, a better doctor, or just a better person, this book is for, and in many ways about, you.

# CHAPTER 2

"**D**OC? HEY DOC." I looked over my shoulder and spotted a short man in disheveled blue scrubs hustling toward me across the waiting room. It was the technician who had just taken my chest X-rays. A paper fell out of the folder he was carrying and fluttered to the floor. "Whew, glad I caught you before you left. Are you going to see your doctor now?"

"No, I already have patients waiting in my office. Why?"

"Uh, if you have a minute the radiologist wants to show you something. Can you come with me? Won't take long."

I followed him into the labyrinthine back hallways. We turned right, then left, right again, and finally reached a dark room, illuminated only by the cold light of a dozen large black and white monitors. The tech said, "Dr. Rotberg," gesturing toward the only other person in the room, "the doctor here wants to tell you about your chest film." He scurried away and a thin man wearing a golf shirt and pressed khakis rose from his desk chair, which spun as he stood.

"Hi, nice to meet you." He was backlit, adding an ominous cast to the atmosphere. "Listen, have you been feeling all right?"

"I came in today because I've had a cough on and off for almost six months. I finally convinced my internist to order a chest film to be sure nothing is going on."

He paused for a deep breath and slowly exhaled, "Well, something is going on. Here, let me show you." As an ophthalmologist, I don't look at many chest X-rays, but the problem here was impossible to miss. There was my heart, my ribs, my left lung, just as they should be. But above the heart, spilling over to the right, was a big white shadow. Something about the same size and shape as my heart, as if I had an extra one sitting in the upper part of my chest.

"Wow, I see what you mean." Taken by surprise, at this point my curiosity was still more academic than personal. "What do you think it is?"

"Well," he said, "you have a large tumor in the anterior mediastinum." The mediastinum is the space between the lungs, inside the chest. Aside from some blood vessels and the esophagus and trachea, the eating and breathing tubes, there shouldn't be much there. Certainly nothing like this. "The most frequent cause of masses in this location is lymphoma, and then there are some other less common things, like thymomas and seminomas, but those would be highly unlikely. It's probably a lymphoma. Good prognosis. But whatever it is, you need to get checked right away."

Oh man. You know you're in trouble when the good news is lymphoma, a treatable, but sometimes deadly kind of blood cancer. "Thanks for bringing me in to see this. I'll call my doctor as soon as I leave."

He shook my hand, mumbled, "Good luck," and pivoted back to his screens.

As I wound my way to the waiting room and then out to my car, it started to sink in that the picture on the monitor really was mine. That was me up there, my chest, my tumor. My tumor!? Those pixels meant that I had a big problem. In an instant I had crossed the unmarked border, well concealed but always nearby, into the 'land of the sick.' Until that morning, I walked into hospitals and doctor's offices as a physician; now it would be as a patient. After years of trying to help others get well, I suddenly needed to focus on a new and urgent project, my own healing.

Life was about to force feed me a lesson on how the other half lives on the receiving end of the healthcare system. I spent years learning to be a doctor and working as an ophthalmologist, but no one ever taught me how to be a patient. Most of what I knew about being a patient came from thirty years of watching, up close but second-hand, people cope with the disruption and distress of their disease, some gallantly, others admirably, many not very well. They had also been ambushed by illness, but some seemed to know how to help themselves, while others flailed around pointlessly or remained passive and in denial. Could my experience as a caregiver help me figure out how to give myself the best chance to navigate the uncharted shoals ahead?

How DID I find myself, late in February 2013, looking at such a threatening picture of my own chest? In thirty years, I never missed a day of work because of illness, shook off colds in a few days, didn't smoke, and exercised several times a week. But that all started to change, imperceptibly at first, several months earlier.

During a routine visit with my internist the previous July, he congratulated me for losing six pounds and asked how I had managed to drop the weight. "I don't know. Maybe I've been working out a little harder, maybe less carbs? But I wasn't trying to lose weight." My cholesterol was lower too, so he was pleased, and I didn't think more about it until a month or two later.

Since I was a kid I have had hay fever, and when my allergies bother me, especially in cold weather or after a fit of sneezing, I cough and wheeze. But my cough became more frequent and productive, with thick, adherent mucus most mornings. And I began to notice my heartbeat. Though hearts pound during exercise or anxiety, they normally work in private, below the level of awareness. But every so often now, I felt a flutter in my chest, or even a sudden deep thump, so strong that I was surprised my shirt didn't vibrate, followed by a slight hesitation before the next beat. This was something new.

My wife, Heidi, and I were planning a two-week trip to South America, to Buenos Aires, Rio, and other more remote places. A few years earlier, one of my partners was sitting in the surgeons' lounge at the hospital when he experienced a sudden irregular heartbeat, ventricular arrhythmia, that led to cardiac arrest. Without warning, his heart stopped. If another doctor hadn't been in the room with him, and if he hadn't been sitting down the hall from the operating room and dozens of people experienced in resuscitation, he would have died. Anywhere else, he could not have survived. So, although I felt fine, the strange thumping in my chest made me worry about what was going on, and I wanted to figure it out before we traveled into the jungle. A fatal arrhythmia in the middle of nowhere would have ruined more than our vacation.

I called my friend, a cardiologist in town who had been my classmate in medical school. When I described my concerns, he asked me to come in. He examined me, listened to my heart and lungs, felt my pulse, checked my blood pressure and ran an EKG. Everything was normal, but to be on the safe side he had me wear a monitor to watch for arrhythmias as I went through the activities of a normal day. Though I felt fluttering in my chest that day, the monitor didn't pick up any abnormalities. But I knew something was going on, so he placed another device to watch my heart rhythm for an entire month.

During those weeks wearing the monitor, I felt palpitations too many times to count, but somehow, after reviewing the results he told me, "It's fine. No problems. Just some PVCs (premature beats followed by a pause), and that's totally normal. Everybody has a few skipped beats. Nothing worrisome. So go on, relax; let's get together when you come home so you can make me jealous about your trip."

Reassured, we had an exotic adventure, the first time in years that I took two weeks off. After a few days in Buenos Aires, we flew to Iguazu Falls, a mile and a half wide waterfall in the middle of the jungle. We saw coatis, toucans, and other wildlife I'd only seen in zoos, hiked under the falls, and ate Pacu and Suribi, exotic Amazonian River fish. The unexpected highlight was our hour in a hummingbird garden in Puerto Iguazu. A dozen different varieties of hummingbirds, kaleidoscopic and gorgeous, buzzed and flitted around indifferent to our presence. It was magical. Sitting together on a bench in this avian paradise, Heidi smiled blissfully and said, "Can you believe this place? How lucky are we to be here?"

I said, "I'm so glad we got to take this trip. If I hadn't seen the cardiologist last month, I would have been on edge every minute."

That was in October. I caught a cold on the flight home, and my cough worsened. Within a few days, I began bringing up dark green sputum, and got a prescription for antibiotics. They worked, and the cough improved. Then, in December, I went to a football game on a cold night, got chilled, the bronchitis recurred, and I was back on antibiotics a few weeks later.

The doctor said, "Your chest sounds clear, but if this happens again, we probably should get a chest film." Once more, the antibiotics did the trick. Just before New Year's Day we visited our daughter in New York. The city felt bone-chillingly cold.

And people started telling me I looked great. "Wow, I don't know what you're doing, but you've lost some weight! What's your secret?" Or, "You've really tightened up. Do you have a new trainer?" I was flattered but mystified. I weighed myself on the digital scale in the gym, and it showed that I had dropped a few more pounds since my check-up in July, but then the scale broke and they replaced it with an old-style doctor's scale with sliding weights. The first time I used it a few weeks later, I weighed even less, but figured it was probably inaccurate. Like seeing a warning light on the dashboard and wondering what's wrong with the light rather than the car.

In January 2013, at my next scheduled, routine appointment to check my cholesterol and blood pressure, my internist said, "You're not trying to lose weight? You're down about twelve pounds since July. That's eighteen pounds in the past year." A couple days later, he called, very concerned. "Your blood tests just came back; you are anemic. I'm worried you might be losing blood. I know your colonoscopy a few years ago was fine, but I want you to get another one soon to be sure everything is OK."

"Well, if you think I should I will, but how about a chest X-ray?"

"I didn't want to expose you to unnecessary radiation because your chest sounds clear. But at this point I'll order it. Just walk into any of the radiology offices. Usually only takes about 15 minutes."

"Let's set up the colonoscopy, but I'm going to get the chest film first. My sister had lung cancer when she was in her thirties, and my wife says my cough worries her. She wants me to have an X-ray to be on the safe side."

"I don't think you have to worry about that. Your breath sounds are normal on both sides, but your peace of mind might be worth a little radiation."

Once the chest x-ray uncovered the root of my problems, the next thing I had to do was to call Heidi. I was still too stunned by the unreality of my predicament to even dread making the call. I had bad news to share, and though too disturbing for me to swallow and digest, it was undeniable, and I couldn't keep it to myself. "Hey, I'm on the way out of the radiologist's office. I'm already late for work." Breezily, as if calling to tell her I needed to stop for gas on the way home.

"Wow, you're done so soon? That was fast. When are you going to find out what it showed?"

I paused, suddenly staggered. We experienced so much together. Our marriage was a start-up, not a merger, two lives entwined. We met the week before medical school while I was scavenging in dumpsters behind fraternity houses, hoping to find free living room furniture for the house I rented in a derelict part of Durham. The first time she visited me there, she howled, "It's freezing in here," looked under the bed, and refused to stay because winter winds gusted through a gap between the wall and the floor. We married when I was 24 and she was only 22, then helped each other through medical school and residency for me, psychology grad school for her, raised two kids, built practices, buried parents, got a house without holes in the walls, and after more than thirty years were still growing closer. But now this.

"Uh, I already know…There's something there."

A split second of silence, "What do you mean?"

"Some kind of tumor in my chest. It's probably what's causing my cough, and my weight loss and anemia too."

"What? A mass in your chest? Oh my God. Haven't I been begging you to get an x-ray? I just kept thinking about your sister." I could tell she was holding back tears and would be crying as soon as we hung up. I felt sadder for her than scared for myself. "What are you going to do now?"

"Well, I'm going to call my doctor. And I'm going to go to work. People are already waiting for me. I took the afternoon off to see about scheduling a colonoscopy."

"You're not going to need that now."

But I did go to work and found the familiar routine of doing eye exams, prescribing glasses, and taking care of people with cataracts, glaucoma, and other conditions absorbing enough that I put aside the morning's bad news for a few hours. After lunch, Heidi and I met at the gastroenterologist's office, executing on autopilot our plan for the day that we had made that morning, propelled for a while longer by the momentum of normalcy toward the unknown and unwelcome changes ahead.

Of course, there was no colonoscopy. The gastroenterologist agreed, "You have more important things to do first." My internist arranged a CT scan for me the next morning. Heidi called our friend, a urologic oncologist, to ask him to recommend someone for me to see. And I went back to the office for two very difficult conversations.

The first was with Chuck Hoch, the long-time administrator of our large practice. We worked closely and well together over the years. I was on the search committee that interviewed and hired him, and as chairman of the eye department, president of the group, and director of both clinical research and of the surgery center, met with him often, respected him greatly, and became his friend. But he was getting ready to retire. This was his last week at work, his valedictory, full of handshakes, sentimental goodbyes, and farewell parties. I called his secretary and said, "I know Chuck is busy, but I need to sit down with him for a few minutes."

As I rounded the corner and headed down the hall toward his office, I heard laughter coming from his open door. I poked my head in, the others scattered back to their desks, and, still smiling, he said, "So what's up?"

"I hate to rain on your parade, but I have some bad news. I just found out I have some kind of cancer in my chest."

The grin dropped from his face. He stood at attention, stared at me, rubbed his brow and said, "That's a real kick in the pants. What is it?"

"I don't know yet, but I need your help. I'm scheduled to do surgery tomorrow, six cataract and two glaucoma cases, but don't you think I better postpone them? People will be disappointed to have to reschedule their surgeries, but I have a CT scan in the morning when I'm supposed to be in the OR. And anyway, I don't know how I could concentrate with all this going on."

"Jeez, that's terrible. But you're right, you have to take care of yourself first. Just let me know what I can do for you," he said, somberly shaking my hand. "Anything at all."

Then I had to talk to my staff, the women who helped me every day, my team, my work family. Carol, who scheduled my surgeries, was by my side for more than twenty years. My three medical assistants, Scottie, Beth, and Michele, were in my life for nearly as long. I asked Carol to summon everyone to in my office at the end of the day. They arrived quiet, somber, nervous. They knew something was up.

"You know I took the afternoon off to go to the doctor." I could barely get the words out. "I was supposed to meet with the gastroenterologist to set up a colonoscopy, but that's not going to happen. Because this morning I had a chest x-ray and it showed I have a tumor in my chest." I could tell they were stunned, silently crying, sad for me, worried for our team, anxious with uncertainty. It was awful to witness the pain I caused.

Scottie gathered herself and said, "We knew something was wrong." The others shook heads in agreement. "You've lost so much weight, and you've looked kind of gray for the last few weeks. And that horrible cough."

"So how come everybody's telling me how great I look?" They laughed. "But here's what has to happen. We need to cancel tomorrow's cases, and I'm not sure when I will be able to reschedule them. Please tell those patients that they can wait for me to do them later or offer to find them another surgeon. I have a CT scan tomorrow, and then I guess I will work on Wednesday. But I'm trying to set up appointments with the oncologist, and I know there will be other tests too, so I really don't know how much time I will have to take off and how many patients we'll have to cancel. For now, please try not to tell too many people about this, OK?"

"We love you, you know," they said. After long hugs, we left for the day, my shoulders moist with shared tears.

Then things began to happen quickly. On Tuesday I had a CT scan. I really did have a big tumor, 3.5 by 5 inches. While working in the office the next day, the head nurse of our surgery center came in for an eye exam. She said, "Why did you cancel your cases yesterday? You never miss a day of surgery. The staff is worried about you."

"You should be," I said, and asked her to keep the news to herself until I knew more.

"We'll be praying for you."

On Thursday Heidi and I met with John Mahoney, my new oncologist, to go over the scan and to make a plan. After examining me, he said, "Well, you seem to be extremely healthy, except of course you have that large tumor in your chest." More ominously, he added, "We really need to get going, there's no time to waste. The tumor is already compressing your vena cava, but luckily it isn't completely closed yet." The vena cava is the large vein that drains blood back from the upper body to the heart. If it becomes blocked, blood backs up into the head, causing tremendous swelling of the face and arms, along with headache and breathing problems. An emergency.

After decades together, Heidi knows that when I have a difficult decision to make my usual strategy is to ignore it, then obsess about it, ruminate over my options, munch junk food, and finally face up to it. On the other hand, her first impulse is to do something. She thrives on the support of friends and family, finds it therapeutic to reach out to people who care for her, and to accept the help they are anxious to offer. For several days, she lived on the phone.

While a few people knew what was bubbling beneath the surface of our apparently normal lives, most had no idea. It was impossible to go out to dinner with friends and pretend that everything was fine, and we wanted to reach out, not cloister ourselves or lie to them. The time had come for us to tell our friends and for me to let my partners know that I was going to have to take a leave of absence, and why. So first, Heidi sent this email to everyone she thought should know:

FROM: HEIDI ROTBERG
DATE: FEBRUARY 28, 2013, 7:44:01 PM EST
TO:
SUBJECT: MICHAEL

Hi—There is no good way to tell you this, so here it is.

Michael just found out that he has a large mass in his chest, between the ribs and the lung. This was discovered on Monday after he had a chest x-ray because of his continued cough and weight loss. He has already had CT scans and met his oncologist, Dr. Mahoney. One of our close friends expedited this appointment.

Until more studies are done (blood work, PET scan, biopsy) the doctors cannot provide a diagnosis. He did say that it does not look like a cyst, and that it is not in the lung. They will be pushing the studies through so Michael can have a diagnosis. The blood work was drawn today, and the PET scan and biopsy will be scheduled soon. Michael will continue to work for now, but will avoid strenuous exercise.

Thank you for being there—sorry for the email but I/we wanted you to know. Michael feels fine, but does not want to talk about this with anyone at this time, especially before knowing more details. I am sure you understand.

I also do not want to talk right now—but we know you care and are there for us. We told the kids over the phone last night, and all three are coming home this weekend. We also have told family, and know we are not on this journey alone.

Heidi and Michael

On Friday, at the end of a work day filled with denial, dissembling, and sense of an ending, I put my coat on, closed my briefcase, turned out the lights, and hit the send button to notify the doctors and nurses who worked with me, my entire Monday to Friday universe, that I was ill, distracted, and soon likely to be disengaged. Then I scurried out the side door before anyone had time to read my email and catch me in the hall. I took comfort in knowing that my partners would be able to look after my patients and that my illness would not leave any without excellent care.

---

FROM: ROTBERG MD, MICHAEL
SENT: FRIDAY, MARCH 01, 2013 3:16 PM
TO:
SUBJECT: HEALTH NEWS

Partners and Friends: I regret that I have some personal medical news that I have to share with all of you. A few days ago I learned that I have a tumor in my chest. Now I am in the process of figuring out the precise diagnosis and what it means in terms of treatment and prognosis. A PET scan and a biopsy are the next steps.

While I hope to be able to return to full participation in group activities, if and when that will be possible is an open question. For now, my job is to take my medicine and push on through to the other side of this unexpected and unwelcome challenge.

Thanks for your support and understanding. No phone calls please. Also, please respect the privacy of my staff so that they have a chance to deal with this in their own way while trying to do their work.

Michael

---

Even though we asked for privacy, we were inundated with incredulous and tearful calls. The phone kept ringing. The avalanche of love, caring, and support was overwhelming, staggering and humbling. It was wonderful to hear from everyone and to be reminded of our important place in their lives, but the volume of calls and emails quickly became a drain on our energy and on our precious, possibly limited, time together. We needed to gather ourselves, we needed to be alone, and we needed quiet.

Our kids flew in for the weekend, our daughter, Emily, from New York with her husband, Josh, and our son David, in his third year of medical school, from Florida. We had a delightful time together eating, drinking, looking at old photo albums, telling stories, momentarily distracted from the somber reason for our reunion. A photographer came by to preserve the moment. After he left Dave and I both put on our old Boy Scout uniforms. I lost so much weight that my uniform from 1970, when I was 16, fit me for the first time in years.

On Monday, after our family weekend, I had a needle biopsy guided by another CT scan, to try to make the diagnosis. I didn't know what to expect, nervous about the procedure and what it might reveal. After sedation, I rolled into the CT room, and while lying inside the big white donut, felt tapping on my chest and heard a mechanical thunk five or six times as a needle painlessly slipped between my ribs to sample my tumor. Then on Tuesday, no longer too concerned about excessive radiation exposure, radioactive isotopes were injected into my vein for a PET scan to be sure the tumor had not spread beyond my chest. Happily, it had not.

On Thursday, while I was at work, Steve Plunkett called. Steve is a radiation oncologist, a good friend, and a caring man. I told him a few days earlier about my tumor and he had offered to help. He said, "Listen, I just saw your biopsy report. Has anyone told you about it yet?"

This was the moment. I took a deep breath and said, "No, what does it show? Do I have lymphoma?"

"Afraid not. I wish you did."

Uh-oh, "What is it?"

"They're calling it a 'poorly differentiated squamous cell carcinoma of unknown origin'. Because of where it's located, they think it's probably from your thymus gland. Can't really be sure where it started, but unfortunately, it isn't a lymphoma." Poorly differentiated is the medical way of saying 'very aggressive'. Thymic carcinoma is a tumor of the thymus gland, a structure involved in the immune system, located behind the breastbone and active in childhood. This cancer is rare and dangerous.

"It's not small cell lung cancer, is it?"

"No, that's a bit of good news; why do you ask?"

"My sister died of small cell lung cancer when she was just 39. I would hate to think something like that runs in our family."

"Well, that's not what you have, so there's one less thing for you to worry about."

"Thanks for that. I'm set up to see Mahoney in the morning. What do you think he's going to say?"

"I've already talked to John. We'll work together. You're going to need several weeks of chemotherapy and radiation, and if we're lucky, maybe the tumor will shrink enough that you can have surgery. But see him tomorrow, and then he'll send you over to me so we can map out your treatment. Probably we'll start treating you on Monday." They were worried; that was only four days away.

It was early in the afternoon. I still had a few patients to see on what turned out to be my last day in the office.

After telling Heidi my unsettling diagnosis, I paused before making another difficult phone call. My niece was scheduled to have her Bat Mitzvah that weekend, and we were planning to attend. But there was no way I would be able to pretend to be in a joyful mood and did not want my presence to shift the focus from her or detract from her celebration. I had to tell my sister that we were going to miss the festive weekend. And the other reason I dreaded making the call was that I knew she would remember our sister's illness and expect mine to follow a similarly brief and tragic course. Her sadness was leavened

by the realization that our mother, 87 years old and demented, would not be able to absorb the news. "Whatever happens,
you better outlive mom," she said.

The next morning Dr. Mahoney laid it all out for us. "Every
Monday, for about seven weeks, we're going to have you come
in for chemotherapy. It will be low doses of Carboplatin and
Taxol, hopefully won't bother you too much. And five days a
week you'll see Steve for radiation."

"Why low doses? Will that work?"

"The chemo will help treat the cancer, but its main role will
be to make the tumor more sensitive to radiation. You're going to get a lot of radiation, and we're going to make you pretty sick. You'll have trouble swallowing, lose weight, won't feel
good at all once we get a few weeks into this. So while you
can, eat lots of calories, okay?" Unlimited donuts and cheese-
burgers! Like ice cream after a tonsillectomy. But when Heidi
asked, "How long does he have?" he said, "Without treatment,
less than a year."

As soon as we got home, the phone started up again, and
Heidi said, "We can't keep doing this. I love that people want
to be in the loop, but we can't call everyone. That's all we'd be
doing. And whenever the next thing happens, if we send out
an email instead, we're going to leave someone important off
the list and include other people who don't want to hear our
problems anymore. It will take hours every day. I want to set
up a Caring Bridge site."

"I don't think I want to put this on the internet," I said.

"Well, sorry, it isn't your choice. I'm doing it for me." She
saw it as a way to get the support she needed without the burden of endless phone calls and emails, a way to keep everyone informed while preserving her energy so she could take
care of me, our grown children, and herself. "It will be great
for keeping everybody up to date. If someone wants to know
about you, they can read it. If they don't, they can unsub-

scribe. And we won't be getting all these calls." She was right. Our Caring Bridge site quickly became our main pipeline for communicating medical news. Eventually, it had nearly 30,000 visits, and the comments people wrote in the guestbook provided us so much love and support. Here is how Heidi kicked it off:

---

**WELCOME TO MICHAEL'S CARINGBRIDGE SITE:**

We've created it to keep friends and family updated. We appreciate your support and words of hope and encouragement during this time when it matters most.

We will keep this site updated as we learn more. Your support and well-wishes are vital, but we also appreciate your understanding that we are fully focused on Michael's recovery.

Everyone is asking us what they can do—right now, love, prayers and thoughts are mainly what we need. We would prefer to use this website to communicate news and updates, rather than updating friends and family individually.

Love—Michael and Heidi

---

Her post continued by summarizing all that had transpired, to lay out the facts and to anticipate and pre-empt likely questions. Now, everyone who cared about us was up to speed. But although the two of us had been through a lot together —births, deaths, broken bones, concussions, major surgeries, other cancer scares, illness in the family—we had never faced anything like this before. Heidi forced a smile and said, "Tomorrow is a big day. Your first day of chemo and radiation." She couldn't hold on, and started to cry, "That's a sentence I never thought I would have to say."

We hugged, and I cried too. "I want to think of this as the first day of killing my cancer, but it's kind of like jumping out of a plane and hoping the parachute opens, you know? Trying not to think about if it doesn't."

"Oh, you'll be a great patient," she said, sniffling and wiping her eyes. "You always have been. You don't complain, you don't stay sick for very long, you'll come through this fine."

"I hope you're right. I have no idea how I'll hold up. It's one thing to be a good patient when it's a broken arm or the flu. But this? I really don't know what to expect," I admitted. "I mean, I might know what it takes to be a good doctor, but nobody ever told me how to be a good patient."

"Come on, you've been watching people deal with illness for more than thirty years. You must have learned something. You should be pretty much of an expert by now. Haven't you worked with some patients who really helped themselves to get better and with others who didn't?"

"Sure," I answered, "some people do everything they need to do. Some act as if they're bulletproof and live in denial. And the ones who try to help themselves usually do better than those who don't."

"So," she asked, "what are the things that make someone a good patient? What are the things you can do to improve your chances of getting better and of living well while you're dealing with this?

Over the next weeks and months, her question echoed as I sat in a recliner with chemotherapy running into my arm, lay supine under a buzzing dose of radiation, or awake in bed. I talked with friends whose opinions I respected and picked their brains. Each had ideas about the characteristics that typify good doctors and successful patients.

And I looked back over my career in medicine to discover lessons that could help me navigate my looming health crisis. To try to wring from my experiences insight into how to give myself the best chance to survive intact. I have been molded as much by my patients and teachers as by my parents and friends. What did they have to teach me?

This book contains stories from my decades as a doctor and my years as a patient, ranging from Durham, North Carolina in 1976 to Charlotte in 2018, interspersed with some of the lessons I have learned along the way. Our Caring Bridge posts, mostly written by Heidi, provide a real-time unfiltered narration of my illness. None of the grammar or punctuation was cleaned up, so they retain their immediacy and raw emotion. Patients' and some of the doctors' identifying details have been changed and stories have been combined and otherwise altered to avoid violating confidentiality. If you think you know any of these people you are mistaken. They live in Florida, Pennsylvania, and North Carolina, and together taught me much of what I know about being a healer, a patient, and a person. I am grateful to have been their student; each helped me immeasurably. I hope I helped some of them as well.

PART TWO

# MEDICAL SCHOOL
# DURHAM, NC 1976–1980

# CHAPTER 3

# INTERVIEW

D URING MY SENIOR year in college, I made the rounds of medical schools hoping to find one willing to take a chance on me. Wearing my only sport coat, a corduroy blazer with elbow patches, my hair curling over the collar, I felt like an imposter. A patchy, slightly pubic, beard barely covered my cheeks and chin; a friend described it as "Jerry Garcia with mange." Probably would have been smart to shave before the interview, I realized too late.

"I see you are majoring in Philosophy. That's an unusual choice for someone who wants to go to medical school, don't you think?" The Director of Admissions at Duke Med School was an amiable thick set man with an extra chin and thinning dark hair. He overfilled his white coat, his belly testing each button.

"Well," I said, "I took philosophy during my freshman year and found it fascinating. But I've always wanted to help people in some way, and being a philosopher wouldn't do anyone any good, me included. I realized I could study philosophy and still take all the science classes I need for medical school. In the next four years I'll learn whatever biochem and pharmacology I need to be a doctor, but won't have another chance at philosophy, history, that sort of thing."

"You're right. Once you start med school your coursework will be pretty intense, and honestly, I think we need more Humanities students to balance all the science and math majors. But do you have a feel for what it is like to be a doctor? Are your parents doctors?"

"My father is a veterinarian and my mother is a school teacher. But my uncle is a physician."

"Oh, what kind of medicine does he practice?"

"He is a hematologist."

"Does he do oncology too?"

"No, I don't think so. Mostly he treats people with leukemia." Oncology is the treatment of cancer, and leukemia is cancer of the blood. Obviously, I didn't know what I was talking about.

He started to speak but stopped himself and looked at me with both pity and piqued interest, as if thinking, 'Hmm, this one might be an interesting project.' He took a gamble on me, and I owe him my career. We all depend on the unearned kindness of strangers.

**GREAT HAVING THE KIDS HOME!**          *Mar 3, 2013 7:52am*

After Michael and I realized that he would be starting the process of diagnosis, treatment decisions, and treatment, we knew we needed to tell the kids even before we knew exactly what we were dealing with. We called David and Emily and Josh last Wednesday, told them what was going on with Michael, and asked them all to fly home for the weekend. All three dropped what they were doing and flew home.

David came up from Boca Raton, and Emily and Josh flew in from NYC. It has been great having them here—very important for them and us. Great especially for Michael. Lots of hugs and love and talks and walks. Big boost after a tough week.

Last night Michael and David put on their Boy Scout uniforms (Michael was an Eagle Scout a LONG time ago) and made a fantastic fire. We drank champagne for Emily's birthday, toasted our family, had an amazing steak dinner. They kids did all the clean-up too! As you know—Michael insists on doing the dishes in this house so this was a big deal.

We know you are there—it means more than we can say. I will write more later.

Love,
Heidi
(PS: I WILL make typos when I write these journal entries!)

Heidi's Caring Bridge post led to an avalanche of supportive notes from friends and family. And for months, each time we updated our Caring Bridge site with new information, we were graced with, and bolstered by, a similar infusion of love, caring, and community. This is a sample:

*"It is indeed remarkable how warm and healing the love and care of our friends is and, from reading the comments in this guest book, it is impossible not to feel that embrace holding you and Heidi and David and Emily and Josh close... now*

*and always. I will add my love and prayers to the growing mass that holds you safe and battles that other 'mass'."*

*"It has taken me 24 hours to absorb your news but was so glad that you chose this practical way to keep everyone informed...You have multiplied your own deep strengths by calling on your family and friends."*

*"Our thoughts, prayers and wishes for a complete recovery are with you at this challenging time. (When we had a similar health crisis) the only way we got through it was by realizing that we need to take it day by day...We were thankful to G-d when we got through the day and braced ourselves for the next day... As we did everything in our power to find the best medical care available to us we realized that ultimately G-d is in charge."*

I was touched by this, and replied, *"Neither of us feel that God gave me this cancer, but we are asking his help in doing what we have to do to have the best chance of healing."*

# CATHETER

WHEN I WAS in medical school, the Durham Veterans Hospital had two Psychiatry wards. The most fragile, dangerous, or violent people went to the locked ward on the Sixth floor. Once stabilized by a week or two of medication, they moved downstairs to another ward where patients had free run of the building. As part of their rehabilitation, many trusted patients worked as escorts, taking others to lab, radiology, or clinic appointments.

I was waiting for an elevator, staring at the unchanging numbers above the door, a restless crowd gathering around me, when a patient and escort ambled over. The escort had a blank stare, facial tic, and shuffling gait. Both he and his patient were unshaven, wearing pajamas, slippers, and a standard issue long, green pinstriped seersucker robe. The patient was holding his hospital chart, apparently heading downstairs to the lab. The escort had his hand on the rolling IV pole, and hanging from it were a half empty IV bottle and a half full Foley bag, both connected to the patient by tubes, one in a vein and the other, held in place by an inflated balloon, in his bladder. Input and output on display.

The bell finally rang, the doors slid apart, and people rushed forward onto the elevator, like a subway at rush hour. It was too crowded for everyone to fit, so I turned away to walk down the stairs, but pivoted when I heard panicked shouting. The patient had stepped onto the elevator while the escort and the IV pole remained frozen on the landing. The doors started to close on the catheters, as if a dog ran into the elevator but the person holding its leash did not.

At the last second, someone jammed a hand between the doors, they sprang open, and I nudged the escort to get on too. He startled, alerted, and stepped aboard. The patient stood trembling, ashen and wide-eyed, aware of how close he came to riding down to the first floor while his bladder catheter stayed behind.


# POWER NAP

"I THINK I am in big trouble," I said.

"What are you talking about?" asked Heidi, who was a few weeks from beginning her Clinical Psychology doctoral program.

"I am halfway done with med school. Second year is almost over. I've been through OB, Psych, Surgery, Medicine and Peds, and I just can't imagine spending my entire career doing any of them. Maybe it was a mistake for me to go to med school."

"Don't say that," Heidi said, "That's not true. You liked some of your rotations."

"Yeah, but not enough to do for the rest of my life. What am I going to do?"

Heidi went into therapist mode and said, "You sound like a little kid who thinks the entire universe of jobs is doctor, lawyer, fireman or cop. There are so many areas of medicine you haven't even tasted yet. You don't know what your options are. Why don't you try something completely different?"

This sounded like a good idea. I had no exposure to anesthesia or emergency medicine. Only one or two lectures about urology, ENT, ophthalmology, dermatology, and allergy. I had a year to pick a specialty. "You might be right. All my rotations had one thing in common. Maybe what I don't like is taking care of patients." So that summer of 1978 I stayed in Durham for a month of autopsy pathology.

My mother said, "What? You're going to spend the summer doing autopsies? Yuck." To most people, autopsies seem gruesome, but they are so helpful for the patient's doctor and family and may be the only way to figure out what went wrong. The old saying is true: 'The pathologist knows everything, just too late.' But for me, doing autopsies was a philosophical and spiritual eye opener. I was blindsided by how a living body's sudden transformation into an empty vessel reified the existence of an animating soul. One moment a living person, and the next a hollow husk. Something more than chemistry changed during that instantaneous transition. The experience was deeper and more enlightening than I expected it to be.

I helped perform several autopsies, and each week wrote one of the official reports. This involved reviewing the patient's hospital chart and looking at the pathology to see if it confirmed the expected diagnosis or uncovered any surprises. Then, in the pathology department library, a small, musty room filled with shelves groaning under the weight of decades of crumbling bound journals, I researched whichever diseases the autopsy revealed.

In the old part of Duke Hospital, the pathology library had a window seat in front of a leaded bay window that looked out onto the West Campus quad. It was a good place to work because it was quiet and usually empty. But sometimes in the afternoon I noticed someone taking a nap on the window seat. I could tell it was a resident because he was in uniform: white pants and a short white coat. But there were few residents at Duke who had the luxury of taking a nap in the middle of the day.

Then one afternoon while I was sitting in front of a sprawling pile of textbooks and journals, he woke up. I couldn't resist asking, "What's the story? How do you find downtime to take a nap?"

He rubbed his eyes, told me his name, and said, "I am an ophthalmology resident."

"Oh, right. I'm pretty sure you did an eye exam on my girlfriend a few weeks ago. What's your secret?"

"For the last few weeks I have been doing the eye pathology rotation. I am assigned to be here full time, but usually there's only enough work to keep me busy 'til noon. If I go back to the Eye Center when I finish each day, they will realize that this should only be half-time and will make me help with afternoon clinic. So, whenever I'm done, I have lunch and then I come up here where it is quiet and comfortable to catch some Zs until it is late enough to check out."

"What kind of resident are you again?"

"Ophthalmology. Why, are you interested in eyes? Have you thought about doing an eye residency?"

"I never really thought about it."

"You should check it out. I'd love to talk to you, but I've got to get out of here; I have a tennis court reserved in 45 minutes."

"Wait a minute, hold on. What's so great about it?"

"Okay, first of all, no other physicians know anything about eyes. Whenever they have a patient with an eye problem they don't want anything to do with it. They don't want to learn about it, they don't want to treat it, they just want to call you to take care of it for them."

"Nobody fights over people with eye problems?"

"Optometrists do a lot of eye care, but no one else can handle really sick eyes. And, even though you would think taking care of eye patients might get boring, it never does. There's a lot of variety: men and women, babies and old people, routine and tertiary eye care, office and OR, medical and surgical. And, even though eyes are really complicated they are also kind of knowable. We're not like family docs who have to send their most interesting patients to specialists. We can handle almost everything ourselves."

I had considered family medicine. He made it sound like I would be a Physician's Assistant with a fancy credential. "I never thought about it that way."

"It's true. I also like that everyone has two eyes and there aren't many emergencies in the middle of the night. Hardly any eye diseases are fatal; I don't have to worry that a patient might die if I make a mistake. It's not about life and death, but if I can save somebody's sight, I've done something really worthwhile."

That evening, I told Heidi about this conversation and she said, "You know, I took a course in Career Counseling. Let me help you figure this out once and for all." In our living room, she interviewed me as if I were her client. "What is most important to you in your career?"

"I was surprised how interesting Autopsy Pathology was, but I got into medicine to help people, so I don't think I'd be happy in a field without direct patient care."

"Okay, so radiology and pathology are out. Do you think you would rather know a little about a lot or a lot about a little?"

"Huh?"

"In Pediatrics or Family Medicine you have to know about almost everything that can go wrong with a person. In other fields, you have to know about just one part."

"With my personality, I think I need to know enough about something to feel like an expert, even if it's a limited area." There went primary care.

"Does the idea of seeing patients over time appeal to you? Do you want long-term relationships with patients?" I did, so Emergency medicine, anesthesia, and general surgery were out too. In this way, we eliminated some specialties and identified others for me to consider. After doing electives in allergy, dermatology, endocrinology, and neurology, I spent a month at the Eye Center and found my home.

And for years, whenever I ran into that resident at national eye meetings we laughed about how his naps, in very different ways, were important to both our careers.

**BIOPSY DONE!**                                        *Mar 4, 2013*

Hi—Just got back from the hospital—Michael had a needle core
biopsy this morning. The radiologist did the procedure, and said
he got a good tissue sample.

Michael is having lunch and is going to spend today resting and
reading and just hanging around.

Love—Heidi

**PET SCAN**                                            *Mar 5, 2013*

Hi—We just got home from the last big test Michael needs, a PET
scan. Thanks to a friend's advice, Michael had the scan at the
Morehead Medical Plaza. The staff and facility were fantastic and
he is glad to have that checked off the list. Michael wanted
breakfast, so we went to the Charlotte Cafe. He had eggs, a bowl of
grits and a biscuit—and ate every bite. We're home now, and of
course will let you know when we hear anything more.

Love—Heidi

# CHAPTER 4

*"It's not having what you want, it's wanting what you've got"*

SHERYL CROW, 'SOAK UP THE SUN'

# GRATITUDE

GRATITUDE MAY BE the key to happiness. The Pirke Avot, an ancient book of ethical teachings from eighteen hundred years ago, says, "Who is rich? He who is happy with what he has." A big house, a Lamborghini, and money in the bank can't make me happy. Plenty of rich people take anti-depressants.

If some is good, more is better, so there can never be an end to striving for material things. How many pairs of shoes do you want? How many guitars? Just one more, always one more. Once you secure basic needs, contentment flows from being grateful for what you have, for who you love, and for what you do.

It is such a blessing that I love my work. Days can be exciting or routine, rewarding or unpleasant, stressful, or discouraging. But I leave in the morning eager to go to work and am happy to come home in the evening. I realize I am incredibly lucky. How difficult must it be for most people to toil for years in jobs that bring them no pleasure, no satisfaction beyond a paycheck. I am so fortunate, and so grateful to have fallen into a career in ophthalmology. It almost didn't happen.

**Michael Rotberg**
*Haverford College*
W. Orange, N.J.
*Neurology*
Med. Center Penn.

# STRESS TEST

LUCKILY, SOMEONE WARNED me that the new Chairman of the Eye department had an unusual way to evaluate prospective residents and fellows.

During my last year of medical school, in 1979, the Duke Eye Center was in transition. The old Chairman, newly retired, had started the ophthalmology department and built the Eye Center. He was a Southern Gentleman, gregarious and bright. His department focused on clinical excellence, but he became an anachronism. I once heard him describe a patient as 'a blue gummed nigra'. Most of the residents were from the South, all were white, all were male, none were foreign born. There were no subspecialty fellows. There was little emphasis on academic research.

The new Chairman was entirely and intentionally different. He was German and spoke with an accent. While on faculty in Miami, he had invented a new operation for several untreatable eye diseases. In his garage, he developed the machine that made it possible, a device that could remove an egg's yolk without breaking its shell. One of the first times he presented his invention a skeptical surgeon asked, "Are you planning to use this on a living human eye?" He did, and it spawned a revolution in eye surgery that helped to save vision for millions of people with retinal detachments, diabetes and macular degeneration. Stern and determined, he arrived aiming to grow the Eye Center into a world class research institution.

On the day of my residency interview, after a morning touring the clinics, labs and operating rooms, meeting faculty, and nervously conversing with other applicants, the final step was a face to face with the Chairman. I sat with the other applicants, my competition, in chairs lined up against the wall in the hallway outside his office. Every few minutes his door opened, a relieved student stumbled out, and his assistant called the next candidate in. The rest of us sat, fidgeting, sweating, and palpitating, pretending to be relaxed and confident.

When my turn came I jumped up and strode into the office. The drawn blinds kept the room in dim light. As much a lair as an office. He motioned me to take a seat on the other side of a low coffee table. This was not my first residency interview, and his initial questions were all standard. "Why do you want to become an ophthalmologist, tell me about the research you have done..."

But then he said, "Your application and transcript only tell us that you are a good student. They do not help us to learn if you will be a good ophthalmologist, and they definitely do not show us if you will be able to do eye surgery. So I have a little test for you." He reached for a paper cup and dumped three pills onto the table. There was a flat white tablet, probably a brand-name Tylenol. There was a small round red pill, like a Sudafed, and a shiny egg-shaped pill, possibly a Motrin. He handed me two toothpicks and said, "Your job is to stack these pills using only the toothpicks."

I took the toothpicks, looked at the pills, then up at him. He stared back unsmilingly with his face tilted forward and one brow raised. "Ja," he gave a quick backhand wave, "any time."

To control my shaking hands, first I swept the pills together so I would not have to carry any of them too far to the pile I was hoping to build. Clearly the white pill would have to be the foundation. The tiny round pill could not be anywhere but on top. One toothpick in each hand, after a couple tries I managed to get the egg-shaped pill onto the white one. The little red pill rolled away each time I tried to grab it, and only was able to corral and then lift it after I pushed it against the edge of the white pill. It teetered but somehow stayed on top. I smiled, handed the toothpicks back to him and said, "That was not as hard as I thought it would be. Good thing I have years of experience with chopsticks."

Without a smile, he said, "People think this is a test of manual dexterity, but just as much it is a way to see how you solve problems and how you function under pressure. When an operation does not go the way you expect, you will have to be able to figure out how to respond, and you must keep your hands from shaking and your mind from freezing. You did a good job."

This small success and freely given praise made me want to do my residency at the Eye Center, and I was fortunate enough to be in his next class of residents along with two southern white men, a woman, an African-American man, and a vision scientist from Iceland.

He was so focused on research and academics that it took a while for him to become a good leader. All his time was devoted to the lab, the OR, and the retina fellows who came from around the world to study with him. Residents never assisted him in surgery and never worked in his clinic unless the fellows were away. Someone finally must have told him that he needed to become more accessible to the residents, so one morning several of us were summoned to a tiny conference room for informal teaching. There was a round table with chairs for each resident and our Chairman.

"I know you all think you know how to use the indirect ophthalmoscope, but I suspect you don't know why you do what you do." The indirect is the headlight eye doctors use to look inside the eye. Looking at one of the other residents, he said, "Tell me how you do indirect ophthalmoscopy. What part of the lens do you look through?"

"Uh, I guess I look through the middle of the lens."

"No!" he erupted. So much for the Socratic method.

"No?" whispered the quivering resident.

"No. You must look through the top half of the lens! This way you will have no annoying reflections. I am surprised you did not know this. I wonder what else you do not know."

If the goal was to become more approachable this was not going well. The only way it could have been more anxiety provoking was if he were in uniform, standing behind a bright lamp with a cigarette between his thumb and index finger. "Now tell me the proper order in which you should do a good retinal examination," he asked the same resident.

Chastened, he ventured, "Well, I guess I dilate the patient's eyes, put the ophthalmoscope on my head, dim the room lights, and..."

"No! First you must clean your lenses. If your lens is dirty you will not be able to see clearly."

The resident looked like he was about to melt. I worried I might be next.

"Do you at least know how to clean a lens?" he asked, in an exasperated tone. Our Chairman was enjoying his time with the residents as much as we were.

"I wipe it with a tissue?"

"Ach Gott. You will go to hell!" Disgusted, he started to get up and leave the room, but calmed himself and then described the proper way to clean lenses. It was the first and last small group learning session to which he ever subjected himself, or us. Knowledge is only useful if you know how to share it.

# CHAPTER 5

T HE DOCTOR-PATIENT RELATIONSHIP is unique and awkwardly asymmetric. Two strangers meet and then quickly become intimate. One retains an advantaged position, holding more medical knowledge, while the other lives with consequences that are infinitely more personal and serious.

A certain asymmetry may be unavoidable but should never be dysfunctional. These people come together only for the patient's benefit, and care needs to be, as much as possible, collaborative. If both participants agree on some ground rules, the relationship can be a powerful framework to promote healing. What question does the patient hope will be answered? What does she want to fix? How serious does she think her problem is, and what is she willing to do about it?

My job is to listen to the patient to learn what she wants, to figure out what she needs, and to do my best to help. When it seems to me that what she wants is different from what she needs, it's on me to unpack the impasse so that we get on the same page. And I need to listen with open ears so that together we can craft an approach, acceptable to both of us, that gets the job done.

It makes no sense for me to propose a treatment plan that the patient doesn't understand or that asks more of her than she is prepared to give. Adherence to a therapy that is too extended, too expensive, or too intrusive will never be as reliable as a strategy we develop together. The trust that underpins our working relationship will fray unless we work, from the start, toward the same goal.

As a patient, it is important for you to choose your physicians wisely. Try to find someone who is both experienced and interested in your problem, up to date and well regarded by other patients and physicians. Ideally, someone to whom you can relate well, whose goals and values are in synch with your own. Someone with whom you can create a healing relationship with you at the center.

PART THREE

# INTERNSHIP
# PHILADELPHIA 1980–1981

# CHAPTER 6

## LEARNING THE HARD WAY

T HE PHONE RANG and my eyes flew open. It was still dark outside. I threw back the covers and jumped out of bed. Heidi squealed, "You broke my seal! It's freezing in here." Shivering, I ran to the living room and picked up on the fourth or fifth ring. Through the window, I noticed it had snowed overnight and was still coming down hard. "Hello?"

"Hi Mike, this is Tom. Tom, your resident? You know, who you work with at the hospital?" I was an intern, a few months into my neuro-psych rotation, and here I was getting an emergency call, just like a real doctor.

"Oh, hi Tom, sorry, I'm still a little out of it. What's going on? You've never called me at home before. And so early."

"You live close to the hospital, don't you? Well, the snow is pretty deep on my driveway. I called the ward and we only have one thing going on today. I'm sure you can handle it yourself."

"Even in the snow, I can walk to the hospital in about 15 minutes. What do you need me to do besides checking on our patients?"

"The only thing on the books is one admission, but it will be easy for you. It is a guy who has been admitted every few months for as long as I have been here. The staff all know him, and he knows the routine too, piece of cake. Can you go in and get him admitted? Then I can see him tomorrow morning instead of coming in today."

"Sure, why's he being admitted?"

"It's pretty much the same thing every time. We tune him up, he goes home, feels good, doesn't believe he really needs his anti-psychotics anymore, never refills them, and then starts to get a little paranoid. When that happens, his wife calls and we admit him again so the whole thing can start over."

"So he's a paranoid schizophrenic?"

"Right, from way back. His parents met on a locked ward. But like I said, he feels comfortable on our hall, almost his home away from home. And the staff are all used to dealing with him too. Just check him in, do the paperwork, start him on the meds that I will call in to the ward clerk, and you'll be back home making snow angels before you know it."

"No problem. Thanks for asking."

"Just a couple things to keep in mind. First, don't go behind any closed doors with him."

"What do you mean?"

"I mean stay in public places where other people are around. Make sure you're never alone with him."

"How can I do his physical exam and draw his blood?"

"Oh God, don't even think about that. Just interview him, write the orders, and tuck him in."

"No EKG, rectal exam, none of the things we always do when people get admitted?"

"Aren't you hearing me? This guy is a black belt, out of control paranoid schizophrenic. He wouldn't be coming in if he was doing well. If you're lucky his car won't even run in the snow. But if he does show up, just check him in, make him feel at home, and leave the rest to me and the staff."

"OK, I'll call if I have any questions. Stay warm. See you tomorrow."

I took a long hot shower, had breakfast, bundled up and trudged down the middle of Schoolhouse Lane to Henry Avenue. The morning was cold, gray, and still except for the white noise of falling snow. Six inches of fresh powder covered the streets, and no tire tracks scarred the hospital driveway. Only emergencies would show up today.

Upstairs on the locked ward everything was quiet. The snow and overcast skies induced a hush over the usually boisterous common room. The TV was on, flickering unwatched and silent. A few people sat on couches and easy chairs, but no one was playing cards or ping pong. Most were still in bed. Our patients were in a good mood, like kids awakening to a surprise snow storm and an unexpected day off school. It was a holiday in the middle of the week. No elective surgeries or tests, no reason to leave the ward or even to get out of bed.

"Hey Doctor Mike, watcha doin' here?" asked one of the aides, a rotund but muscular guy, dressed in white smock and pants.

"Tom can't get his car out of the garage, so I came in for him. Not much going on anyway, just one admission."

"Today?" He looked at his calendar and said, "Aw, he probably won't come in the snow. But if he does, keep him in the hall where other people are around."

"That's what Tom said too."

"Yeah, I know this guy. We all know this guy. He jumped one of the aides last year and it took three of us to get him under control. Nice guy when he's on his meds, but when he's not...."

I sat down and filled out as much of the admission paperwork as I could so there would be less to do in case he showed up. A little after 10 o'clock the ER called to say he had just arrived. A few minutes later, he appeared at the locked door at the end of our hall with a duffle bag and two security guards. The aides let him onto the ward, then stood aside while I introduced myself.

"I am working with Dr. Tom. He is stuck in the snow, so you won't see him until tomorrow. Why don't you come on in and we can get you settled." I turned to the side and with a sweeping motion of my arm welcomed him into the hall. A row of plastic chairs lined the wall, "Let's sit right here and get you checked in, OK?"

He took the last seat and I sat sideways, facing him, with an empty chair between us. He was a white man in his early thirties who looked as if he had not shaved or showered in a week. Standing 6'2", solid except for a beer belly, his lumberjack arms were covered with amateur tattoos. I had already read his thick hospital chart to record his medical, family, and social history, but still needed to interview him to get him admitted. After answering my first couple questions he stopped responding. "How long ago did you run out of your pills?" Nothing. "Did your pills give you any problems?" Just a blank stare, chin down, and then he began to rock back and forth, shokeling, his instability manifest.

"All right, listen, don't worry about that. Just a few more questions and we'll be through here." He reached into his bag, rooted around for a few seconds, and drew out a small Bible. He held it by the spine like a TV preacher, its floppy, black, well-worn cover draped over his hand. Silently he opened it, flipped to the right page, and began mumbling quietly, every so often raising his eyes to peer at me over the book to see if the incantations were working. Disconcerted to find that I was still there, his rocking increased in frequency and amplitude.

"Well, all righty then, I guess that's about all for this morning. Let's go into the Day Room while they get your bed ready for you, OK?" I got up and offered a handshake, but he just stood, lifted his bag, and strode down the hall without me, turning left toward the Day Room. By this time a few other patients were there, playing cards, watching TV, or looking out the wire-mesh windows at the unfamiliar snowy landscape. He hesitated in the doorway, scanning the room, unsure where to go. There were lots of empty seats, so I said, "Just sit anywhere and they'll be right with you."

I took a step forward to lead him in when suddenly he wheeled around and punched me in the face. My glasses took most of the force and went skittering across the floor. I was stunned, staggered but stayed on my feet. Before I could blink three of the biggest aides, moving impossibly fast, bolted out of the nursing station and jumped on his back, swiped his feet out from under him and knocked him to the floor. He roared and bucked, and they struggled to hold him down. Only when one of the heaviest aides sat on his back and another pinned his legs were they able to put him in restraints, lift him to his feet, and drag him to the padded room down the hall. One aide stayed behind to check on me.

"Aw, look at you, you got off easy. He busted your glasses, but you ain't even bleeding. Last time he hit somebody here the guy needed surgery."

"Wow," I said. "Lucky for me you guys were on him so fast or he might have really hurt me. I didn't even see that coming."

"Naw, I bet you dit'n. But since he put one of our aides in the hospital last year we all were ready for a little payback this time. He won't bother you no more. Course, you probably shouldn't get near him again neither."

I called my resident, and he apologized for putting me in that situation. "Oh man, you really have to be directive with this guy. He must have freaked out trying to figure out where to sit…" The hospital bought me new glasses. And for years every student and intern who passed through got a 'what not to do' lesson based on my getting cold cocked by a black belt paranoid schizophrenic on the locked ward. I realized I would never be good enough at martial arts to become a Psychiatrist.

# BE OBSERVANT

SHERLOCK HOLMES NOTICED everything. The dog not barking in the night, the number of steps in a stairway, the vintage of champagne. He always paid attention because he knew that, "…the little things are infinitely the most important." In life and in medicine, there is a difference between hearing and listening, between looking and seeing.

Often, the complaints that lead a patient to my office have nothing to do with the condition we really need to address. There may be another disorder underlying the most obvious, salient, one. My ability to diagnose and treat is, like a detective's, based on both knowledge and experience. But mostly, it rests on being able to observe, to see who really is sitting there in the exam chair, and to be mindful that first impressions may be misleading.

It helps to know a patient over time, so as a glaucoma specialist whose patients come back every few months for many years, I have an advantage in detecting subtle distress compared to an ER doc who first meets patients during a crisis.

But powers of observation can be learned and fostered. Practicing mindfulness, training the habit of alertness, of trying to see beneath the surface, can be rewarding for both doctor and patient. If I had been more experienced and observant, I might have done a better job noticing the previous patient's agitated state of mind, saving him from trouble and myself a trip to the optical shop.

PART FOUR

# OPHTHALMOLOGY RESIDENCY DURHAM, NC 1981–1984

# CHAPTER 7

# WHICH IS BETTER?

H EIDI'S SISTER CAME to visit us in Durham a few weeks
into my residency. She needed an eye exam, so I took
her to the Eye Center on Saturday afternoon when the clinic
was closed. I had just learned how to check eyes and still had
to consciously tick off the various elements of a complete eye
exam (pupils, motility, external, vision with refraction, visual
fields, pressure test, slit lamp exam and dilated retina) to be
sure not to leave anything out.

Her pupils were normal, her eyes were aligned, she did not
have any lid malposition, cranial nerve findings or facial asymmetry. Her vision was good with her glasses and contacts but
she wanted new ones. After putting her prescription in the
phoropter, the big mask-like device we use to check vision, I

dimmed the room lights, covered one of her eyes, and asked her to look through the machine.

I started flipping between lenses. "Which is better, one or two?" I asked. No response. "Just see which one looks clearer. They might be pretty much the same, but if you can tell a difference let me know which one you prefer." Still nothing. I tried again, but then she started to laugh. I recognized that laugh. It was the same laugh Heidi has when she is nervous or thinks she has done something wrong. "What's the matter?"

"I think you are checking the wrong eye," she said, then giggled again. "When you change the lenses, I hear the gears clicking, but nothing looks different. You're working on the eye that's covered."

I was mortified but glad she spoke up. Doctors make mistakes too. Happily, though boneheaded, this one was harmless except to my pride.

# FIRST CASE

THE PATIENT'S HAND trembled holding a nearly full emesis basin, his vomit sloshing back and forth to the rim. He reached out to pass it to me. "Here, would you take care of this?" he asked. I threw a glove on, grabbed it before he let go, then dumped it into the biohazard bag. When I turned back he was moaning, his palm pressed to his right eye, as if he had taken a face full of pepper spray. He reached for the emptied basin and used it again, panting, perspiring, hyperventilating.

His intraocular pressure, which should measure in the teens, was over sixty, but he couldn't relax enough for me to get an exact reading. Not that it really mattered; whatever the pressure was, this was an emergency situation. He was in trouble, and I had no idea what to do.

I went to the next exam room where Jake, my senior resident at the Veterans Hospital, was with another patient. "Can you come next door. I need your help with someone." A few minutes later he popped in and said, "Oh boy."

"Have you ever heard of neovascular glaucoma?" he asked. I had, but never cared for anyone who had it. This is one of the most difficult to treat forms of glaucoma, and usually happens to people with bad circulation due to diabetes, high blood pressure or inflammation. The blood vessels that nourish the eye get so damaged that it becomes ischemic, starved of oxygen, and sprouts new blood vessels. But rather than helping, these bring a new set of problems. They don't grow only where needed, but proliferate wildly, everywhere, on the surface of the retina, into the vitreous, even on the iris. And they grow over, and block, the eye's drainage channels, so the intraocular pressure rises painfully high.

Since drops and other medicines give only temporary relief, most people need laser treatment or injections inside the eye to make the abnormal vessels dry up and go away. But if the drainage pathways scar permanently closed, the eye becomes like an overflowing sink. Water continues to pour onto the floor until someone turns off the faucet, unplugs the drain, or both. Advanced neovascular glaucoma can only be controlled by either surgery to make a new channel for fluid to leave the eye or laser or freezing treatments to reduce the eye's ability to pump itself up.

"What meds have you already given him?" he asked.

"About an hour ago I gave him timolol and Diamox, but they didn't help much."

"No, he's going to need laser, but his eye is way too hot. And his pressure's so high his cornea is cloudy, so nobody could see in to focus the laser anyway. We need to get that pressure down ASAP. Have you ever done a cyclocryo?"

Me? We stepped into another room and shut the door. "Uh, I'm a first-year resident, remember? I've only been here a few weeks. I haven't done anything yet. I haven't even watched anyone do this."

"Well, this is going to be the first surgical case of your career."

"Where can I read about how to do it?"

"No time for that, you can read about it later. I'll walk you through it." I started to sweat. He said, "Don't worry, it's the easiest procedure you will ever do." He told me to go to the operating room and get the cryo machine, which uses liquid nitrogen to freeze a probe that can be applied to the surface of the eye to shut off the fluid that raises the pressure. When I wheeled it into the clinic, he helped me set it up and test it. "You gently press the tip of the probe against the white of the eye a couple millimeters behind the cornea. Like here, here, here. Step on the pedal and hold it for about a minute at each spot, and treat halfway around the eye, six clock hours."

"That's it?"

"Yup, easy. Nothing to it."

Okay. I tipped the exam chair back so the patient was in astronaut position, instilled a numbing drop, and placed a lid speculum to keep him from squeezing his eyes shut. He fought me and I said, "I know your eye is really sore, but this should help make you feel better." Then, as Jake watched, I touched the probe to his eye and depressed the pedal.

"Ow! Holy crap!" He jerked his head to the side and threw up again, this time onto my shoes.

"Sir, this is for your own good. Please let us give you this treatment. It won't take but a few minutes," said Jake taking charge. Once the patient settled down, I did it again, and he bucked and roared. Jake scolded, "Listen, you're a veteran.

You've been through a lot worse than this. Only a few more times, just suck it up."

I was shaking. "Should I really keep going?" I asked.

"We need to get his pressure down or by this time tomorrow his eye will be permanently blind, so yeah, keep going. And I'll help hold him still."

It was an ordeal for all of us, but I quickly completed the treatment, removed the lid speculum, placed a patch, and admitted the patient to the hospital for overnight pressure and pain control.

That night, while I was home, the phone rang. It was Jake. "How's our guy doing?"

"The nurses just called to tell me that he's still in a lot of pain. Is that normal?"

"Uh, not really. His pressure should be coming down by now." He paused, "Listen, remind me, how did you numb his eye?"

"Before I put the lid speculum in I gave him some drops."

"Right, but what else?"

"I guess I put the drops in twice."

"That's it?? Didn't you give him an anesthetic injection behind his eye?"

"You were there. I just did what you told me to do. You didn't say anything about a retrobulbar block. I don't know how to do that yet either."

"Oh Jesus, oh my God, I feel terrible. Cyclocryotherapy is probably the most painful thing you can do to an eye. You have to numb it up first. Oh man, what a screw-up. It's on me. I'll call the floor and tell the nurses what to give him."

"Yeah, I read about it when the office quieted down, and I wondered why we didn't block his eye."

"Poor guy," he said, flagellating himself, "but I bet you learned a lesson you'll never forget."

The patient ended up doing fine. Although his vision was damaged by high pressure and his underlying disease, within a few hours his pain improved and he became calm and comfortable. But I was distraught. My first case, my first complication, left me a with humbling dose of regret and the resolve to do better.

Residency was a time of intense learning. Memory of this first case serves as a spur to read, to learn, to be honest about what I do and don't know, to be prepared, and never to be complacent.

---

**JUST A NORMAL DAY**                                    *Mar 6, 2013*

Hi—Michael and I went to work today—just a normal day. (Really?)

We are waiting to hear from Michael's oncologist, Dr. Mahoney, and will post what we learn at that appointment. We remain quite optimistic. At this point the pathologists and radiologists are going to provide some answers, and once there is a diagnosis we can proceed with treatment.

Thank you for your support, prayers, offers of help and messages on Caring Bridge.

Love—Heidi

# CHAPTER 8

# KNOWLEDGEABLE AND COMMITTED
# TO LEARNING

A FEW DAYS into my treatment, I told Heidi, "We were
talking about what makes good doctors and patients. Remember Don Gold?"

"Who?" Heidi asked.

"Don Gold. He was one of the three family docs who
founded Doctors' Clinic." This was the multispecialty group
in Vero Beach, Florida that gave me my first job after my residency training ended in 1984. He was almost retired by the
time I joined them. Kind of a jowly curmudgeon with a few
strands of white hair, a big belly and red face. Used to wear a

barber's smock instead of a white coat. "I'll never forget what he told me on my first day there."

"What did he say?"

"He called me to his office, and I figured he just wanted to crow about how his little practice had grown or to wish me good luck or tell me how happy he was that I chose to join his group, something grandfatherly and welcoming like that. But instead, he leaned forward and pointed his finger at me, 'You just finished a fancy residency up at Duke and I bet you think you know what it takes to be a successful doctor. Well, if you're like all the other rookies that come through here, you don't have the first clue.'"

I was taken aback and a little insulted, so I said, "I hope you'll tell me what I need to know."

Without a smile, he interlocked his fingers across his belly, sucked in his cheeks and chewed a few times before saying, "Just remember the three A's and you'll be fine. A, A, A. If you're available, affable, and able, you will do well throughout your career. And it's no mistake I said them in that order. You do have to know what you're doing, but if you're not available to your patients and if you can't get along with people, you can forget about being a success in practice."

"Do you think that's right?" Heidi asked.

"When he said it, I thought he was an out of touch old man who probably still treated his patients with leeches. Now, I'm pretty sure he knew what he was talking about."

To be a good doctor, it is necessary to be knowledgeable and intelligent. That should be assumed. But it isn't nearly enough.

I had the good fortune to train at Duke, one of the best hospitals in the world, surrounded by internationally famous professors and by outstanding students and residents who aspired to join their ranks. During my internship year in Philadelphia, my senior resident boasted, "This hospital has the best neurologist in the whole city." In contrast, when I was in medical school, only a faculty member who was one of the best in the world would have merited similar praise.

I was encouraged to model my behavior on the highest standard of patient care and academic medicine. In practice, even though I always worked in community settings, my goal was to remain worthy of the trust that patients placed in me by trying to be as good as anyone in a teaching institution. There is a local standard of care in small, isolated communities that makes it acceptable for a family doctor to deliver babies, even though in a bigger city quality and liability concerns limit this service to Board Certified Obstetricians. In the same way, in little Vero Beach, it was fine for a general ophthalmologist like me to do retinal laser treatments, because the nearest competent retina specialist was more than an hour away.

But when I moved to Charlotte I handed those patients off. I was trained to do all sorts of eye surgery, but in my new city I found others with years of extra training in each subspecialty. How could I justify straightening crossed eyes a couple times a year when someone better was down the hall? It was not in my patients' best interest for me to keep doing occasional blepharoplasties, macular lasers, or temporal artery biopsies. As I got busier doing cataract and glaucoma procedures, I began to refer these cases to others. Doing more and more of less and less, I got better and better at the procedures I continued to perform. I needed to be confident that when patients entrusted me with their care we both could be sure they were making a good choice.

Complacency is deadly for physicians and the love of lifelong learning is critical. Reading medical journals, attending continuing education meetings, and discussing tricky cases with colleagues are all important. My participation as an investigator in clinical trials enabled me to gain early familiarity with new drugs and procedures before they became available.

Going to investigators' meetings, presenting studies at conventions, and exploring new treatments with my patients, was the creative spice that seasoned my day to day clinical practice.

And while it may be true that, 'The only way to avoid having complications is to avoid doing surgery,' I tried to learn from cases that didn't go as planned. Every bad outcome is traumatic for the patient, but the silver lining is that, if I pay attention, each complication makes the same thing less likely to happen to someone else.

# DISSERVICE CONNECTED

CHRIS, MY FELLOW resident at the VA, sat back and studied the man in his exam chair. The patient had a plethoric complexion, a bulbous nose, and three days of stubble. A whiskery silver rim circled his shiny dome, a bald man's buzz cut. He wheezed and smelled of smoke. Nervously, the patient asked, "Did you figure out what's making my eye blurry?"

"Your cataract surgery went fine last year, your lens implant still looks good, everything is OK, but your eye is blurry because a film has grown behind your pupil."

"What went wrong?"

"Nothing went wrong, it happens all the time, just takes a couple minutes to fix, won't hurt at all. It's called a capsulotomy. You lean forward, put your face in a machine like this, I give you some numbing drops, push a button, and in a few seconds you'll be able to see a lot better. No cutting, no needles, no patch, no recovery time, simple. But the VA doesn't have the laser we need, so we have to use the one at Duke."

"When can I get it done?"

"I already checked; it's available right now, so as soon as we get you over there we can take care of it. Let me call VA transport to set up your ride." But when he did, all their drivers were busy, and it would be more than an hour before they could carry the patient to the Eye Center. He looked at his watch and hung up the phone. "You want to get this done today, right? It's getting late. Why don't we just walk across the street?"

"How far is it?"

Chris raised the blinds and pointed out the clinic window, "See, it's right over there."

"Uh, OK, whatever you say." They walked out of hospital, turned right across the parking lot, and waited in the scrubby grass and dried mud at the edge of Erwin Road to let cars pass. Chris jogged across the two lanes of pavement and his patient shuffled behind, stopping to catch his breath once safely on the other side. He paused and gazed warily at the rutted, grassy embankment that rose between him and the edge of the Eye Center's parking lot.

It started to drizzle. "We better get going!" Chris said, then turned and jogged up the short hill, looking back down from the top to urge his patient onward. Lightning flashed and the skies opened up, and he ran across the pavement to the porte cochere. After laborious trudging, the patient's head appeared, followed by the rest of his body. At the top of the hill he stopped and bent over, rested his hands on his knees, panting with one hand on his chest, soaked and unable to continue.

One of the nurses inside the Eye Center looked out, saw the patient struggling in the rain, and burst from the front door with a crash cart, passing the young doctor, who was standing under the shelter of the overhang waving and shouting, "Come on, come on already, hurry up, can't you see it's raining?"

In the MASH-type atmosphere of a training program, people say all kinds of things. *'First you try a new treatment on animals, then Veterans, then patients.' 'You can't make a 20/200 brain see 20/20.' 'The average person is pretty stupid, but half the people are even dumber.' 'That patient was uglier than a hatful of assholes.'* But justifying this sort of language as 'just locker room talk' is inexcusable. Internalizing a disrespectful attitude at the formative stage of a career led to behavior that was geared for the doctor's convenience to the detriment of the patient. This resident was nearly thrown out of the program for selfishly putting his patient at risk.

Whether due to my training as a Boy Scout to 'Do a Good Turn Daily' or to my father's example of volunteering as veterinarian for the Humane Society, service has always been a powerful motivator. Later, when I got sick and had to leave my full-time practice, I began to visit an eye clinic for indigent patients every week, treating the kind of people who go without glasses for years because they cannot afford new ones. It allowed me to keep my hard-won skills intact and provided me a way to be of service even in retirement.

**THANKFUL**                                    *Mar 7, 2013 11:48am*

*"THE VERY FACT THAT YOU KNOW ABOUT SOMEONE WHO IS IN TROUBLE MEANS THAT IN SOME WAY YOU ARE ABLE TO HELP." MENACHEM MENDEL SCHNEERSON*

I wanted to take today's update as an opportunity to say thank you. First, thank you to everyone who has visited and posted here. Your words, thoughts, prayers, hopes, care and love mean more than we can express. We have so many family members, friends and colleagues who care—please know that while I am not mentioning you by name you ARE very important.

I want to thank some people who have already helped Michael—again I don't have the words to express how much they mean to us.

Michael's staff: Carol, Scottie, Beth and Michelle. When Michael called you in on Monday, you told him he was FAMILY and that you would do ANYTHING he needed. Once he had you on his team he was able to focus. Michael felt awful about telling Chuck Hoch in Chuck's last week at work, but Chuck took care of what Michael needed, and was there for him.

I don't know how I could have gotten through the first week without Dick Blackwell. Sharing an office, and knowing you are there for me and Michael, is tremendously important.

I am not going to mention MY close friends by name—you know who you are and how much I value and love you. Michael's friends—same. Knowing you are there makes all the difference. Thank you.

Hoping we have news—good news—for you soon.

Love,
Heidi

# LONG WAY FROM HOME

I PUSHED THE phoropter aside and the patient exclaimed, "Jeez, doc. That was tough. I mean, you kept asking me which is better, one or two, three or four, nine or ten, but sometimes it's impossible to tell them apart. Like, fuggedaboudit."

This was her first eye exam at the Duke Eye Center. She was a 400-pound New Yorker, enrolled in one of the weight loss programs in Durham. There was a community, an in-gathering of the obese diaspora, who arrived in town hoping to stay several months, remake their bodies, and then return home. But while few kept the weight off, some enjoyed the company of other obese people, accepted because of, rather than in spite of, their size. It was an exhilarating experience for a 300-pound woman to be the thinnest person at the pool, and many stayed after failing their diets. Never accepted in their home towns, they were embraced by welcoming and empathetic new friends who found themselves together in an unfamiliar and exotic place.

"No problem, that's normal. The way this test works is that when you get to the point where you can't tell the difference between two choices that means we've found the right prescription. So don't worry about it, you're going to love how you see with your new glasses. Now let me take a minute to be sure your eyes are healthy, all right?"

"What, we ain't done?"

"Not yet. That was just figuring out your new glass prescription. Now I'm going to examine your eyes. Please lean forward and rest your chin on this little shelf and tip your forehead forward so it touches this bar, OK?"

"Uh, Doc, somethin's in the way, know what I mean?" She shifted her shoulders side to side. "Two somethin's, really."

"We can make it work. This machine is one size fits all. Just scoot up to the front of the chair, I'll lower the table a little, and you can lean forward. There, that's better. Think you can sit like this for a couple minutes?"

"I can hardly breathe, but yeah, sure, go ahead and do what you gotta do."

I turned on the slit lamp and shined the light at her right eye. "Everything looks fine so far. Now let's take a look at your other eye." From the waiting room, through the closed door, I heard the overhead intercom, "Paging Dr. Beauregard. Paging Dr. Beauregard. Dr. Beauregard, please call Dr. Anderson's office."

She lurched back from the slit lamp. "What the hell was that?"

"What do you mean?"

"That announcement. Did I really hear them say, "Paging Dr. Beauregard?" Is there really somebody here named Dr. Beauregard?"

"He's one of our eye doctors, a resident, like me."

"That's un-fuckin' believable. The South really is different." She laughed, "Do you all, 'yawl', happen to have a Dr. Stonewall Jackson and a Dr. JEB Stuart too?"

"Uh, his first name is JEB. How did you know?"

"You're shittin' me doc, right? Where the hell am I anyway? A long way from New York, that's for damn sure. My friends back home won't believe this. I gotta get back home!" It is hard to build rapport outside your comfort zone.

# CHAPTER 9

## UNCONVENTIONAL

**"I** CAN FEEL myself starting to hyperventilate whenever I think about it," I said to Heidi. "How can a first-year resident stand in front of the entire eye department and give a lecture without getting murdered?" Every year, each resident had to give a Saturday morning talk to all the residents, fellows and professors. It was an audience of people who, if they were feeling uncharitable, could easily expose my ignorance and humiliate me for the fun of it.

Heidi said, "You get to pick what to talk about, right? So, don't do cataracts or glaucoma or diabetic eye disease. Choose a topic nobody knows about but that you are interested in and want to learn about. Try to make it fun, explore something new."

Great idea; that's what I did. The first year I talked about non-compliance, when patients miss appointments, fail to take their medicine, fill prescriptions, or follow medical advice. Back then, this subject had been largely ignored by ophthalmologists. Fewer than a dozen papers had been published in eye journals. Research on non-compliance in medical conditions, like diabetes and hypertension, was further along, but most studies had been published in psychology journals, which no one in the department read. Now everyone recognizes that what is currently called non-adherence is pertinent to every interaction with every patient. It is not enough to make a brilliant diagnosis and to prescribe the right treatment if the patient never comes for follow-up visits or swallows a pill. But in 1982 this was big news. The talk was well received, I was able to teach my teachers something new, and no one asked any questions I couldn't answer. What a relief.

The next year I found an even more obscure topic. While on the eye pathology rotation I examined a specimen from the eye of a premature infant who died only a couple days after birth. The child had something called 'Potter Syndrome'. I had to look it up. Babies with Potter Syndrome are born without functioning kidneys, so they cannot survive, which is why I had never seen a child with this disorder. If I hadn't heard of it, maybe my professors didn't know about it either; another good subject for my annual Saturday lecture.

The eye had abnormal blood vessels on the surface of the retina. How could a baby who only lived two or three days have had enough time to develop retinal vessels that looked like those of an infant who had been on oxygen for weeks? The ocular pathologist was giddy with excitement. This subject turned out to be a trifecta. It was the topic of my annual lecture, it won me a free trip to a meeting in Sarasota where I presented the case. And I published both an article in the American Journal of Ophthalmology and a chapter in a book about diseases of the eye and kidney. For a while I was the world expert in a disease that no living person has.

My third year's lecture arose from a presentation I heard at the same research meeting. A scientist gave a talk about the levels of clotting factors in aqueous humor. Aqueous is the transparent fluid that fills the front part of the eye, between the lens, iris, and cornea. It nourishes these structures, helps control the intraocular oxygen level, pressure, and temperature. This researcher wondered why the iris does not bleed much when it is cut during surgery. It has plenty of blood vessels but if the iris begins to bleed it stops quickly on its own. He was the first to measure clotting factors in normal and inflamed aqueous humor.

What could be more obscure that this? I searched the literature and found nothing about clotting factor levels in aqueous. And the study presented at the meeting had not yet been published, so the only people who knew about it had been in the audience with me. I went back to Duke and found a researcher interested in coagulation, told him about this, and asked if he wanted to become world renowned in aqueous humor clotting factors. I convinced several cataract surgeons at the Eye Center to draw off, with the patients' permission, a tiny sample of aqueous from healthy eyes having cataract surgery. I placed these syringes on ice in a cooler and ran them over to the research lab, where they assayed the samples for clotting factors and vitamin C. This got me another free trip to Florida.

Later that year, the head of the residency program called me to his office. "Why aren't you going to do a fellowship?" he asked, curious why I was not planning to spend an extra year of academic training in an ophthalmic subspecialty like retinal disease, glaucoma, or cornea.

"I don't want to confine myself to one small part of eye care. And I'm anxious to start helping real patients," I answered.

He said, "What a shame. You are so creative, I wish you were going into research. You always come up with ideas no one else has thought of." I was flattered, but also happy that he never figured out the real reason I looked for such obscure topics.

I have always enjoyed coming up with creative ideas. My mind is not data driven; I have never been interested in statistical analysis or in adding incrementally to knowledge. Rather, I like synthesizing disparate fields, finding previously unappreciated connections. Sometimes this gets me a free trip to a meeting in Sarasota. Most of the time it just is fun.

For example, one night during sophomore year in college, a friend and I were brainstorming while giggling under the influence. I had a kazoo, and he was blowing bubbles. Eureka! Why not attach a bubble wand to the end of a kazoo, so that when you sing into the kazoo the flowing air also produces bubbles!! Why hadn't anyone thought of this before? We rigged up a prototype and named it the 'Hummabubble.' But there were some technical difficulties. Humming into the kazoo did not produce any bubbles. I had to shout for anything to happen. Also, even our friends didn't want one.

Oh well. Our next inspiration was the 'Mobius Trip.' He had just learned about mobius strips in an advanced math class and was fascinated that this form, contrary to its appearance, has only one side. I went to a garden store and got a green foam Christmas wreath. Using a knife, we carved it into a four-sided mobius strip. Actually, it had only one side, but its cross-section was square, so to get back to the starting place I had to drag my finger along the surface of the circle four times. We marked the wreath into sections and figured we had an unusual game board. But though we had the board, we never devised a game to play on it.

Many years later, during a Sunday morning bike ride with my friend Andy, after riding for a couple hours, we had exhausted any meaningful conversation and were saving our breath for the last few miles until home. It was a perfect Carolina winter day, with crisp air, blue skies, and brown corn stubble in the fields. I already heard about his kids, his week, and where he went to dinner the night before. He had heard the same from me. We were disinhibited, drained, dehydrated, and delirious. At the top of a hill we passed a small country cemetery in the village of Wesley Chapel. The sign said: 'W ley Cha el Cem t y.' Some of the letters had fallen off.

He said, "Cem T Y. It looks like it says, Cem TV. Wouldn't it be weird to have a TV station in a cemetery?"

I said, "Coming to you live from Wesley Chapel Cemetery, it's Cem TV!"

"What kind of shows would it have?" he asked.

"Mostly obituaries, I guess. People would be dying to get their names on TV."

"That's bad. But you have something. People might actually pay to get their relatives on the air."

"How about if there was a cable station that really did that? My mother reads the obituaries every day, but lots of people don't get the newspaper anymore. What if there was a station that did on TV what the paper has always done? You could have local obits, you could have celebrity obits, you could have features about important people who passed away on this date in history. It could be a whole station. I mean, who ever thought there would be a station about weather, fat surgery, or shopping?"

"Or a station that only shows people remodeling their kitchens. People will watch anything."

"And with this viewing audience advertisers would line up; life insurance, Viagra, Depends, estate planning, reverse mortgages, Metamucil. Could be a gold mine!"

We called it 'The Memory Channel' and trademarked the name. But we were just eye doctors and dreamers. We did not know anyone who could make it a reality. Too bad, because I still think it's a great idea. This was just idle fun, but it can be useful to nurture a habit of playful creativity.

# CREATIVITY

WHEN YOU SHOP for new shoes, it isn't enough to measure your feet. You need to try on a few pair before you buy. Choosing the right ones ends up being more subjective than objective, more based on how they feel than on whether they are the 'right' size. If they don't feel right, they don't fit right. In the same way, auto-refractors, machines that measure the strength of the eye, are no substitute for checking vision the old-fashioned way. Only by asking a patient, 'Which is better, one or two?', giving her a chance to choose her own lenses, can we both end up happy with the outcome.

Computers cannot fit shoes and they cannot prescribe eyeglasses, at least not well. Similarly, 'preferred practice patterns,' cookie cutter national guidelines for treatment, are no substitute for care designed around individual needs and circumstances. Clinical decisions need to be based on science, but treatment recommendations cannot be based on science alone. Experience, respect for individual differences, intuition, and creativity also play an irreplaceable role.

The best quality care demands creative thinking, making connections between what is known and what might be. The art of medicine is the synthesis of knowledge and imagination, of the general and particular, for each patient's benefit. Sometimes, what the manual prescribes for most people is not the correct approach for a certain individual. Existing treatments, creatively seen with fresh eyes, can be applied in new and exciting ways. Imaginative people have said, 'I just read about a new medicine for colon cancer (Avastin); I wonder if it might be helpful in treating macular degeneration too (it is).' 'I just heard of an injection that can relax muscle spasms (botulinum toxin); I wonder if it might also be useful for wrinkles in the forehead (it is too, as Botox).' 'Oh look, when my patients use this eye drop (Lumigan) for their glaucoma, their lashes get longer (Latisse).'

In my practice, I try to foster my own creativity by being an investigator in clinical trials of new drugs and surgical devices. While never a 'first adopter' of untried techniques, I have often been the first in our area to offer innovative treatments. At work and at home, I enjoy thinking outside the box, especially when it leads to creative solutions for the patient.

---

**TEST RESULTS**                                    *Mar 9, 2013 9:32am*

This is the first time I have contributed to this journal, but I have been reading everything, and I have to start by thanking all of you for your support, your kind words, your offers of help, and your prayers.

This entire experience has been kind of like watching a movie —I see what is happening but it seems to be someone else's story. Unfortunately, it is mine, but it remains kind of unbelievable. Two weeks ago I was working full time, doing surgery, giving lectures to other doctors, sweating in spin class, and now I have a serious medical problem that is going to dominate the next several months and years of my, and my family's, lives.

This week I found myself in the bizarre position of hoping to learn that I have lymphoma. Who hopes to have cancer? The chest X ray and CT scan suggested that lymphoma was the most likely diagnosis. Although it is cancer and requires intensive treatment, the outcomes are usually good, so that is what I was hoping to have. Unfortunately, that is not what I do have. I have 'poorly differentiated carcinoma, possibly squamous cell origin, of the anterior mediastinum.' Don't bother looking it up, there is not much written about it. It was a surprise to everyone who had seen the scans. But the bottom line is that I am going to need several weeks of intensive daily radiation combined with weekly chemotherapy. No work for at least the next several months.

I will start both chemo and radiation on Monday and feel very lucky to have been able to assemble such a good medical team. Dr. Mahoney, the oncologist, is a straight shooter and is very patient with questions that he cannot fully answer. And Steve Plunkett, the radiation oncologist, aside from inspiring great confidence in the care plan they have developed, is simply one of the best men I know. I am sure that I will have excellent and attentive care. So again, I thank you for your love and your support and for respecting our ongoing need for privacy as events unfold. Michael

# NUCLEAR OPTION

A FEW MONTHS before the end of my residency, in 1984, I started to look for a job. Heidi and I wanted to stay in North Carolina, but with our first baby on the way, we decided to head either north to be near my family in New Jersey or south to hers in Florida.

The best opportunity up north was near Harrisburg, PA. A busy ophthalmologist was looking for someone to help his practice grow. He had his own surgery center and a gorgeous new office. I spoke with him, visited, and was pleasantly surprised by the city. Even better, it was only a few miles from Hershey; when the wind was right the air smelled like chocolate.

In February, with Heidi 8 1/2 months pregnant, we traveled together to check out the place and the practice. Right away she knew something was wrong. The doctor was distracted and had pressured speech, very different than he had been during my first visit. She whispered, "I don't care if this is the best practice in the world, I don't care if this city is paradise, I don't want you to work with this guy." He was acting strangely, but when I met him before he had been fine. I liked the town and could imagine our having a nice life there.

Back in our hotel room that evening we digested the day and our disparate reactions to it–hers strongly negative and mine lukewarm but still favorable. We took a break from arguing to watch the evening news. The first story was about a big demonstration protesting the Three Mile Island Nuclear Plant, which was about to reopen five years after a near-meltdown.

Heidi said, "Why are they protesting here? Where is Three Mile Island, anyway?"

I pulled back the curtains and said, "See that glow above the trees?"

"No way!" she cried.

"I think we can see the cooling towers from the parking lot if you want to go outside."

Just then, the TV camera backed away from the reporter and scanned the hundreds of angry people chanting and holding posters protesting the nuclear plant. 'No More Melt-downs,' 'Keep TMI Closed,' '2,4,6,8, We Don't Want To Radi-ate.' Suddenly it zoomed in on a demonstrator shaking a large sign that read: "HELLO FROM HARRISBURG—CITY OF DEATH!"

"That's it. That's it," she yelled, "A really bad omen. I've seen enough. We're out of here." I called the doctor and told him I wasn't interested. Early the next morning we left to drive back to Durham and ended up moving to Vero Beach.

A few months later, soon after joining the practice in Flori-da, one of the senior partners shook his head solemnly, and said, "I feel so sorry for you. You missed out on the Golden Age of medicine. You're starting your career when medicine has already gone to hell." How disconcerting, but I bet some-one said the same thing to him when he was freshly trained, and I know many of my contemporaries feel the same way now. Every generation thinks the gravy train has left the sta-tion.

When my son was applying to medical school, one of the surgeons I work with asked, "You didn't encourage him to go to med school, did you? If mine asked me, I would talk him out of it."

How sad. "He surprised me when he told me that's what he wanted to do. I didn't talk him into medicine, but I sure didn't try to talk him out of it either."

"Why not? The hassles with insurance companies, regula-tion, and malpractice keep getting worse."

"He will have a career that challenges him, that encourages him to keep learning, lets him to do good for people every day, and brings him the respect of his community. He'll have a good reason to get out of bed every morning. How many bet-ter ways are there to make a living?"

PART FIVE

# FIRST PRACTICE
# VERO BEACH, FLORIDA
# 1984–1992

# CHAPTER 10

## NAME IN VAIN

O N THE MATERNITY ward in April 1987, I held Heidi's sweaty hand while she was in labor, our second child on the way. As her contractions intensified her grip strengthened too, crushing my fingers. With each painful wave, she shouted my name in an accusatory way, the words 'MichaelMichaelMichaelMichaelMichael' pouring out blame for her miserable and, if not for me, avoidable predicament.

Shifts changed during her hard labor, and the nurse who had been with us through the night wished us well and left. A few minutes later, just as Heidi began to have another contraction, a fresh perky nurse took her place. "MichaelMichaelMichaelMichaelMichaelMichael…"

"Top of the morning," she greeted us, "my name is Pat. I'll be your nurse the rest of the way. It's going to be an exciting day for the two of you!"

No niceties for Heidi. Her face was contorted: "MichaelMichaelMichaelMichaelMichaelMichael…"

So I said, "Hi Pat, this is Heidi and my name is Fred." Pat did a double-take. Poor girl. Heidi glared, roared, and tried to break my hand. Might not have been the best time for a joke.

---

**TODAY**                                      *Mar 10, 2013 10:54am*

I am not a great writer or blogger, but I know that when I had friends with Caring Bridge sites (and you know who you are!) that I would check the site lots because I wanted to know what was going on. So I'm trying to post for me, Michael and for you.

Michael and I are having a quiet weekend before he starts treatment tomorrow. I feel like we are 'squeezing the juice' of life—and just being together this weekend. We are taking walks, eating good food, and talking. It is beautiful weather and we are enjoying just being outside. Last night we went to Flemings for a jalapeno/cilantro margarita and a great steak. Then we came home to watch the Duke-Carolina game and stayed up too late.

Michael already took a walk, and we'll go to the greenway for another walk this afternoon. Later we will go to Minyan at Temple Israel. Tonight we are planning on doing one of Michael's favorite things to do on a Sunday—Chinese food and ice cream.

Love—Heidi

# MEDICAL ADVICE

"My nose has been driving me crazy since I saw you last week," I told my allergist. "I hope you figured out why I sneeze so much."

"No wonder," he said, "Your skin tests show you are allergic to so many things."

"Like what?"

"Well, you are very allergic to orange blossoms…"

"Wait, we live in the middle of an orange grove."

"I know. That's going to be a problem. You really are allergic. And you're also allergic to the usual things, like dust mites, mold, cats, dogs…"

"Hold on. I know I am allergic to cats. Whenever a cat owner comes into the office I get a sneezing fit and my eyes water. But my father was a vet, we always had dogs, how can I be allergic to dogs?"

"You have always had dogs but you have always been allergic too, right? Didn't you tell me that when you were a kid you even had to get your sinuses vacuumed out a couple times?"

"Wow, I can't believe it. What am I supposed to do?"

"We could do allergy shots; that would help. But this is a tough one, because you still have something in the house that you are allergic to. I know you love your dog, but if I were you I would find him a new home or you might never get better."

"Oh man, I love him and our kids do too. I really have to think about this." But I didn't think about it for long; Eno was our first child. My allergies didn't bother me nearly enough to break up our family. It surprised and annoyed me that my allergist, otherwise a sensitive guy, would casually give such upsetting advice.

A few days later I told him, in a morose tone, "I thought long and hard about what you said, that I should get rid of our dog. So this morning we took him to the vet and had him put to sleep."

He looked stricken. "You did what?? That's terrible."

The poor guy didn't get it. "I thought so too. I'm just pulling your chain. But you really should think twice about what you tell your patients."

Being a patient, I learned a lesson about being a doctor. People take seriously what we say. Words have an impact. I have to be careful that the treatment I prescribe and the advice I give is not more disruptive than the disease I am treating, or people will neither appreciate nor benefit from my attempt to help.


# REUNION


I WAS WADING through yesterday's mail before the first patient of the morning when someone knocked. "Yes?" It was Marie, from the reception desk.

"Doctor Rotberg, there's somebody here to see you."

"But our first appointment isn't for another fifteen minutes."

"I know, but it's not a patient. It's just some old lady who wants to see you."

"Did you tell her to make an appointment?"

"No, I told you, she's not a patient. She's here with another lady who came in to see one of the other doctors and wants to say hi to you. Can't you just come out and see what she wants?" She curled her index finger to get me moving.

"Oh, okay." I followed her down the hall to the front desk. Standing there was a tall, elderly woman with a wrinkled complexion and a tightly curled perm of thinning silver-blue hair, wearing a floral dress and thick glasses. When she saw me, she glanced toward the waiting room and nodded over her shoulder. Another woman, even older, gripped her walker, rocked back, and with obvious effort rose from her chair.

Before I could speak she barked, "Are you Michael Rotberg? Michael Rotberg from West Orange, New Jersey?"

"Uh, yes, that's me."

"Do you know who I am?"

I had no idea. "Can you give me a hint?"

"Do you remember the name of your fourth-grade teacher?"

I looked again. "No way. Are you Miss Schauwecker?" She smiled and nodded excitedly. "What are you doing here?"

"I am visiting my good friend Eleanor Noyes," and pointed to the little lady slowly sliding her walker toward us. She was my Principal at Pleasantdale School.

"Wow! I haven't seen either of you since I finished sixth grade. Miss Noyes lives in Vero Beach?"

"She does. And here she comes now."

I felt twelve years old. No way could I hug these women, so I shook their hands and asked, "How did you find me?"

"We didn't even know you were here. We weren't looking for you. Eleanor hurt her knee last week and has an appointment to see an orthopedist. We've been sitting in the waiting room with nothing to do, noticed your name on the wall, and had to find out if it was you."

"I can't believe it. Of all the gin joints in all the world, you walk into mine. And I'm flattered that you remember me from more than 20 years ago."

Miss Noyes said, "Do we remember you? Of course, we do. We still talk about that map you made on the blacktop behind the school when you were in fifth grade. It was amazing, it was perfect. We couldn't have paid someone to do a better job." Our class painted maps of the state, the country, and the world on the pavement behind the school. I was in charge of New Jersey. I drew a grid on a AAA road map, made a larger grid on the pavement, and then got kids to paint the map, square by square. "That's why we left it there for so many years."

"Well, I remember you too. Once you sent me to the drugstore to pick up Lomotil for you. I didn't even know what it was for." They laughed.

"And Miss Schauwecker, your fourth-grade class turned out to be so important for me. You taught us Braille and took us on a field trip to the Overbrook blind school, remember? You found a student there to be my pen pal. That was my first exposure to people with eye problems, so maybe you're why I became an eye doctor."

She beamed, but the reverie ended when Miss Noyes said, "Great to see you and all, but we've been sitting her so long my back is killing me. What I really want to know is if you can get my doctor to call me in already."

# CHAPTER 11

## FLYING LESSONS

"H ELLO?" I SAID, picking up the phone.
"Hey Mike, this is Terry, how ya doing?" He was a cardiologist in Vero Beach. Heidi and I were friendly with him and his wife.

"Oh hi. We're going to be seeing you two this weekend, aren't we?"

"Yeah, that's what I'm calling about. Karen and I are supposed to come over for dinner on Saturday night."

"Don't tell me you won't be able to make it."

"No, we really are looking forward to it. But I have something I have to do Saturday morning and thought you might want to come along for the ride."

"I'm wide open. What's going on?"

"I have to take the plane up to Sanford Airport to get the seat reupholstered. They told me if I show up by ten in the morning they will have the work done in a couple hours. It's only an hour each way, so we could be back in plenty of time for you to have the afternoon free to help Heidi get dinner ready."

"I didn't know you got your license already. And I sure didn't know you had a plane. I thought you just started to take flying lessons."

"No, I finished my lessons and got my license a couple months ago. I have more than fifty hours solo. But we do have to go during the day."

"Sure, if we have to be there by ten."

"Well, not only that. I still don't have my IFR.'

"Your what?"

"IFR, my instrument flight rating. It means I can only go when it is light out and I don't have to depend on instruments. I can't get my IFR for a few more months, but no problem. It's a short ride. Ever been in a small plane?"

I never had, so we agreed to meet at the Vero Airport at 8:30 on Saturday morning. I parked three spots from the terminal, walked in the front door and out the back right onto the tarmac. There was no security; the gate agent barely looked up from his book as I passed. Though the airport was busy with private and flight school traffic, the next commercial arrival wasn't due for hours. Squinting into the morning sun, I saw Terry walking around a small yellow plane. More than doing a preflight checklist, he was petting the machine.

"This Piper was built right here. I got it used, and it is good as new except for the seats. We might bounce a little on the way up, but the ride home should be very cushy," he boasted. "Ready to go?"

Climbing into the cockpit was like getting into a minivan with bad shocks. We closed the doors, started the engine, and stopped talking. The noise was physical, more felt than heard, like riding inside a lawnmower. After I put on my headset I could only see his mouth moving until he turned the intercom on. He smiled, gave me a thumb's up, and shouted, "We're cleared to take off."

The plane rolled onto the runway, turned and accelerated, and with a bounce was lifted airborne. The Piper was like a bumper car with wings. The sensation of speed as we hurtled down the runway and suddenly jumped into the air, the feeling of flying FLYING! was exhilarating. Terry dipped the wings left and right and then banked north when we crossed the beach. It was a sunny and cloudless day. I spotted our house, the bridges, the beach, and was entranced enough I didn't think about the flimsy machine encasing me.

After an hour or so, Terry pointed ahead to an airport, descended, and landed smoothly. He taxied to a hangar surrounded by derelict planes without wings or windows. He killed the engine, and once my ears stopped ringing, I heard him say, "All right, wasn't that cool?"

I had to agree. I had been on hundreds of flights, but none where I could see the runway as we took off and landed. He said, "I'll be right back. I have to make sure they start our job right away."

The airport was even smaller and quieter than the one we had left. Aside from an occasional prop plane coming or going, the moist breeze carried only the sounds of birds and bullfrogs. He returned from the upholsterer, "They are a couple guys short today, so it's going to be about an hour before they get to work on our seats."

There was nowhere to wait but a large quonset hut with a concrete floor, a couple of molded plastic chairs, and a soda machine. In the corner a black and white TV with rabbit ears produced audible conversation and visible static, radio in a snowstorm. Holding on to the antenna, we got enough of a picture to keep us occupied for a while, but after nursing our Cokes and pretending to be interested in the invisible golf tournament, we walked back to the shop. Still, no one was working on his plane.

For several more hours we tried to watch TV and strolled around the airport to check out the other planes. Every hour we returned to the upholstery shop, and finally at about three they pulled out the seats. It took two and a half hours. By the time we were ready to leave it was nearly 6 o'clock and the sun was setting. The new seats were more comfortable, but Terry was not. "Let's get out of here quick," he said. We strapped ourselves in, taxied and took off, and only when we climbed was there sunlight. "I think we'll be okay if we go straight home."

"Yeah," I agreed, "We probably won't be too late. Heidi will start the grill and maybe Karen will come over to meet us so you don't have to go home first."

"No, I'm not talking about being late for dinner. I'm talking about landing."

"What?" I shouted, hoping I had misunderstood him through the roar of the propellers.

"I have never flown in the dark, and I sure as hell have never landed in the dark. I'm pretty sure I can find the way back to Vero as long as we get there while there is still a little light to navigate by."

Just then, the ground disappeared under a cloud. We popped out, and he said, "I've never flown through clouds either." We pierced the clouds again and found ourselves flying above a solid gray layer that stretched away in all directions.

We flew Southeast in silence for about forty-five minutes when Terry said, "We should be pretty close to Vero now. Can you see the airport?"

"I can't even see the ground."

"If I get on the radio and ask the airport for a bearing they'll know I'm not IFR. Let's look for a clearing to pop through first."

"What if we don't find one? What if another plane doesn't see us as it climbs out of these clouds?"

"That won't happen. Everybody flying now has radar."

"Everybody but us, you mean."

He looked over and after a few minutes said, "I think if we go out over the ocean the clouds might break up." This did not reassure me.

"Where is the ocean? And, I thought you weren't supposed to take single engine planes out over the water, especially at night."

"Hey, we have a full tank and a working radio. We'll be fine."

What we did not have was a GPS or a cell phone, so Heidi was at home wondering where we were. Karen rang the bell expecting to be peeved at Terry for not calling before coming to dinner, but her anger flipped into worry that we had neither returned nor checked in. They talked for a while, then fired up the grill, put the steaks on to cook, and sat down to dinner without us. "They probably stopped off for a couple drinks at the airport bar and lost track of time," said Karen, not believing her words.

Meanwhile, late for dinner, we were still aloft. "Let's turn north toward Daytona and then out over the Gulf Stream. Somebody told me the weather pattern changes over there. We'll probably find a break in the clouds."

Far as I could tell, turning back and heading out to sea did not represent progress. "How is our fuel holding up?" I asked, prodding him to call air traffic control for help and directions.

"No problem," he responded airily. "We could probably fly another hour or so if we had to, and we're only a few minutes from home."

Soon, we did spot a gap in the cloud layer, held our breath, dove through it, and were surprised to emerge over Melbourne Airport, about thirty miles from home. So much for Daytona and the Gulf Stream. We flew low, under the clouds, and soon were on the ground in Vero.

In the car on the way to a late dinner Terry turned to me and said, "That was fun until the clouds came in, wasn't it? I have to fly to Okeechobee next Saturday. Wanna go?"

# CONFIDENT, NOT COCKY

SELF-CONFIDENCE AND COCKINESS are separated by a fuzzy line, but one is empowering and the other dangerous. Some doctors on the wrong side of that line carry their character flaws with them outside the office. Physicians are bright, curious, work long hours, and are tempted to pack intensive recreation into their limited free time. In combination with exaggerated self-confidence, this might be the reason doctor pilots have a reputation, possibly unfair, as being reckless in the air. One study years ago did find them to have a higher fatality rate than non-medical private pilots. But I witnessed firsthand the trouble that baseless confidence can cause. Trust has to be earned, and Terry lost mine.

People expect health care providers to be thorough and tenacious, resilient and hard-working, with confidence based on experience and expertise. Confident but not cocky. Physicians who are arrogant, self-important, or conceited may be skilled, but are incapable of the kind of clear eyed self-criticism that breeds excellence. They can also be unpleasant, even dangerous, company. Society holds doctors in such esteem that the praise and status make it easy to lose perspective.

One of my medical school classmates said, "Med school never turned an asshole into an angel, but it's sure changed some nice guys into jerks."

# CHAPTER 12

## ACUITY

THE PATIENT WAS in the office for her first post-op visit after cataract surgery. My assistant removed her patch, checked vision and pressure, and then escorted her back to the waiting room.

She didn't notice me watching as she grinned, giggled, and excitedly covered one eye, then the other, while looking around the room. When she spotted me I said, "Okay, why don't you come on in?" She popped right up and followed me down the hall. In the exam room, I asked, "How did it go last night?"

"I really did great. I was so nervous before the surgery, but just like you said, there was no pain when you were doing the operation and no problems last night either. I am so relieved I was finally brave enough to get this done."

"I am glad it's been a good experience. Let's take a look and then we can talk about how to care for your eye so it heals up perfectly."

She leaned forward to put her chin in the slit lamp and then suddenly pulled away. "You know, I guess you hear this from patients all the time, but this whole experience is totally amazing to me."

"You mean that you had an operation on your eye and didn't have any pain?"

"Yeah, that too. Definitely. But what I really can't believe is how much better I can already see this morning. People told me how cataract surgery makes colors so much brighter, but until it happens to you it is impossible to really get what they are talking about. It's not even 24 hours after surgery and already I see so well."

"That's great to hear."

"Like, you may think this is crazy, but would you believe that until today, when I went back to the waiting room after your assistant took my patch off, I always thought the carpet out there was kind of a drab gray color. But now I can see that it is royal blue. How did I miss that? I was seeing it totally wrong. I just can't get over it."

"That's great. I am so happy that things are going well. And the best thing is you are just starting to improve. So please lean forward and let me look at your colorful new eye."

I didn't tell her that the night before, workmen had pulled up the old gray carpet and replaced it with a new blue one.

That was dishonest but harmless fun. Other times, too much honesty can get a doctor in trouble. Without lying about what happened during surgery, the surgeon in this next story might have chosen his words better when he wrote his operative note after a difficult procedure.

# OP NOTE

EVERY MEDICAL STUDENT learns the importance of good documentation. If you didn't write it in the patient's chart, it didn't happen. I was saved from a malpractice suit by three little words I scribbled as an afterthought.

A local politician came to me because her eyes were red. That evening she was going to be interviewed on the news and didn't want to look sick or hungover. I gave her allergy drops to whiten her red, allergic eyes. Worried about the blinding TV studio lights, she didn't let me dilate her eyes that day, but never came back for a complete eye exam. Only because I ended my office note with the words, 'needs full exam,' was I blameless when a few months later another doctor discovered a tumor inside her eye that might have been present when I saw her. But sometimes even complete and candid records can cause problems.

"Hey Ed," I asked, "Have you ever been sued?" Ed Branigan and I, along with some other friends, had a standing Sunday morning bike ride when I lived in Vero Beach. We met at 10AM, or earlier in the summer, rode north through orange groves, over the Wabasso Causeway, down along the beach on A1A, and then back home across the 17TH Street Bridge. The bridges were our only hills, but we faced headwinds that could be even more challenging. Ed was an excellent ophthalmologist, a few years older than me, and we passed the miles talking about patients, politics, and college basketball.

"You mean malpractice? Never," he said.

"Long as you've been working and as many operations as you have done, that's amazing," I said.

"Well, there is a certain amount of luck, I guess, but I learned my lesson early about how important it is to keep good records."

"What do you mean?"

"I have a friend who is a retina specialist. Might be the world expert in endophthalmitis. You know, the terrible infections that sometimes happen after cataract surgery."

"Yeah. Did he get sued?"

"No, but he sees other people's complications. Whenever something goes wrong with an eye surgery in South Florida, chances are at some point he's going to get involved."

"What's the story?"

"Well, this was a patient he didn't even see. The insurance company wanted a second opinion about whether to defend a case. The surgeon wanted to fight it, but the company had a bad feeling, so they asked my friend to look at the chart. He called me to vent. What happened was, this guy got sued. He did cataract surgery, had some complications, and the patient ended up losing most of her vision in that eye."

"Did he lose the suit?"

"Oh yeah, that's what I'm telling you. He dug his own grave. They couldn't defend him. The case never even went to trial and his insurance company made him settle."

"What happened?"

"It was his Op Note that got him. He dictated it right after the operation ended. It started out normally, you know, 'First I did this, then I did that,' a normal Op Note," and Ed started laughing, barely squeezing out the words. "And then it said, 'but after the nurse dropped the cornea onto the freezing cryoprobe the entire operation turned to shit.'"

# INSCRUTABLE

MR. CHANG WAS A lab tech in our office. One day he button-holed me in the hall and told me that his elderly father, who lived in Taiwan, was planning to visit. Mr. Chang was tired of hearing his dad complain that he didn't see well, suspected he had cataracts, and asked me to take care of them while he was in town.

Several weeks later they came to see me. I could tell that it had taken some coercion to get him there and would take yet more before the senior Mr. Chang would agree to let me do anything. He looked like a Chinese version of American Goth-ic, bald, thin, and severe. His dark gray suit, starched shirt, and tie perfectly knotted over a loose collar projected formali-ty and suggested recent weight loss, but as the minutes passed he relaxed, smiled, and even laughed.

His son had to translate every step of the exam. If I said, "Look up," several seconds passed before the younger Mr. Chang said the Chinese equivalent, and even longer be-fore his father heard and responded. Checking him for glasses took forever, between translating every 'which is better,' the uncertainty caused by poor hearing, and the indecisiveness common to anyone whose poor vision makes seeing fine dis-tinctions difficult.

ME

"Mr. Chang, please ask your father if he sees better with the first lens or the second."

SON

"爸爸，你看到第一种镜片还是第二种镜片更清楚?"

(Dad, did you see the first or second way better?)

FATHER

"我都看不太清楚" (I can't see too clearly)

SON

"爸爸，不要读。只要告诉我哪个看的更清楚" (No Dad, don't read, just tell me which one is better.)

FATHER

"Da, Ah, Oh, Pa."

SON

"He sees fifth line."

ME

"No, he doesn't have to read yet. I just want him to tell me which way makes the letters easier to see."

SON

"这一次，请你告诉我哪一个更清楚" (This time, please tell me which one is better.)

FATHER

"Eh, Ge, En, Da, Ach." Etc, etc, etc.

He didn't seem to understand anything I said. The exam moved at a glacial pace, but by the end it was clear that he did have cataracts and was having a hard time reading, watching TV, and doing the things he needed to do. After explaining what cataracts were and what their removal entailed, I knew I was going to need extra help in the OR.

"Mr. Chang, please ask your father if he would like you to be in the operating room with him during his surgery. Having you there to translate would help him relax and would also make it easier for me to make sure he is comfortable and that nothing is bothering him."

After another prolonged exchange, he said, "No problem."

On the day of the surgery, I waited expectantly in the operating room. Finally, the nurses opened the door, and in rolled the elder Mr. Chang lying on a stretcher, followed by his son, wearing shoe covers, a mask, a bouffant cap, and a puffy white bunny suit over his clothes.

The nurses wheeled the stretcher next to the surgical bed, stopped, looked at me, and wordlessly asked, 'How is this going to work?' I said to the son, "Mr. Chang, please ask your father to move from the stretcher onto the bed." He leaned over, put his mouth a few inches from his father's ear, and paused. I expected several minutes of animated Chinese.

But instead, he shouted, "PA, GET ON BED!!" and without hesitation his dad slid right over. He had been sandbagging me. Later, when I asked the anesthetist if the patient was sedated enough for me to get started, the elder Mr. Chang's eyes popped open and he anxiously exclaimed, "Not Asleep!"

Language is rarely an insurmountable barrier, so effective communication depends on how information is presented. How much, if at all, should the discussion be skewed to make the decision turn out as the doctor thinks it should? In my opinion, not much. I try never to be a salesman but, as much as possible, an expert explainer and interpreter working for the patient's benefit.

# CHAPTER 13

## MAGIC WAND

A FTER SEVEN YEARS in Vero Beach I was bored. My patients seemed to appreciate me and work was often gratifying, but it was like practicing medicine on a desert island. In the 1980s there was no internet, no medical library, no medical school, no continuing education meetings, and no eye subspecialists nearby. I felt out of touch, isolated, and understimulated, and had no way to reassure myself of the quality of my work. The daily routine became repetitive and unexciting.

Also, my group practice began to implode. It was a large group with physicians in specialties ranging from family practice and pediatrics to cardiology and orthopedics. The business model favored some at the expense of others and fostered hostility and discontent. Group dynamics were toxic and going to the office was unpleasant. Seeking outside help to solve our problems, we sold the clinic to a practice management firm, but they didn't know what to do either. As they siphoned revenues for their investors, the atmosphere worsened, and one by one the best doctors began to leave.

When I came home from one of my weekly Sunday bike rides, Heidi could tell I was upset. She asked, "What's wrong? What's bothering you?"

"During the ride Neil told me that he's going to quit the group tomorrow."

"Oh no," she said. "He's your best friend in the group. But he has been unhappy for a long time."

"Yeah, but I hate that he's going to leave. I don't know what to do. So many of the best doctors have already left. Who's next? I don't want to be the last rat off this sinking ship."

She asked, "So what do you want to do?"

"Well, if good docs keep resigning, I guess at some point I will quit too. I will leave town, maybe go to Stuart or Melbourne and work until my 18-month restrictive is over, and then come back and either open a practice or maybe join Ed. I better figure it out."

"Is that what you really want to do?"

"What do you mean?"

"Well, if you could wave a magic wand and do anything at all, what would you want to do? Would it really be your first choice to commute to another town for 18 months?"

"I never thought about it that way, but no, I would just do that so we wouldn't have to move. But I never want to be in a group like this again, and I think Vero might be too small for us anyway. If you're really asking, if I could wave a magic wand, I guess in my fantasy I would use the time to refresh and recharge, do a fellowship in glaucoma and then join a group of good eye doctors, maybe back in North Carolina. That's where we met, we know lots of people there, and it would be halfway between our families in Florida and New Jersey."

She said, "Then poof, that is what you are going to do!"

"What are you talking about? I can't do that. I'd have to find a fellowship to get extra training, I'd have to leave town for a while, where will you and the kids be? I probably wouldn't have any income until it was over. And we'd have to move and uproot the kids." Our children were four and seven years old, had good friends, and were happy; I was reluctant to disrupt their stability.

"Well, that is why we've been working and saving all these years, to have the resources to do what you want. If that's what you want to do, go for it. We'll figure it out. You're 37 years old. Life is too short for you to be unhappy every day at work."

"You don't think this is just some kind of midlife crisis? Think I really should go for it?"

She smiled, "You surprised me. When I asked what you would do if you had a magic wand you actually had an answer. You didn't even hesitate. You've obviously been thinking about it. If this is a midlife crisis, I'm happy that what you want is more education and not a red sports car or a hot nurse."

With so many moving parts, it was an easier decision to make than to implement. Until I actually had a fellowship and job lined up, we couldn't tell anyone in Vero. We went to a medical meeting at Duke, where I ran into some friends from my residency. When I told them what I wanted to do I was shocked how excited and encouraging they were, and by the end of the weekend had informal offers to join several practices.

Next, I contacted the three teaching programs in Florida to see if any had openings for clinical fellows. At University of South Florida the Eye Department was in turmoil. The chairman had been forced out and now, in private practice, for the first time in his long career he was without anyone to teach. The new glaucoma specialist who took his place had to shoulder the entire burden of glaucoma care, surgeries and consults by himself. Though they wondered why someone with a thriving practice would leave it to work as an unpaid fellow, they welcomed me aboard.

After arranging the Fellowship, I decided that when it was over I would join a group in Charlotte and work, once again, alongside several of the best doctors from my training program. We had already worked together as residents; I knew them and they knew me. This gave me confidence that I was joining a high quality, ethical practice; I didn't want to make a mistake and have to move again.

The day I signed the contract, I resigned from the job in Vero Beach. We finally told our friends, and they were sad to lose us but supportive of our decision. I worked my notice period in Vero, Heidi continued to see therapy patients, the kids stayed in school. But we sold our house, moved into a rental, and prepared to cast off.

For the next six months, I spent weekdays in Tampa, drove home on Friday afternoon, and then back again on Sunday night or early Monday morning. While away, I was lonely and missed Heidi and the kids. But I had nothing to do except study and learn. I read in the medical library every night until it closed, helped staff the resident clinics, and assisted them with surgery. I even taught my professors modern cataract surgery.

Several of my doctor friends in Vero said they envied me. One admitted, "I'd love to go back and do a fellowship, that would be a dream. But I could never do what you're doing. I have the golden handcuffs; way too many expenses to take that kind of time off."

It was a thrillingly invigorating and rejuvenating experience and laid the foundation for my subsequent career in Charlotte. One of the most loving gifts Heidi ever gave me was the magic wand and the freedom to dream. It is always better to live your dreams than your fears.

## SEEK HELP

No one knows everything. No one knows everything about anything. Even experts sometimes need to ask for advice. During medical school, I noticed that full professors were more likely to say, "I don't know," than were junior faculty or residents. Back then, if I said, "I don't know," I was confessing that I didn't know something I should have. But when professors said, "I don't know," it really meant, "This is something that is not known," and rather than being an embarrassing admission, indicated secure command of their fields.

One of the nicest things about practicing in a large group was the easy access it gave me to second opinions. This was good for my patients and good for me. If I was puzzled by a patient or unsure what I was seeing in her eyes, I did not have to inconvenience her and delay care by sending her to another doctor's office or out of town. All I had to do was walk down the hall and ask one of my partners, "Hey, would you take a look at someone for me?" Rather than making the patient uneasy that I didn't know what was going on, it usually made her feel good to see me taking her complaints seriously enough to put my head together with another specialist for her benefit. More than once, I had a conversation that went something like this:

"Uh, don't take this wrong, but would you mind if I got a second opinion about this surgery you say I need?"

"Of course not. I wish you would."

"Really, that's great. When I said that to my last eye doctor he said, 'What's the matter? You don't trust me anymore?'"

"Well, the way I see it, if you get a second opinion, consultants will either tell you that what I advised you to do was right, and you'll be able to have surgery knowing that it's the right thing. Or if they disagree, you'll avoid surgery and I will learn something that might help me with other patients in the future. I'm happy you asked for a second opinion; we can set it up if you like."

A confident doctor welcomes the opportunity to learn and to enlist help in offering state of the art care. And just as I rely upon consultants at work, I also look to friends and family, especially my psychologist wife, for wisdom and guidance when dealing with uncertainty outside the office.

---

**DAY 1 OF TREATMENT**                    *Mar 11, 2013 4:01am*

Today is the first day of Michael getting better.

He has 4 hours of chemotherapy this morning at Dr. Mahoney's office, then late this afternoon he has his first radiation treatment at Dr. Plunkett's office. Both are in outpatient settings.

The chemo is TAXOL & CARBOPLATIN. The chemo is once a week for 6–7 weeks.

The radiation is 5 days/week for 6–7 weeks.

I am going to recommend a website—it is from the foundation run by Scott Hamilton, the Olympic skater. A strange but fun thing that Michael and I do—after the winter Olympics we go to Stars on Ice (or whatever it is called that year) to see the skaters on tour. I LOVE Olympic ice dancing, and am mesmerized by the whole skating thing. Michael totally indulges me in this, and makes comments like "Look how fast they go!" The website,

Chemocare.com, has excellent info about chemo, because I know you may want more information than I am providing.

Love—Heidi

---

**Gorgeous spring day in Charlotte**        *Mar 12, 2013 5:20pm*

It is gorgeous today—crisp, clear, sunny. Michael was outside in his new sun hat (the chemo can make him sensitive to the sun) enjoying just taking a walk and sitting on the back deck. He drove himself to radiation, and took a walk on the Greenway too.

Both chemo and radiation went really well yesterday. He was at the chemo center for about five hours, then we came home for lunch and then went to radiation. He will be at chemo every Monday morning, and radiation M-F at 4pm.

I don't think I'll be writing daily, as the pace of new events has slowed down (YAY!), but I really wanted to write about something important today.

This Caring Bridge site, and every single one of you who have visited and posted, is love. When we read the posts we feel loved, and I believe—I KNOW—that this love is part of Michael's healing. I recently read the book Proof of Heaven by Eben Alexander (who was a classmate of Michaels at Duke Med School). Eben had an experience of near death, and when he recovered he came back to this life to share with all of us that love is "the single most important emotional truth in the universe."

We all want to love and be loved. Thank you for loving Michael and me.

Love—Heidi

**SECOND OPINIONS**                                    *Mar 15, 2013 1:15pm*

Another beautiful day in Charlotte! It will be in the 70s here
tomorrow! I will probably set up my hammock in the morning, and
then lying in the shade slathered with sunscreen will read in the
hammock (in other words, take a nap while pretending to read).

Many people have reached out to us and asked us about 'second
opinions'. Since it was only a few days between the first inkling of a
problem and the start of treatment some people seem to be
concerned that we did not take time to consider other options. I
know this comes from a place of caring, so let me try to bring you
some peace of mind about this.

My CT and PET scans were reviewed by at least 4 radiologists in
Charlotte. Some were affiliated with CMC and some with Novant.
That was before the pathology came back with the diagnosis. Once
the path report was in, another 5 Radiation Oncologists reviewed
the pathology, labs, and the scans to discuss the best way to
approach this disease.

I am fortunate to have college and med school classmates who are
taking this further. One friend runs a hospital, another runs a med
school, and another is the head of oncology at a major medical
center. My records have already been Fed Ex'd and are being
reviewed. In addition, I personally called the pathologist who
made the histological diagnosis and she is sending my slides to the
guy she described as 'the world expert.' I want to be fully focused
on my treatment and recovery—not getting more info at this point.
I am allowing others to help me, and us, by doing all the opinion
gathering for us. There is no need for me to personally go
anywhere else to be examined since my exam remains totally
normal —the tumor is only apparent on the scans and the lab tests.

So we have gotten other opinions and continue to wait for more doctors to weigh in.

But the most important thing I can convey is that I have total confidence that I am getting the best care here in Charlotte. We have an excellent medical community, one that I am proud to be a part of. My doctors are excellent, up to date, and compassionate. While we await the reports from out of town, I am convinced that this is the treatment that I need right now. There is no room for doubt in our minds; we are totally committed to getting me well.

Michael

# PART SIX

# CHARLOTTE
# 1992-TODAY

# CHAPTER 14

# RUTABAGA JACK

J UST BEFORE I started practicing in Charlotte, the head of Human Resources explained, "Usually new doctors start out with one employee to help with patients and another to schedule surgeries, lab tests, and that sort of thing."

I asked if she had any candidates in mind. "Well, I have somebody I think you will really like for the secretarial position. She has worked in one of our other offices for a few years and is very good, but has a new baby and wants to shorten her commute. From where she lives, it's about 45 minutes each way. The doctor she works for hates to see her go, but understands she wants to work closer to home."

"OK, when can I meet her?"

"Well, I should tell you, she is African American. You don't have a problem with that, do you?"

"I'll work with anyone who does a good job." That was Carol, and it worked out more than fine for over twenty years.

"Now, for your medical assistant, I have someone who is new to the practice. She just graduated from her training program and does not have much experience but seems personable and willing to learn. Sort of a blank slate. It might be good for you to be able to teach her the way you like the office to run rather than having to retrain someone who is used to another doctor's style."

She appeared for the interview with heavy makeup, a tremulous, country voice, and dark hair swept, windblown, above her forehead. I hired her, but it was a mistake. Her hands shook when she took blood pressures. I had to double check prescriptions when she read glasses in the lensometer. She never even figured out how to use the pinhole. God forbid she should try to refract.

Although my new office was not busy, she couldn't keep up with our low volume of patients, wasn't able to learn new skills, and had no common sense. One day I heard her calling a patient from the waiting room. She shouted, each time more loudly, and finally came back into the office saying, "I don't know where this person could have got to. He signed in, but I called and called, I walked all around the waiting room yelling his name and nobody answered." As you imagine her voice, think Barney Fife.

I said, "Well, maybe he went to the bathroom. Wait a few minutes and try again."

The next time she held the door open so I was able to hear as she called out, "Mr. Jack. Mr. Jack. Rutabaga Jack." Some joker had signed in with a fake name, and she had no idea she was being pranked. Exasperated, she came back inside, oblivious to the snickering people in the waiting room. "I can't find

Mr. Jack anywhere." But soon she did find a new career. Patients rightly judge me by the quality of my team.

# ITCHY

EVERY YEAR OUR practice hosts more than a hundred optometrists for a day of continuing education. We give talks on eye care and new research and invite patients with unusual eye problems to come in to teach as well, by being examined.

My first year in Charlotte I was excited to present one of my surgery patients. I had just started doing glaucoma implants, tiny tubes that drain excess pressure from the eye. Since no one else in town performed this procedure, I figured none of the optometrists and few of my partners had ever seen an implant tube in person. A couple weeks before Grand Rounds I operated on a man in his 40s, an unemployed, poorly controlled diabetic with neovascular glaucoma. He neither took his eye drops nor controlled his sugars, drank too much, and came to appointments in dirty clothes, unshaven, looking as if he rolled out of bed directly into his car. He switched to me when the eye doctor in his home town, an hour away, refused to see him anymore. I arranged his two-week post-op visit for early Saturday morning before the optometrists arrived.

Surprisingly, he showed up right on time. He looked great; the eye was healing well. I was proud to show him off to visiting doctors who might start referring patients to me. Martin, our most senior partner, cracked the door and asked, "Do you have a patient here for Grand Rounds?"

"I do. It is a guy with a Baerveldt implant that I placed a couple weeks ago."

"That's great! I've never seen one of those. Let me take a peek before it gets crowded." He introduced himself, "OK sir, please lean forward and put your chin right here so I can take a look. I bet you have been through this a few times before, haven't you?"

Martin flicked off the lights, picked up a Q-tip, and used it to raise the upper lid. "Very nice suturing, looks like it is healing well. Nice deep anterior chamber. And the tube is in perfect position! Isn't that amazing. Who would believe you could do that to an eye?" He paused, "Wait a minute, oh boy, what do we have here? Will you look at that?"

I stopped feeling so proud of myself and asked, "What? What do you see?"

He pushed back from the slit lamp, handed the Q-tip to me, and said, "Go ahead and check out the lashes on the upper lid."

I guided the patient back into position, raised the upper lid slightly, everting the lashes. Something moved. What? Then something else moved. Oh no! He had lice in his eye lashes! My head started to itch. I looked at Martin and he smiled. We excused ourselves and went into the hall.

"Martin, you have to help me out! I can't have a hundred optometrists look at this guy. They will never send me another patient. And if they get lice I'll have to leave town. What a disaster!"

"No problem," he said as we went back in to see the patient to tell him what we had found.

The man said, "Oh, I had lice on my head a few weeks ago." Martin took him downstairs to an exam room, plucked the lice off one by one with a forceps, prescribed medicine, and sent him home. And I had to make up a story about why my surgery patient failed to show up for Grand Rounds.

# HUMILITY

RESPECTED BY PATIENTS, deferred to by nurses, courted by sycophantic salesmen and hospital administrators, and pursued by mothers for their single daughters, some doctors find it hard to keep their heads on straight. But trying to remain humble and to avoid taking myself too seriously is as important to being a good physician as it is to being a good person.

I love the New Yorker cartoon with two angels talking in heaven. One has a huge halo, and sheepishly admits to the other, 'Ironically, it's for being so humble.' It would be oxymoronic, and just plain moronic, to claim that I am good at being humble. My obvious failings make it impossible for me to get too full of myself.

My father was a bright and hard-working man, who was a veterinarian but always wished he could have been a physician. Rightly or not, he felt he was denied admission to medical school in the 1940s because of religious quotas that many universities used to restrict the number of Jewish students. When my first acceptance letter arrived, he told me he was surprised how dramatically standards must have slipped.

While in college, I spent summers working in factories, one that made lighting fixtures and another that repaired factory motors. In comparison, seeing patients is easy. In medicine, I never had to spray toxic solvents, lie in a grease pit, or get my hands so filthy that it took three months to get them clean. While wearing a white coat, I never had to duck a razor knife tossed by a co-worker. That was real work, hot, exhausting, dangerous, and underpaid.

So, no matter how long my hours, how sick my patients, or how afflicted by insurance companies, I never doubt that I am one of the lucky ones, privileged to do what I do. I may feel put upon, but I realize that plenty of people work a lot harder for a lot less money, status, and recognition. And if I ever forget I'm not such a big shot, my patient's lice reminds me.

# TUESDAY

As MUSIC PLAYED in the background, I pushed my stool back from the operating microscope, placed the ultrasound handpiece on the Mayo stand, and asked the scrub nurse, "Christie, this singer has such a beautiful voice. What did you say her name was?"

"She's the one I told you about last week, remember? Eva Cassidy. I can't believe I finally found some music that you never heard before. Isn't she great?"

"Can I borrow this disc? I need to make a copy of it."

"She only made three or four CDs. It's such a sad story. She died a few years ago. Melanoma, I think. Really young, too."

"Well, what a voice." The patient laying under the drapes snorted and quaked. "Everything all right down there, Mr. Fitzgerald?"

"Sorry doc, I think I fell asleep. But nothing hurts. How's it going?"

"The hard part at the center of the cataract is already out, and everything is going fine. Just stay awake, hold still, and we'll be done pretty soon. Christie, can I have the I/A now?" I was ten minutes into the second cataract surgery of the day, a few steps from inserting the lens implant and the end of the case. Focusing through the microscope, a suction probe in my hand, I concentrated on the delicate maneuvers required to safely remove a cataract through a tiny incision. I heard the door opening and peered over the eyepieces to see that a nurse had poked her head into the OR. When I took my foot off the pedal and looked up she said, "A plane just flew into the World Trade Center in New York."

I thought of King Kong. "What was it, a little Piper Cub?"

"I don't know, but there's a fire up near the top of the building."

"Whoa," I said as she turned and left. "Did you hear that Mr. Fitzgerald?"

He didn't respond, so I put the instrument back in his eye and resumed the business at hand. Just after I inserted the lens implant the same nurse came back into the room, this time throwing the door open more forcefully. "Another plane just flew into the other tower. That one is on fire too."

"What?"

"Oh yeah, and they weren't little planes. They were airliners." No one said a word. The only sound was Eva Cassidy's spectacular voice.

We looked at each other, and I said, "Let's concentrate on what we're doing, finish this case, and then figure out what happened, all right?"

Within five minutes the case was over and we wheeled the patient into the recovery room. There, the TV up near the ceiling, which normally droned on unwatched, was the focus of attention for three patients and a dozen staff standing, faces tilted up to the screen, somber, silent and tearful. One of the nurses said, "I just heard the other hospitals in town are cancelling elective surgery in case they need the ORs, you know, if something like that happens here. Nobody knows what's going on."

"Are we shutting down too?"

"Only the inpatient ORs. They didn't tell us to clear the schedule here."

"I guess this outpatient center isn't really set up to handle major trauma, but who would want to have elective surgery today anyway? I bet the rest of my day is going to cancel. I kinda hope they do."

In the next room two more cataract patients were already dilating. CNN was on their TV too. I said to one of them, "You know what's going on in New York and Washington, right?"

"Yeah, terrible, just terrible. I feel awful about this. Those poor people on the planes and in those towers."

"So, you don't want to do your surgery today, do you? Wouldn't you rather just go home, hunker down, and come back in a week or two?"

"No way. I got up real early to come here today, got my neighbor to drive me, they already started an IV and gave me drops. Let's just get it done."

"This is like having surgery on Pearl Harbor Day. Are you sure?"

"If you'll do it I want to get it done."

The rest of the day's patients felt the same way, could not be dissuaded, wanted some good to come from this historically awful day. Their impulse was affirmation that life goes on, that there will be a tomorrow, and that tragedy needs to be acknowledged but transcended. The staff and I endured the rest of the schedule and the patients did well. But that night our practice called off its monthly meeting. No was in the mood to haggle about the call schedule or which equipment to buy. None of that seemed important. We needed to be home with the TV off, hugging our kids.

The nurses and I did not want to continue as if it was a normal day. None of us was interested in doing routine cataract surgery, which could safely wait, when the fate of our country and the safety of our families were at risk. But the patients took off work, arranged transportation, and had psychologically prepared themselves and their families for surgery. Having cataract surgery was by far the most important thing they were planning to do that day, so to postpone for our own comfort would have been selfish and wrong. They could have chosen someone else to remove their cataracts but had honored me by trusting me to do their surgery. I was grateful that they had, did not want to take this gift for granted, and owed it to them to be a good steward of that trust.

Fortunately, we managed to focus on the task at hand well enough to take care of everyone who happened to be scheduled on that memorable day. Patients' needs come first.

## BE SERVICE ORIENTED

MEDICINE IS A calling, a profession, an intellectually challenging career, an academic discipline, a way of life. But while it is all of that, the essence of clinical practice is service. Taking care of patients is a unique service industry, because to satisfy my 'customers' I sometimes have to walk the tightrope between doing what they want and giving the advice and care they actually need, often two very different things.

Medicine does have some characteristics common to other service businesses: I need to be courteous, must be available to our clients, need to respect their privacy, and should take their concerns seriously and explain things understandably. I should not aggressively sell services or products. Their interests must remain my only concern. Sometimes, as Steve Jobs said, they may not really know what they want until I educate them about their options, but selling medical services is different than selling iPhones. It is done face to face, one on one, person to person, and involves decisions with life changing consequences. I cannot abuse their trust, and patients need to know that the advice I am giving is based only on their welfare.

Still, keeping the patient happy is impossible with limited office hours, long wait times, shabby furniture, or harried staff. Do patients complain about the front desk, billing department, or poor customer service? Do they feel valued and welcome? Do I adjust my staffing and design my facility for the type of people who are likely to come through the door? When I go to my own doctor's office do I enjoy the experience? What's different there?

A few years ago, one of my partners, who is bilingual, told the Eye department, "You know, our population of Spanish speaking patients is growing so fast it's getting to be a problem for my office. The switchboard only has one operator who speaks Spanish, and if she's tied up the calls get shunted to me. I'm always being interrupted, and it's becoming a real burden. If we're going to serve our Hispanic patients properly, we need to upgrade our phone answering services."

Everyone agreed it was the right thing to do, and we decided to hire more bilingual operators and front desk receptionists. But I couldn't waste the straight line, and deadpanned, "I take care of a lot of patients from the Jewish community. If we're going to serve them properly, we need to upgrade our complaints department too." Only I can tell a joke about my mother.

SUNDAY 3/17                               *Mar 17, 2013 6:41am*

Hi—we are having a fantastic weekend. It feels like we have been given a gift of a perfect little space this weekend. It was 76 degrees yesterday—and the air felt soft like spring. I went out for fresh bagels and coffee (NOT a typical event!) and we had breakfast while watching the birds. After a long walk we went to the library and Michael stocked up on books. The hammock went up after lunch—and it was a PERFECT hammock afternoon. In addition to doing some visualization[1] and relaxation practice, Michael also had a massage—then went back to the hammock. Dinner with friends and a little college basketball—great day. Michael still feels great but as he goes into his second chemo treatment tomorrow we just don't know what to expect. So we are trying to be mindful and stay in this moment and accept this gift of time.

So today looks like another beautiful day to spend together, enjoying.

**WEEK 2 OF TREATMENT OFF TO A GREAT START**

Hi—Michael had his second day of          *Mar 19, 2013 7:02am*
Chemo+Radiation yesterday. Here is how the day goes. We check into the Chemo center before 9am, and then after Michael has his vitals checked we see Dr. Mahoney. He said he knew Michael would tolerate the chemo well as he is so strong physically. Then we go into the infusion room and MIchael gets into a recliner. The RN starts an I.V., and draws blood to check Michael's counts. Once that comes back (30–45 min) the chemo starts. First premeds—things to make the actual chemo drugs easier like a strong antihistamine and a steroid. Then the Taxol for an hour, then the Carboplatin. Michael reads, does relaxation and

---

1. Also known as guided imagery, a way to influence mood and healing through the imagination. In sports, visualizing yourself making a putt or foul shot rehearses the event, helps calm the nerves, and may improve the odds of success. It is unclear if imagining a tumor being nibbled away actually makes it dissolve, but does it make the possibility of healing more plausible and optimism seem more justified.

visualization, drinks lots of water and juices, eats salty snacks so he drinks more water and juices. If he wants to move around he can unplug the I.V. Yesterday we left at 12:30 and when we got home Michael had a turkey sandwich on a bagel, a side of stuffing and more water.

It was cold and rainy here yesterday, so the afternoon nap was perfect. Then to Matthews for radiation at 4 pm.

The best part of yesterday for Michael was he went to his monthly Men's Group meeting. This is an interfaith group of men that has been meeting for about 6 years, started by one of Michael's partners and facilitated by a minister. The men have dinner together, then talk about a topic involving faith/values/morals/life and death. No sports, work, or car talk. Michael was a philosophy major and really loves this group—and the guys who are now friends. After a wonderful dinner the guys had an evening together talking about all kinds of spiritual things. Michael felt very loved and supported. He came home at around 9:30 and was still smiling.

So it continues. Even falling down the rabbit hole into this alternative universe of Michael having cancer, life is sweet.

Love—Heidi

# CHAPTER 15

## PASSING GRADE

B Y THE TIME patients roll in to the operating room, their nerves, insomnia, and pre-op sedation have unpredictable effects. Under local anesthesia some people clam up, others become talkative. Many are so afraid that speaking might make them move and interfere with surgery that they don't make a peep until the case is over. Then, flooded with relief, all the words that were dammed up pour out in a torrent. Others become disinhibited and ramble, tell jokes, sing, and display their stream of consciousness. The microscope magnifies tiny movements; an unpredictable twitch or sudden jerk of the head can be disastrous, so during the most delicate parts of a procedure, I ask patients to be quiet, but they don't always listen.

One man repeated, "I'm driving in darkness, yes I am driving in darkness," throughout his cataract operation. He must have said it twenty times. I was curious what he meant, but hesitated to encourage conversation, and never found out because by the end of the case he didn't remember saying it. Another called me over to the bed when she rolled into the room, grabbed my arm, looked right at me and pleaded, "Dr. Rotberg, please save my sight!" Not helpful.

Dr. Miller was my son's high school calculus teacher. She was a bright person with a logical approach to her cataract surgery. She asked good questions in the office, understood what to expect, and in the pre-op area was quiet and relaxed. In the OR the nurses cleaned her face, I placed the sterile drapes, leaving only the operative eye exposed, and repeated the exact words I already said at her recent office visit. "You will feel me touching you, you will feel cold water, and you will see bright colorful lights, but nothing will hurt, nothing will bother you, and this will be over before you know it."

This is the script I use with every patient. In the office I look people in the eye as I say these words, and when I get to, "You will feel me touching you," I touch their forearm to add a sensory component to the message. Repeating the same words in the operating room serves as both a reminder and a subtle hypnotic suggestion. One of the nurse anesthetists, having heard this hundreds of times, once gave a sarcastic, backhand, circular wave, and echoing Obi Wan Kenobi, softly muttered, "These aren't the droids you're looking for."

But Dr. Miller was immune to my hypnotic suggestions. When I sat down to start the procedure, from under the drapes she announced, "Doc, just one more thing; better do a good job today or your kid won't get an A."

She was disinhibited by drugs, insomnia, and anxiety, and used humor to make sure I was paying attention. You should be a forceful and informed self-advocate, asking for more information or a second opinion if that's what it takes to wrap your head around your situation and to understand your options. Come to the office organized, think in advance about the appointment and write down a list of questions to bring with you. If my answers don't make sense, keep asking until they do, or I may be fooled into believing that I have done a good job of explaining a complicated situation in an understandable way. Don't be ashamed of what you don't know; you've never heard of congenital glaucoma or macular pucker before. So don't hesitate to ask questions, but also be sure to listen to the answers.

# BE ACTIVE PARTICIPANTS

NO DOCTOR EVER cares as much about you as you do, so you need to be your own best advocate. Learn about your condition. Go online to reputable websites and become an expert. Find out if there are patient support groups in your community. Don't avoid information, seek it out, learn about relevant clinical trials, get second opinions. Keep track of your appointments, your treatments and medications, your test results, and any procedures you've had. Doesn't matter if you keep a paper file or do it online, just be sure to collect and keep the information.

Delegate some authority to your doctor, but don't allow yourself to become overawed or intimidated. It is important to be an active participant in your care, and you are more likely to be on board with a treatment plan if you understand and have collaborated on its development. Inevitably, there is an imbalance in all doctor-patient relationships, because no matter how many websites you visit, the physician should have more medical knowledge and experience than you do. But on the other side of the partnership, you have an infinitely greater personal stake in your doing well. No one should care more for your welfare than you do.

# PROSTHESIS

SHANQAVIA HAD A homemade name, an unmarried 16-year old mother, and ambiguous paternity.

But, as if three strikes were not enough, the unfortunate kid also had a serious eye disease. When she was only a week old her grandma noticed that bright light made the child cry, and wondered why one of her eyes was red, watery, and larger than the other. The pediatrician realized that the large eye also had a hazy cornea and sent her to us to figure out what was wrong.

A pediatric ophthalmologist and I put her to sleep in the operating room for an exam under anesthesia. The pressure in the large eye was high, in the 40s, the cornea was swollen and translucent. We could not see the optic nerve but by the way the pupils reacted we could tell that it was damaged too. This was congenital glaucoma, which effects about one in every 10,000 infants. Luckily, the other eye was fine.

Surgery can cure this kind of glaucoma. Unfortunately though, the operation went well but didn't work; the pressure remained high. A few weeks later I took her back to the operating room to insert a glaucoma implant. The pressure normalized and the cornea cleared. A few weeks after surgery she stopped coming back for post-op visits. Her mother did not answer our phone calls and certified letters to arrange ongoing care.

She didn't return for several years until, while running around at home, she tripped and hit her bad eye on the corner of a coffee table. Her eye exploded, a ruptured globe. The doctor on call repaired the eye wall but could not salvage any vision. Weeks later the pressure spiked again. We only care about high eye pressure because it damages vision. In a blind eye, like this one, elevated pressure cannot do further harm. But her pressure was so high it was painful. An eye that is totally blind, intractably painful, and visibly damaged needs to be removed.

Finally, after weeks of trying to control the pressure and the inflammation, I sat down with Shanqavia and her mother. She was now almost 4 and mom was 20.

"You know we have tried everything. She's never going to get vision back in this eye. Even to partly control the pain she will have to be on three or four different kinds of eye drops every day for the rest of her life. That gets to be expensive and irritating and most people can't keep it up for long. You will be hassling with her and her drops several times a day, and for what? I think that a blind painful eye is like an abscessed tooth. Did you ever have a toothache?"

"Yeah."

"I bet you didn't feel good again until the dentist pulled your bad tooth. If we remove your daughter's bad eye she will be comfortable and won't have to use most of her drops anymore."

"But won't it look really bad?" she asked.

"It looks pretty bad right now, doesn't it?" Her eye was red and watery, she squinted in bright light, and the cornea was gray. Anyone could see she had a sick eye. "The surgery will make her look so much better. Within just a few weeks the eye will look normal again."

"How does that happen?"

"After she heals for a month or two we can fit her with a prosthesis, an artificial eye, that is handmade to look exactly like the other eye. Nobody will be able to tell that there is anything wrong unless they do an eye exam."

"Then she can get glasses too?"

"She can, and she should wear shatter proof glasses all the time anyway to protect her good eye."

"Well, I hate to think about it, but it sounds like that is the right thing to do. It will be so good for her to have two good eyes again. I don't think she sees right with just one."

"Uh, no. Her new eye will look good, but it is a glass eye. It looks normal, but it cannot see."

"Well give her the kind that looks good and also can see, OK."

"I better explain this again."

Your doctors need to be sure the message gets through. You need to ask for explanations in clear language. Once you understand where you stand, try to stick to the plan. Take your medicine. Keep your appointments. Do what you need to do now and put less urgent tasks on the back burner. And above all, be resilient. There are bumps and potholes in every road, but that doesn't mean you won't get where you're going. Keep your eye on the journey and remain thankful for the help you get along the way.

# COUNTING ON A MIRACLE

"I KNOW IT is hard to remember to take your eye drops. You wish you didn't have to. Sometimes they sting, and they're not cheap either. But if you don't use them reliably you will slowly lose your vision, and then it will be too late to do anything about it."

"Well Dr. Rotberg, my mother lost her vision, my auntie did too, so I think I am just going to leave it in the hands of the Lord."

"I bet they didn't take care of themselves either. Maybe they didn't have insurance. Maybe they didn't get to the doctor in time. But you have a chance to hold onto your sight for the rest of your life if you will only take your drops. With glaucoma, like with so many other things, it's a lot better to try to stay out of trouble than to try to get out of trouble, don't you think?"

"If the Lord wants me to see I will see and if he wants me to go blind I won't complain either."

I paused, and said, "Okay, I hear you, but listen. I am going to tell you a story. Did you ever hear the one about the lady who bought a house by the river?

"Uh uh."

"It's such an old one I don't think anybody knows who came up with it, but here goes. There was a lady who told her friend that she was going to move close to the river. When her friend heard where it was, she said, 'Don't buy that house. Whenever it rains hard it floods down there.' But she bought it anyway, and told her friend, 'The Lord will protect me.'

"A few weeks later she was watching the news and the weatherman said, 'We are expecting heavy rain and flooding tonight. If you live in low-lying areas near the river you should move to higher ground now.' Police cars cruised her street announcing the evacuation order through loudspeakers. But she stayed put, because she knew that the Lord would take care of her.

"The next day the river overflowed its banks, her house flooded, and she climbed onto the roof. A neighbor came by in a rowboat, but she sent him away. A helicopter came to rescue her, but she waved it off, knowing that the Lord would protect her.

"Then she drowned. She couldn't believe it. When she got to heaven she was angry. She said, 'Lord, I am so upset with you. I trusted that you would be there for me, and now look where I am.'

"And he said, 'Lady, calm down. What did you want me to do? I told your friend to talk to you, I put it on the news, I sent the police car, I sent a boat, even a helicopter. What were you looking for, a miracle? I did my part, why didn't you do yours?'"

"Yeah, I've heard that story. But what's it got to do with me?"

"What I am saying is, the Lord will help you hold onto your vision if you do your part too. The Lord helps those who help themselves. That is why he helped the drug companies figure out how to make medicine to control your glaucoma and that is why he brought you to my office. But you have to use the tools he put in this world, the everyday miracles He made for you. If you take your drops and keep your appointments, you won't need to split the Red Sea to save your sight."

# CHAPTER 16

## DOCTORS: MIND/BODY/SPIRIT

I LOVE TO see families riding bikes in the park. This whole-some activity combines the joy of exercise with the enjoy-ment of being together. So why do many parents make their children wear bike helmets but ride without wearing their own? Will their kids grow up believing that bike helmets are important, or are they more likely to dream of the day they can ride like grown-ups, with the wind blowing through their hair and their skulls unprotected?

How about parents who drop their children off at Sunday School and then go out for coffee instead of to worship? Ad-vice is cheap if you don't walk the walk.

Similarly, will patients listen to an obese physician who lec-tures them about the benefits of weight loss and exercise? Will people stop smoking if the doctor still does? To be a good physician I have to be a good role model. Not a saint or an angel, not a teetotaler or triathlete, but someone who tries to embody the advice I give, whose lifestyle sets an example that patients can admire and to which they can aspire. Word and deed need to be aligned, body and mind in harmony.

Effective healing also needs to recognize the limits of medical knowledge and to acknowledge that the patient's wholehearted participation is indispensable to healing. If patients believe that treatment cannot work or that they are impotent to improve themselves, the odds are longer than if they know they can effect a change. Superstitious, unfounded, negative beliefs and mindsets can subvert the doctor patient relationship and inhibit recovery.

Imagine an elderly man with glaucoma. He knows he might go blind if he fails to take his eye drops and keep his appointments. If his mother also had glaucoma and ultimately lost her vision, he might be even more inclined to take his disease seriously and to compulsively care for his eyes. But as in the story of the patient resigned to a poor outcome, sometimes the opposite is true. Several patients have told me, "Nah, to be honest, I don't usually take my drops. Why should I? My mom took hers and still went blind anyway. If it's God's will, there's nothing I can do but pray on it." These people need an attitude adjustment. They need to see that their approach is neither helpful nor appropriate. They can overcome their illness. Treatment can work. There is another way to interpret their family history. Rather than learning hopelessness and fatalism, they need to absorb a different lesson, the importance of being active, proactive, and hopeful. I like that old story about the house in the floodplain to drive the message home. Sometimes the message gets through; often it does not.

# ANSWERED PRAYERS

Caleb was legally blind due to Toxoplasmosis, a rare eye problem that was diagnosed in infancy. His vision was poor because of scarring in both retinas. Never able to focus, his eyes constantly danced, jiggling side to side and up and down, a condition called nystagmus. He also had glaucoma due to iritis, recurrent inflammation inside his eyes. We met when, in his fifties, his glaucoma escaped control and threatened to erase what little vision remained.

Seeing him over the years, we got to know each other well. I admired his competence, optimism, and 'just go ahead and get it done anyway' attitude. In spite of many challenges, he graduated college, married, and built a career as a programmer. He was articulate, caring, and very religious; life revolved around his work, his family, and his church, where he taught Sunday school. His faith gave him strength and solace to deal with his illness and build a productive life.

When iritis heated up, Caleb's eyes became red, painful, and sensitive to light. Steroid drops controlled the inflammation and made him comfortable but sometimes caused his intraocular pressure to rise, which was dangerous since glaucoma had so badly damaged his optic nerve. He barely saw well enough to walk around and recognize faces and needed a magnifier to read. Treatment became a balancing act between giving just enough steroids for comfort yet not so much that the pressure would rise and risk his vision, which was hanging by a thread.

He rarely complained, but one day said, "My eyes hurt so much I think I am going to need those steroid drops again. I hate to get started with them, but I really need some relief."

"OK. I am going to put some ointment in your eye now. It will make you a lot more comfortable within a few minutes."

"What's that?"

"Atropine. Pretty soon the light won't bother you. And here is a prescription for a steroid drop that you should put in every hour while you are awake and a couple times during the night too."

"Every hour!? I don't think I can do that."

"I know it's hard, but if you can you will feel better sooner."

"What drop is it this time? Is it Pred Forte?" he asked in his syrupy drawl. I laughed, and he asked, "What's so funny?"

"Your belief is so strong it colors everything you do and say! You asked me the name of the drop, and the way you said it, it sounded like, 'Is it "Prayed For It"?' Let's hope it does turn out to be the answer to your prayers." He smiled, and from then on always made a point to insist, "I don't want generic steroid drops. I want the real thing. I want the brand name. I want 'Prayed For It.'" Treatment worked because when he needed help he took his drops religiously.

Other patients hold surprising beliefs that can get in the way of timely care.

# DANGEROUS AGE

THE ELDERLY MAN said, "I think I better wait a few months to have my cataract removed."

"Okay, no problem. It's never a rush as long as you're happy with the way you are seeing."

"I'm not happy. I really need to see better, but I'm 79 now."

I asked, "What's that have to do with anything?"

"It's a dangerous age. Just look at the obituaries. Almost every day there is somebody in there who was 79."

Really? "Is it like the 27 Club for rock stars?"

"The what?"

"You know, Jim Morrison, Janis Joplin, Jimi Hendrix, Curt Cobain, Amy Winehouse were all 27 when they died. Robert Johnson too. None made it to 28."

"Well, there you go," he said. "That's what I'm saying. If I need surgery, I better wait until my next birthday."

Some people have belief systems that invite a me into a productive therapeutic relationship. Others, like this man, have a kind of fatalism that can be a roadblock to healing. I need to remember the impact that mindsets have on confidence and compliance, and to identify, confront, and correct them. I need to offer more constructive ways for them to interpret their facts.

Patients who don't believe that treatment can work or fail to realize that they can be the agent of their own recovery are swimming upstream. The body heals better when the spirit is enlisted to help. And magical thinking usually evaporates in the light.

**LOTS OF STUFF GOING ON**                    *Mar 21, 2013 9:02am*

Hi—No news about Michael—he's handling the Chemo+Radiation really well. He drives himself to radiation and is still taking long walks and doing his visualization/relaxation. His sister is coming on Saturday.

Last night we had a dinner party—really! Michael's staff came over. Carol, Scottie, Beth and Michelle brought dinner and mail and news from the office. Michael has worked at there since 1992, and Carol has been with him from day one—his staff has made every day a good day for Michael.

Some other news—I am officially on Family Medical Leave from my practice. I have referred out most of my clients. And the support from the therapist community here has been wonderful. I will continue to work a very very limited schedule —we'll see how it goes. I want to be with Michael.

David is coming home on Friday and wants to be here and be with both me and Michael. Emily and Josh are coming on Sunday and staying for a week. We are really happy E&J are coming.

So we are laying low today—just being around and having a quiet day.

Love—Heidi

In this post, Heidi told our Caring Bridge friends that I handled my treatment well, and she was right, but I don't want to give the impression that chemotherapy and radiation were no more taxing than taking Tylenol for a headache. After the first week or two of treatment, while my energy remained good, my stamina did not. I could still walk a few miles at a good pace but needed a nap afterward. I could fantasize about returning to work but had to admit there was no way I could be productive.

My immunity was reduced, so I tried to see my friends one or two at a time. The chemo caused numbness and tingling in my fingers and toes. Toward the end of treatment, damage to the nerves in my neck sent an occasional electric jolt flashing down my arms, something called 'L'Hermitte's sign.' But most distressing was what happened the time I drank a milkshake.

One afternoon after chemotherapy, my doctor gave me an encouraging report, so to celebrate, I left his office and got a chocolate milkshake. I watched them make it: three scoops of ice cream, chocolate syrup, milk. I gulped it down. About an hour later I began to feel queasy and worried if I was going to be able to keep from throwing up. 'Oh no,' I thought, 'is the chemo finally getting to me?' The feeling passed within the hour, but the next time I had ice cream it came back, and I realized that chemotherapy had, as antibiotics also can, disturbed my intestinal flora and made me lactose intolerant. I had to avoid ice cream, one of my favorite treats, until after the end of treatment.

But these were all minor complaints. When I told Steve Plunkett that it hurt to swallow taco chips, he laughed and said, "You have no idea how lucky you are. I have another patient who is getting the same treatment as you, and he is in the hospital now being fed intravenously because he hasn't been able to eat for a week." I am not sure why, but I really was fortunate to tolerate my treatment so well.

# CHAPTER 17

## EYE OF THE BEHOLDER

IT WAS DARK outside as I walked into the Emergency Room. The receptionist buzzed me into the back. The ER was quiet, and I found one of the nurses typing at a computer. "Hi, your doctor called me about somebody with an eye injury."

She looked up and shook her head. "Oh right. You better talk to him before you go in there."

"What is it?" Without looking up, she twitched her head and eyes to the left and I turned to see two policemen standing outside one of the rooms. I asked, "Is that where the eye patient is?"

She nodded, "Here comes the doctor. Talk to him," and she resumed typing.

I put out my hand, and he said, "Gee, listen, I am really sorry we had to call you in so late. This is a big mess." He put his hand on my back and gently guided me around the corner, out of earshot of the rest of the people in the ER.

"What's going on? How come the police are here?"

"Well, it's kind of sensitive. It seems like an abuse situation; they think his roommate in the group home might have hit him. But the patient says they're friends, and since no one is sure what really happened, he's sitting in there too."

"So the cops…"

"Yeah. The police are waiting for you to tell them what the eye looks like before they arrest the other guy. You know, what charges to bring."

"Oh man," I moaned.

"I know. Like I said, I am so sorry to get you involved, but wait 'til you see this eye. His lids are so bruised and swollen he can hardly open them. He has no facial or orbital fractures; we got a scan before I even tried to examine him. And then when I did, I didn't want to force his eyes open, so I didn't get much of a look. But what I did see was pretty ugly. Hardly even looks like an eye anymore."

I sighed. "Is the slit lamp in the room?"

"Yeah, I think you have everything you'll need. And we gave a little sedation, so he'll be easier for you to examine."

I gathered my things, and as I approached the room I nodded to the police. They opened the curtain and stepped aside. On the bed was a small, rotund man, snoring. He had dark, disheveled hair, like an aging troll after a sleepless night. His fingers were truncated and overstuffed, five Vienna sausages on each hand. A metal shield covered his right eye. A scrawny man with a sun damaged complexion, long, scraggly, unwashed hair, John Deere cap, and sparse beard sat slumped in a chair in the corner. Like a dog expecting to be beaten. He looked up at me, then broke eye contact and mumbled, "Hey."

Gently shaking the patient's shoulder to rouse him, I said, "Hello Mr. Peppers, I am Dr. Rotberg, I am the eye doctor the ER called in. They said you hurt your eye. Can you tell me what happened?"

The man in the corner started to answer. I raised my hand and said, "Let me hear what he has to say first, OK?"

Quietly, the patient said, "My eye hurts awful bad. I can't see anything out of it. And I think I lost my contact lens when I fell."

"You fell? That's what happened to your eye?"

"Right. I was walking in the common room and I must have tripped over something, I don't know what. Next thing I know I'm lying on the floor messed up like this."

"What do you think hit your eye?"

"Maybe the edge of the coffee table or the arm of a chair. It all happened so fast."

I felt a tap on my shoulder. One of the policemen had been eavesdropping, and he motioned me to follow him out of the room. "Doc," he whispered, "that's not what he said when we went to the house with the EMTs. He told us that his roommate hit him with his fist, maybe even with brass knuckles. They were having an argument, he was drunk, and all of a sudden just hit him. It wouldn't be the first time; we know this guy pretty well. He sometimes makes a scene at the home, but never anything like this. And now you're getting a totally different story."

"Maybe you should get him out of the room while I'm taking the history. Aren't there any more questions you need to ask him?"

"We'll keep him busy for a few minutes," he said. They returned to the room, and a few seconds later left with the roommate to confer in an empty treatment room.

"I am going to take this patch off and see what your eye looks like, OK?" I put on gloves, peeled off the tape, and aimed the surgical light at his face. There were no lacerations, but the lower lid had clearly taken the impact. It was swollen and tense, the color of eggplant. "Can you open your eye at all?" I asked. He opened his left eye widely but was only able to show me a couple millimeters on the right. "Do you think you can sit up for a minute so I can look with this machine over here?"

He nodded, sat up unsteadily, both pudgy feet dangling several inches from the floor. The nurse helped him to stand and shuffle across the linoleum to a stool. Once we were both seated he rested his chin on the slit lamp and I looked through the binoculars. I had to force myself not to gasp when I saw the severity of his injury. The conjunctiva was elevated by blood. Mixed in with the blood was something darker on the temporal side. His cornea was clear, but there was a total hyphema, blood filled the eye and made it impossible to see anything inside. He couldn't see out, I couldn't see in. And the eye was soft, deflated, terribly damaged.

I put the shield back on and led him back to the bed. "Listen, you have a very serious eye injury. Whatever hit your eye caused a lot of bleeding both inside and outside your eye. I am also pretty sure that you have what we call a scleral rupture."

"What's that??"

"It means that your eye is like a flat tire because the wall of your eye is torn. But I can't be sure since there is so much blood in the way. Did you have anything to eat or drink in the last few hours?"

"Not since about 1 o'clock. Just some water in the afternoon. Why?"

"You need surgery tonight, because if there is a scleral rupture I need to fix it right away. Or else there is a good chance you are going to lose your eye."

He began to sniffle, "He hit me, you know. He hits me sometimes. But this time he really went too far." He was sobbing. The nurse, jaded, shook her head.

"We can talk to the group home to make sure they make it a safer place for you, but this is an emergency, this has to come first. I will repair the main injury and put your eye back together. But understand that there is no way I can tell you how well this eye will be able to see or even if it will end up seeing at all. Almost for sure you will need another operation to get the blood out and fix injuries in the back of your eye that I can't examine yet."

I called the surgical eye team to let them know what was headed their way and waited almost an hour while they readied the room.

In the OR, once the patient was asleep, I saw the full extent of the trauma. His eye was collapsed. "Look how soft this is. He must have a big defect in the sclera," I said to the scrub nurse. I incised the conjunctiva at the limbus and carefully opened it all the way around with a small scissors, wiping with sponges to allow pinpoint cautery to create a blood-free field. The temporal edge of the cornea was torn away from the sclera and his iris was laying in the defect. "Oh man, he got hit so hard the pupil blew out of his eye!" I said, and lifted the brown, thready tissue off the surface with a sponge, which snagged some vitreous as well. I slowly removed the exposed vitreous and then closed the wound with a dozen sutures until it was watertight.

Before tying the last sutures, I inflated his eye with saline and flushed out some of the blood, but the vitreous was still full of it. With a spreading scissors, I explored the eye wall in all four quadrants. "Well, look at this," I exclaimed. Something on the surface of his eye was poking out from behind a pool of blood at the eye's equator. Using some dry sponges, I milked it forward, and finally it popped into view. "It's the lens! His natural lens got ejected from the eye too!"

These were such awful injuries, I had little hope for the eye and didn't expect it to regain useful vision. Then over the next few weeks it got even worse: his retina detached and the pressure in the eye climbed dangerously high. Somehow though, after two more operations, he made a remarkable recovery. Three months later, during his last post-op visit, I was incredulous, "I cannot believe it. That line you just read was 20/20! With the right prescription your bad eye can see great. It's amazing."

"Thank you Dr. Rotberg. Thank you and the other doctors for everything you have done. My roommate is in jail, and I'm making my way on my own with the help of other people where I live. Time for a fresh start, so I can't thank you enough."

"I am so thrilled with this. Let's make you a date with the best contact lens fitter I know. Your eye is unusual because of your injury, but if she can fit you with a lens I think you will be able to see well enough to do anything you could do before."

A month or so later when he returned his attitude had changed. "My vision is terrible," he said. "It is hard for me to see the computer or to read the papers at work. And the glare is awful." He was still 20/25 with his contact lens.

"I know this exam room is not the real world. In real life, you have to do more than read black letters on a white background in a dark room. It's not a true measure of your vision, but you are seeing so much better than I had any right to expect," I repeated.

"You keep saying that, but what about the glare?"

"Have you tried sunglasses at work?" He worked in the sheltered workshop affiliated with the group home.

"I hate glasses," he replied. "I can barely see to do my work. I think I might get fired. Oh, I'm so unhappy with the way my vision turned out."

I pushed my stool back, sat up, and took a deep breath. "I know you have been through a terrible time. Your friend attacked you and almost blinded you. But he didn't blind you. You are seeing unbelievably well considering what happened."

"But I can hardly see."

"Your vision is a long way from how it used to be. You wish it was better and I do too. But while you keep focusing on the fact that your vision isn't perfect, all I see is the miracle that you're able to see at all."

The next time I saw him was about six months later as he was recovering from surgery on his other eye. His roommate never came back to the group home, but a few weeks after he got out of jail they ran into each other. They argued, they fought, and he punched Mr. Peppers in the other eye. Someone else was on call that night.

---

**FAMILY GATHERING!**                    *Mar 22, 2013 7:33am*

It is still amazing to me that this all started just in the past 2 weeks. Two weeks ago we knew Michael had a mass in his chest but did not yet have a diagnosis or a treatment plan. WOW.

I am the oldest of 5 kids. When I called my family EVERYONE wanted to be here—to help, to give us support, just to show love. My whole family is coming for Passover. My Mom, sisters and their kids, my brother and brother-in-law Charlie, as well as our kids and Michael's sister.

Michael will lead the Seder. The 'fam' starts arriving today.

I feel so lucky and blessed!

Love—Heidi

**PROOF OF HEAVEN**                    *Mar 23, 2013 8:52am*

Last night friends invited us to their church to hear a talk by Eben Alexander. He was a classmate of mine in medical school and became a neurosurgeon in Boston, but now is widely known as the author of the best-selling little book "Proof of Heaven." I read the book when it first came out a few months ago, mostly because I was interested in learning his personal story, and had no idea that the subject of life after death would soon become so much more interesting to me.

His book concerns the wisdom that he gained during a serious illness. He had a type of bacterial meningitis that is usually fatal, and when not fatal leaves the patient with severe deficits. He had no cortical activity for several days. Yet when he miraculously recovered neurologically intact he recalled some amazing experiences. His disembodied soul traveled to 3 realms, one sort of like purgatory, the next very beautiful and loving, and the last a place where he was taught deep lessons about the soul, the nature of the universe, etc. Although he is on an extensive lecture circuit these lessons are hard for him to articulate since they were transmitted to him without language and in a non-earthly context.

Sounds very 'woo-woo' but the underlying message is powerful and comforting. The soul persists after death, the soul is eternal, the universe is loving and welcoming, and heaven is available to everyone. No religion has a full picture or explanation, but the parts of all religions that promote love, compassion, and care for the less fortunate are true and the parts that separate the world into believers and infidels are false and the result of human, not divine, inspiration. Underlying all religions and most mystical traditions is a well of common universal wisdom that different people in different cultures have described differently and imperfectly over the centuries.

The book is not great literature, but its message takes its place in a long tradition of similar deep wisdom. It never hurts to be reminded that our understanding of existence is limited and in some important ways mistaken. Many smart people over the millennia have known this and we need to remember it too.

Michael

# CHAPTER 18

# BATTERIES

O N MONDAY MORNING, I opened the garage door and got in the car. I turned the key and stepped on the gas, but nothing happened. Just a fast tapping sound. The dashboard was lit, the dome light was working. I tried again. More clicking, now a little slower, like screwing the gas cap too tight. Crap. Dead battery. The car worked fine yesterday. Did I leave a door open last night?

I went back inside, and there was Heidi's Aunt Irene, in her robe, sitting at the breakfast table. She looked up from the newspaper and said, "I thought you were leaving."

"I thought so too, but my battery's dead. The car won't start. It might be under warranty, so I think I'll call Triple A to see how much it would cost for them to come out to try to jump it."

"What?"

More loudly, I said, "I can't go. The battery's dead."

"No," she said. "It's not the battery. I didn't even put in my hearing aids yet."

Even using the most basic vocabulary isn't enough when patients don't understand, or cannot hear, the words. Now we use sign language interpreters for hearing impaired patients and a phone-in translation agency for people who don't speak English. But it isn't communication if the message doesn't get through.

# MUSHROOM

ANGIE SPENT A semester learning American Sign Language. Her teacher showed the class how to sign the alphabet, all the numbers, and the most commonly used words. She read her textbook, studied pictures, watched videos, and trained with the other students. After a while, she felt pretty good about her ability to use her hands to communicate without speaking.

Near the end of the term, the class pretended to go to a restaurant to order a meal using only sign language. For several days, she practiced ordering a pizza with extra cheese and mushrooms. She was ready. When her teacher, posing as a waiter, came to her table, she signed, "I would like a pizza."

He smiled and signed back, "What kind?"

She placed her palms together with the fingers of one hand pointed to the left and the other to the right. She rotated the base of her palms together like a cheese grater, and then cupped her left hand over her extended right index finger, meaning "Extra cheese and mushrooms."

He shook his head no.

She tried again. "Extra cheese and mushrooms."

Again, more emphatically, no.

She grimaced, shrugged her shoulders, pursed her lips, scratched her head. What was the problem? Then she smiled, and raising one finger, signed, "extra cheese." He signed back, "OK," so once again she asked for mushrooms, cupping one hand over the index finger of the other, tapping the palm onto the tip of the finger.

The waiter started to sign a reply, but then broke character, laughed, and said out loud, "No, you're going to get yourself in big trouble if you keep asking for mushrooms that way. Here is how you sign the word mushroom. Take your index finger, point it upward, and put it in the center of the palm of your other hand."

"That's what I was doing," she said.

"No, you have to keep your hand open. That's mushroom. What you were doing, cupping your hand over the finger, that's not mushroom. That's blow job." Then he showed her, "Mushroom, blow job, mushroom, not mushroom. Get it?"

She got it.

## BURYING THE LEDE

In 2005, well before my diagnosis, I had my first colonoscopy and asked to be awake so I could watch. Lying on my left side, I was fascinated by the moist, pink images of my own colon on the monitor.

"Can you see all right?" asked the gastroenterologist.

"Yeah, this is amazing."

"Glad you can see what's going on." Then he said, "Whoa, that's a big polyp. More juice please." Next thing I knew, I was sitting in a recliner in the recovery room and he was talking to me. "That was pretty cool wasn't it? Could you see the polyp?"

"I think so, but nothing after that. What happened?"

"Everything looked good, you had a good prep, we got a great look and only found two things. The first little one you were awake for, and then we found a polyp. We knocked you out for a minute while I removed it. It was big but looked OK to me. We'll call you in a few days when I get the pathology report. Just take it easy today, back to normal activities tomorrow, and you'll hear from me soon."

I went home, took a nap, had something to eat, and quickly felt fine. My office was busy the next day and, absorbed in work, I forgot until ten days later that no one had called with the results of my procedure. That afternoon I was examining a patient when someone knocked on the door.

Scottie poked her head in, "Dr. Rotberg, I have to interrupt you for a minute. It's a nurse with that phone call you've been expecting. She said she needs to talk to you RIGHT NOW!"

I quivered from a burst of adrenaline and dread. Palpitating, I excused myself and, eyes fixed on the floor, charged down the hall, shut my office door, and picked up the phone. "Hello, this is Dr. Rotberg, can I help you?"

"Hi Dr. Rotberg, this is Joanne, from your gastroenterologist's office. I was just looking through our pathology reports. Has he called you yet about your results?"

"Uh, no, he hasn't," I replied, feigning casual curiosity.

Silence. "Oh my…hold on, I'll get him right away, just hang on."

I was ready to faint. After a couple minutes he came on the line. "Hi Mike, how ya' doin'? How's Heidi, how are the kids?"

"Fine, what's up?" Come on already.

"Well, uh, yeah, we got the pathology back. Uh huh. Remember I removed two lesions? Well, the first one, that was nothing, just what they call lymphoid hyperplasia. See it all the time, nothing to worry about. But the second one was something completely different…"

My heart stopped, sweat trickled down my forehead. Had it already spread throughout my body? Would I need surgery? Chemotherapy? How could I work with a colostomy bag?

"…the second one was something completely different. That was an adenomatous polyp, larger than average, but also nothing to worry about. Just get another colonoscopy in 3 years, OK?"

"So you mean both things you removed were benign?"

"Yeah, you're fine."

"Well, that's a relief, but c'mon, couldn't you have given me the headline first?"

"What do you mean?"

"I mean, that was torture. You said, 'Well, the first one was nothing to worry about, but the second one was different.' And I'm thinking, 'Oh shit, I have little kids, do I have enough insurance, will Heidi be OK, how much time do I have left before I have to stop working?' Why didn't you just get to the point and start by saying, 'We got the pathology back and everything's OK. Want to know more details?'"

After this experience, I always make a point to give the headline first. Even during an eye exam, rather than leave the patient hanging for a few minutes, I often say, "Everything looks great so far. I'll explain everything as soon as I finish my notes, OK?" And at the end of the exam, when I deliver the promised report, it usually starts with, "Here's the headline. I don't see any trouble in your eyes. All you need is some new glasses." The patient exhales, relaxes, and then is better able to hear the rest of what I have to say. Even if the news is bad, after gentle explanation, I still try to get the message across as promptly as possible.

# MILLIONS AND MILLIONS

FOR NEARSIGHTED PEOPLE it was a dream come true: a new laser to evaporate the outer layers of the cornea to correct myopia. People who grew up needing glasses and contact lenses could lie down under the laser and, by investing a few minutes and a couple thousand dollars, see more clearly than ever. It seemed miraculous.

But it was so expensive many could not afford it. Because laser vision correction is rarely medically necessary, insurance companies consider it cosmetic surgery and do not pay for it. I chose to avoid doing other kinds of cosmetic surgery, but after a few years it was clear that laser vision correction was here to stay. Plenty of people were thrilled with their results, and most problems could be traced to overly aggressive surgeons operating on inappropriate eyes. Also, compared to the cataract and glaucoma operations that I had been doing for years, it was comically easy to perform. Why shouldn't I do it too?

After a few years and many successful laser vision correction procedures I realized that I had done enough to be able to give informed advice to my patients about it and had no interest in making it a bigger part of my practice. I figured it would be smart to quit doing LASIK before any patients had a bad outcome. My conversation with one patient convinced me to stop dabbling.

She was a middle-aged woman who wanted treatment for the right reasons. She was bright, had realistic expectations, and her eyes were perfect candidates. After a long discussion of LASIK, what it was, how it worked, what risks it carried, and how well she could expect to see, she said, "I hear you telling me that LASIK is so great. If it is, why are you still wearing glasses?"

"Well, I'm glad you asked, because I'm not selling anything here. LASIK is surgery. It can be amazing for the right person, but you don't have to have it. I still wear glasses because glasses don't bother me. If your glasses or contacts don't bother you, then maybe you shouldn't have LASIK either."

"No, I really want it. I would love to wake up in the morning and be able to see clearly without fumbling around for my glasses."

"Right. After your LASIK there is a very good chance that, for the first time in your life, you will be able to drive without glasses. Remember though, you'll probably need reading glasses."

"No I won't. I don't need glasses to read now."

"But you will after the LASIK. Can you read through the upper part of your driving glasses?"

"No, that's why I take them off to read."

"After LASIK, you will probably see to drive as clearly without glasses as you now see when you wear them. It will be like you are always wearing your driving glasses, but you won't be able to take them off to read anymore. That's why you will probably need reading glasses for detailed close work."

"So you mean I will just be trading distance glasses for reading glasses?"

"That's pretty much right. But most people spend a lot more time looking away than up close. And not having to depend on glasses to drive, to watch TV, or play sports can be wonderful."

"Yeah, I would love to be able to walk in the rain and not have my glasses fog up. I think I want to do it."

"Good, do you have any other questions?"

"I feel a little funny asking, but why should I let you do my LASIK?"

"I would be happy to do it, but if you want me to I'll give you the names of some others who could do a good job for you."

"No, I know you are a straight shooter and I've heard you're a good surgeon. And I have already talked to a couple other offices. But what worries me is maybe I should go to Dr. Spielvogel. I see his billboards all over town; they say he has done thousands of LASIKs. He does so many, doesn't that mean he is the best?"

I took a deep breath and considered what to say. I knew the doctor. He was a very busy refractive surgeon, advertised constantly, and had many unhappy patients. Oh, why not. I said, "Let me put it this way. Have you ever noticed the big sign in front of McDonalds that brags about 'Millions and Millions Served?' Does that mean McDonalds has the best hamburgers? Is that where you are going for lunch today?"

She smiled, "I get what you are saying." She came back in a few days for her LASIK and had an excellent result. But I stopped doing LASIK a few weeks later.

---

**WEEK 3 OF GETTING WELL**                    *Mar 25, 2013 11:56am*

Michael is getting his chemo this morning. While sitting in his recliner he does relaxation and imagery to enhance the potent effects of the chemo. He has his iPod and new iPad and a book to play with while we are here. He drinks lots of juices and eats all those salty snacks—he has settled into a routine that we both wish he never even experienced.

My thoughts today are with family. Our kids are here for a long visit. My whole family was here for the weekend. Lots of love, talking, hugs, laughter, news, eating and just being together. They came for the Passover Seder—really one of the highlights of our year.

This year we had Seder a day early—Michael's chemo+radiation schedule made today questionable. We will do a Seder tonight too—just much smaller. Last night was GREAT—16 of us and my family took care of every detail. We started the evening before the Seder with champagne (I love champagne!). My mom had gifts for EVERYONE. Then the Seder, followed by the festive meal. It was wonderful! And the message of redemption was so powerful.

Michael and I felt such love and support and happiness—just what Pesach should be. We really are blessed. From our family to yours—we wish you movement from bondage to freedom, from illness to health, with Gods mighty outstretched arm and love.

Happy Pesach.

Love—Heidi

# CHAPTER 19

## COMMUNICATE HONESTLY AND EFFECTIVELY

W HY EVEN BOTHER talking about honesty? It is essential. But dig a little deeper and it gets more complicated. When talking to patients, how honest should I be? Completely honest, laying out all the facts dispassionately, then stepping back to answer questions and to let the patient decide which way to go? Or should our discussion emphasize some facts and edit out others?

This is what inevitably and necessarily happens. I curate the facts I present to the patient. Full disclosure of all the possible outcomes and every reported side effect is both impractical and unhelpful, drowns the patient in irrelevant facts and fails to distinguish important from distracting considerations.

Which facts to present and which to ignore depend on the complexity of the situation, the ability of the patient to understand, and his personality. Some crave information while others cover their ears and are happy to defer to me. In explaining the pros and cons of an upcoming surgery, 'information seekers' want to know as much as possible and others, called by some 'information avoiders,' hold up their hands as if to say, "That's enough. I trust you to do what's best for me."

So how do I decide what to tell and what to leave out? This is where scripts come in handy. Over the years, I developed a few prepackaged tools to help me explain common surgeries, treatments, and diseases to make sure I always use understandable language, hit the high points, and don't leave anything out. I try to deliver these explanations in a way that sounds fresh, as a stage actor, tired of reciting the same old lines, needs to remember that each audience is seeing him for the first and only time. Here is how I tell patients what to expect on the day of cataract surgery:

# PRE-OP INSTRUCTIONS

"OKAY, HERE IS how it's going to go. Surgery will be right upstairs; you don't even have to go to the hospital. On the morning of your surgery you shouldn't have anything to eat or drink. You can have water until about 3 hours before the scheduled time, and you can take your medicines with a sip, but that's it. No eye makeup, no makeup on your face at all.

"The Surgery Center will call you a couple days before to tell you the exact time you need to be here. When you arrive, they'll check you in, put you in a bed, ask your name and your birthday and which eye you are having done and what kind of surgery you are having. Remember, it's cataract surgery with a lens implant in your left eye. They'll start an IV, wash your face, and put drops in your eye to dilate your pupil; antibiotic drops and numbing drops too. I'll come by and put a mark on your forehead to be sure everybody knows it's supposed to be the left eye. But you should also make sure they only put the drops in the eye we are planning to do, OK?

"When you're ready they'll take you back to the operating room. The nurses will make sure you are comfortable and then we'll get started. You'll be awake the whole time. You'll be able to hear me talking, you'll see pretty colored lights, and you'll feel things. You will feel me touching your forehead but nothing that you feel will hurt. Like you feel me touching your arm now but it doesn't hurt, right? There's a difference between feeling and hurting. You will feel things but nothing will hurt, nothing will surprise you, nothing will scare you. Ten minutes will go by like it was a minute. During surgery, sometimes people even ask, "When are you going to start?" when I'm almost finished. Anyway, when your surgery is over I'll take the drapes away, clean the soap off your face and put a cover over your eyes. You'll be able to see but it will be blurry because of the ointment in your eye. Then you'll go back to recovery to relax in a recliner for a few minutes before they send you home.

"That first day you can be up and around but take it kind of easy. Leave the shield on your eye all day and all night except when you take it off to put drops in. I'll tell you more about that afterwards, don't worry about remembering now."

"Will I be in pain that day?"

"No, your eye won't hurt but it will probably feel a little scratchy or burny like you got soap or a hair in your eye, nothing bad enough to worry about. If it does bother you, please call. Your vision will gradually improve as the dilating drops wear off and the ointment dissolves. The next day I'll see you back here so I can check how you're doing and explain more about what drops to use. One thing you will notice the first day is that things will be brighter and colors will be much more vivid than they have been for years. You won't believe how blue blue is or how white white is. Just wait. And your vision should keep improving for a few weeks."

"Do I need somebody to stay with me?"

"If you want to that's fine, but there are no restrictions on your activity after the first day except you don't want to rub your eye really hard or swim for a few days. So it's up to you. Usually I'll see you here the day after surgery, and then a week and a month later, and that is when, if you need glasses, I'll give you a prescription to get some new ones made. If you want to take care of your other eye soon we can make a date now to do it a couple weeks after the first or you can wait as long as you like. Do you have any questions?"

It isn't enough to simply recite these words. The job isn't done unless I also solicit feedback and ask open ended questions to be sure the message is received. To be even more certain, in the operating room I repeat the relevant part of the script just as I sit down to begin the procedure.

"You will feel me touching you, you will feel cold water, and you will see bright colorful lights, but nothing will hurt, nothing will bother you, and this will be over before you know it." I try to follow the classic advice to 'Tell them what I'm going to tell them, tell them, then tell them what I told them.'

While talking to patients, I do my best to avoid medical jargon and to use normal conversational English. Sometimes we forget that most people don't know the terms hypersensitivity reaction, rhegmatogenous detachment, or pellucid degeneration. Esoteric medical terminology is precise but sometimes just showy, and may not help patients understand what is happening to their bodies. At the risk of sounding like a world-wise grandpa, I try to find colorful ways to make complex concepts comprehensible. Very often, patients say, "You're the only one who ever took the time to explain this to me," implying, "in a way that makes sense." Here are a few that come in handy:

- "Pray as if your healing depends on God but take your drops as if healing depends on you." (a line adapted from St. Augustine.)

- "It is better to stay out of trouble than to try to get out of trouble."

- "If you call the fire department before there is too much damage you can still live in your house. But if you wait until flames are coming out the roof you'll need to move. It's important to find and treat glaucoma early too, because you can't move."

- "Deciding when to have cataract surgery is like getting a haircut. Your hair grows a little bit every day. But one morning you look in the mirror and it's a hair emergency. Cataracts also worsen gradually but bother you suddenly."

- "If LASIK was the only way to correct nearsightedness and then people invented glasses or contact lenses, they would get the Nobel Prize." (borrowed from my teacher, Dr. Banks Anderson)

- "The only place in your entire body where anyone can examine your blood vessels is in your eyes. If the circulation looks healthy there, then the blood vessels in your kidneys and toes are probably in good shape too."

- "It's as if you are standing on the roof of a burning house. You are afraid to jump off because you might break your leg. But if you stay where are, the fire might get you. By delaying your decision, you are making a decision you may regret later."

- "I don't know what to do. You're the doctor. Why can't you just tell me if I need cataract surgery?"

"Here's why. Do you think anyone can tell you when to wear a sweater?"

"No way. I'll wear one if I'm cold and if I'm comfortable I won't."

"But if you were cold the sweater would probably help, right? Same here. You have a cataract and removing it will make you see better. But I can't tell you how much your vision bothers you. You have to tell me

- "At this point, there isn't anything we can do to make your vision better, but there are still plenty of things we can do to make your life better."

- "You are the one with the eye problem. Why do you expect me to care more about your vision than you do?"

- "Your prescription has hardly changed, but your glasses are all scratched up. Your feet stopped growing, but you need to get new shoes once in a while."

- "Know how new shoes don't feel natural even if they're the right size? It might take a few days to feel comfortable with your new glasses too."

- "Doc, I think I'm too old to have cataract surgery." "So just wait and do it when you're younger."

- "Your waiting room is so full!" "You wouldn't go to a truck stop without trucks, would you?"

- "When you have cataracts, getting new glasses is like focusing a camera through a dirty window. You won't be happy with the picture."

- "Why are my eyelids drooping like this?" "Birthdays and gravity."

---

**GOOD NEWS**                                    *Mar 27, 2013 8:58am*

Yesterday, before my 12th (of 37 scheduled) session of radiation, I had a CT scan to find out if the treatments were showing any early results. And the news was good. The tumor has gotten smaller by 20–25 percent! This is great not only because it shows we are on the right track but because it will allow the radiation fields to be adjusted to avoid treating surrounding normal tissues. Very encouraging early results.

Michael

---

# CHAPTER 20

# CRISIS & OPPORTUNITY

IN 1998, MY sixth year in Charlotte, our practice was in a
bind. The office building we leased was thirty years old and
needed to be refreshed. We hoped to see patients there during
renovations even though it meant living through months of
dust and noise. But that plan became unfeasible once we discovered asbestos. We also learned that couldn't get a building
permit because new zoning rules required more parking for a
building our size. We needed to move.

We faced other issues too. Our group owned an old house
across the street that was valuable overflow space, but the
property was too small and poorly located to sell.

And at the same time, we wanted to open a surgery center.
Even though we had fifty surgeons, we couldn't build operating rooms on our own. North Carolina, like many states, re-

quired a Certificate of Need (CON), to control proliferation of medical facilities. In effect, this allowed hospitals to limit local competition. We did all our surgery at the hospitals in town. Why would they partner with us on a surgery center when it meant we might move our cases to the new facility?

So, we had three problems that seemed unrelated. We needed a new building. We wanted to sell surplus property near our current office. And we wanted our own surgery center. The first was tricky enough. After looking at dozens of locations, we found a medical building in an attractive part of town. It had been empty for more than a year, and the owner was anxious to sell. We voted to buy the building, but what about our unneeded property? And how could we build a Surgery Center?

Heidi reminded me of something her father did several years earlier. After retiring, he moved from New York to a little town in Florida. Bored, he joined the commission that ran their municipal airport, used mostly by student pilots from a nearby college. It was surrounded by pine forest. The college wanted the tree line moved back from the end of the runway to make take-offs and landings safer. The airport administration, short of funds and worried about losing their main source of income, couldn't figure out where to find the money to remove thousands of trees. But he saw an opportunity. "We don't have to cut those trees down. Someone will pay us to do it." With a few phone calls, he found a timber company anxious to harvest trees. By reframing the situation, crisis became windfall. He solved the airport's problem and earned some revenue as well.

Heidi said, "You can do the same thing here. Just show the hospital how it is in their interest to buy your property. The hospital owns your old office building and may not realize they won't be able to rent it without using your property for overflow parking. And if they buy it, you might give them the opportunity to partner with you on operating rooms. They already have extra CONs, and you can work out a deal to own the Surgery Center together. It's good for everybody. The hospital gets new ORs, gets your loyalty, gets to keep using your old building, and you get a great new place to work, a piece of a surgery center, and you can unload that crappy property. Just don't smile when you make the offer."

At breakfast with our group's attorney and Chuck, our administrator, I scribbled this plan on a napkin. They never knew the kernel of the idea was Heidi's. A few weeks later we met with the head of the hospital. We told him that he had a big problem. We were going to vacate his building, and zoning issues might force him to tear it down and replace it with a smaller building on that site.

But we could help each other out. We'd sell him the property we owned next to the building we were getting ready to vacate so he could place extra parking there. In exchange, we agreed to reserve space in our new building for a surgery center that the hospital could partly own. We would not invite other hospitals to develop this center if he promised to joint venture with us and help get regulatory approval. After a few minutes of back and forth, he said, "That sounds like a win-win to me. Let's do it."

We left his office suppressing incredulous smiles. Until you ask, the answer is always no. Creatively reframing the dilemma helped us get to yes, and the surgery center became an asset for the hospital, our practice, and our community.

When doctors think creatively, it can help patients too. Whether painting, wood working, knitting or welding, whether playing a musical instrument, reading or writing, a doctor's creative activity outside the office brings personal pleasure and also inclines the mind toward more inventive patient care.

> **One Month of Treatment Completed!**      *Apr 5, 2013 4:25pm*
>
> Today is 4 weeks of Chemo/radiation treatment completed! It went so fast—still seems unreal. Michael has no negative effects from the treatment—which is amazingly wonderful! He feels great, and is back at the gym in addition to his daily walks. Another part of Michael's daily routine is relaxation and the visualizations he worked up.
>
> Michael had a CT scan with contrast dye today—and the tumor continues to shrink—at this point he is NOT worried about too much radiation!
>
> We are going out to the Gallery Crawl and dinner tonight—just the two of us. It looks like it will be BEAUTIFUL this weekend: we hope to do some long walks and maybe even a bike ride. It's the 20th Anniversary of the Charlotte Blues Society and we plan on going to the concert Sunday night. While Michael is still avoiding large crowds, we are venturing out to smaller venues. His white counts are lower, but he is still able to be out and about.
>
> I'll update the journal when there is news—promise! Have a wonderful weekend and enjoy this great Spring we are having! Every day is a good day....
>
> Love—Heidi

# BE HONEST

As a patient, I need my doctors to be honest with me, to level with me, to tell me the truth in a humane, caring, understandable, and hopeful way. But I need to be honest with my doctors too. I have to give a complete and accurate history, un-filtered by worry that they will judge me when tell them I for-got to take my medicine, ate a candy bar, or drank a six-pack.

I also need to be honest with myself. Am I doing all I can to get better? Am I doing anything harmful? That's not blaming the patient; that's stepping up to be part of the solution.

Honest information is the foundation of good care. If I don't know my own patient's problem by the time I finish taking his history, it is going to be much harder to reach an accurate diagnosis and begin treatment. When patients mis-lead, omit important facts, or are embarrassed to tell the truth, they hurt only themselves. Withholding uncomfortable infor-mation leads to unnecessary needle sticks, prescriptions, and office visits. A misleading or incomplete history can send me down the wrong path, delay diagnosis, and cause unneeded testing. Only by facing up to reality can patients overcome de-nial and self-delusion. Only when doctor and patient are both honest and candid can care be both compassionate and effi-cient.

Since patients come to me for help, my inclination is to be-lieve what they tell me, at least at first. But some stories are so transparently false they don't fool anyone.


# SOME DUDES


As I WALKED down the hall to my office one morning, I ran into one of my partners, who yawned as I approached. He said, "I'm a little out of it this morning. I got called to the ER in the middle of the night to see a guy with an eye injury."

"What happened?" I asked.

"The usual. He told me that some dudes did it. He was just walking down the sidewalk near his house at two in the morning, minding his own business, and for no reason out of the blue some dudes started beating him up. He doesn't know who they were, he didn't say anything to piss them off, and never even saw them coming."

"Some dudes, huh? You believe that?" Every doctor who covers the Emergency Room has run into patients injured by 'some dudes' or a 'brick that flew out of nowhere.'

"Oh yeah," he said, disinhibited by exhaustion. "When I was an intern in Philly, some dudes jumped a guy for no reason and gave him orbital and facial fractures. And when I was in residency and fellowship, some dudes were there too."

Whether an illness is inconvenient or potentially blinding or fatal, facing facts with yourself and your doctors gives the best chance of healing. Until you admit you have a cold and stop telling yourself 'it's just allergies,' you won't drink chicken soup and get the rest you need. Until you accept that you have a serious illness, you won't be willing to put your normal life on hold to do what needs to be done. Unless you acknowledge that your illness has imposed a new normal on your day to day routine, you will continue to make decisions based more on nostalgia and wishful thinking than reality. If you don't tell the truth, your doctor cannot help you. Nobody believes that 'some dudes' did it anyway.

# CHAPTER 21

# TRUST AND TRAIN STAFF

N<small>O ONE WORKS</small> alone. We all depend on other people, so a good doctor also must be a good colleague and a good boss. My only formal training in how to lead people was in the Boy Scouts, so I had to learn on the job. And I guess I did, because by the time I left my Charlotte practice after 21 years, I had a wonderful team working together for the benefit of our patients.

Carol, who scheduled surgery and lab tests, joined me my first day. Beth and Scottie came aboard soon afterward, and even Michele was with me for more than ten years. They were my work family, and I spent nearly as much time with them as with my family at home. We shared laughs, tears, grew and lived together and had the chance to help people every day.

Gradually I think I figured out how to be a good boss and to become worthy of my staff's time, effort and devotion.

Clear boundaries were crucial. We were friendly, but I treated my team as the professionals they were. At work, we maintained a certain amount of distance that reflected our different roles. Outside of work, once or twice a year we could drink a beer and blow off the steam generated in the hothouse of our shared experiences, but work was work.

Our relationship was based on mutual trust and respect. I respected them for doing their jobs well, for having pride in their work and taking it seriously. I respected them enough not to expect them to run non-professional errands, like picking up my laundry. And I know that they respected my competence and demeanor and enjoyed being with other skilled and diligent people.

I strived for a stable work environment. If office rules needed to change, we met, each had our say, and then moved ahead as a team collaborating in the best interests of our patients. Since each woman always gave her best, on the rare occasion one of them fell short, it was usually because I had not done a good job explaining what I expected. I criticized my team in private but praised them in front of patients, who needed to see the confidence I had in the talented and caring people who worked with me.

# GLOVES

ONE OF OUR doctors was notoriously hard to please. He was a fickle and demanding boss, voluble and incapable of introspection. A good talker and disinterested listener.

One day, Michele was filling in with his office, sitting behind the counter, on the phone with a pharmacy. Across the
hall, he cracked the exam room door, popped his head out,
said, "Can you get me some gloves?" and then retreated just as
quickly. She finished the call and brought him a box of medi-
um surgical gloves.

She sat down to do paperwork when something whizzed
past her head, missing her by inches before smashing into the
wall behind her. It was the box of gloves. He shouted, "Didn't ·
I tell you that I wear small?!"

This disrespect for a co-worker was stunning. She was startled, but recovered, muttering, "I don't know if you want to be
broadcasting that."

Learning never ends, so if a patient presented with an interesting or unusual problem, I called my staff in and discussed
the differential diagnosis and management options in the hall
afterwards. The more I showed them the more they wanted to
learn and the more invested they became in our work.

Another part of my job was to protect them from difficult
patients and to ensure a healthy work environment.

# FANBOY

WHEN HE CAME in for eye exams this man only wanted to
work with Michele. He always made appointments on Mon-
days and Tuesdays, when she worked with me. He asked personal questions and took unusual interest in hearing about her
life outside the office. Finally, after months, she told Scottie,
"I'm getting a little weirded out. He keeps trying to grab me
and I don't want to work with him. When he comes in tomorrow, can you pick up his chart and start his exam?"

The next day, when Scottie fetched him from the waiting room, he stood and asked her, "Where's Michele? Isn't she here today?"

"Oh, she is here, but she is busy right now with other patients."

"Can I wait for her?"

"She is going to be tied up for a long time and you are just having a quick recheck today. I don't think you will want to wait so long." Reluctantly he agreed, entered the exam room with Scottie, and then I came in to do his follow-up visit. When we finished, I shook his hand and opened the door to the hallway. He stepped out, stopped and smiled.

"Michele!" he called and ran to where she was filing papers. She turned her head, and as I watched he grabbed her, spun her around, hugged her, and kissed her cheek.

"That is so wrong!" she squealed, as she pushed him away and wiped her cheek with her sleeve. "I told you not to touch me!"

I scolded him, "What do you think you're doing? My staff are here to help you. They don't want you to touch them. That is unacceptable; it makes all of us uncomfortable. You need to find yourself another doctor." He was as apologetic as a serial batterer. Michele felt supported and valued when I fired him from the practice and stood up for my family.

# CAROL'S NEW CAR

A NATTILY DRESSED man in his sixties noticed Carol as he walked by her office. After his eye exam, he ambled over to her desk, invited himself to sit down and started chatting her up. He did not need to schedule a test or surgery but liked the way she looked and wanted to hang out with her for a while. But after a few minutes, I overheard him say, "You so fine, what you doing here? You got a man who is good to you?"

She replied, "I am happily married, but thanks for asking."

This was not even a speed bump. "I think I am going to get you a present. A girl like you should have a pink Cadillac. How would you like that?"

Hearing this, I went to her door and said, "Carol, as soon as you are finished helping this man with his appointment I need to see you in my office." She ushered him out and thanked me for rescuing her.

A few days later I stood by her desk and told her, "Carol, you are so fine. I have a present for you," and gave her a Match-box toy model of a pink Cadillac. She laughed and said, "You are just not right," but it parked on her bookshelf for years. Humor can be a way to defuse a situation, as well as to show someone you care.

Controlling my emotions showed respect for myself, my staff and my patients. I am even tempered, but if I ever felt hassled by emergencies, by problem patients, or by being late for a plane, I tried never to blame those around me, and did my best to keep my own agitation from spilling over in their direction. These women were much more than my co-work-ers. We depended upon, loved, and respected each other, and shared some of the most sublime and tragic events of our lives.

**WEEK 5**                              *Apr 8, 2013 5:17pm*

Hi—Michael just finished his 5th Chemotherapy treatment and his 20th Radiation session. He and David went to Chemo today—David met Dr. Mahoney and kept Michael company during the 4 hours of treatment. Dr. Plunkett also examined Michael today and is really pleased with his response to treatment. YAY!!

We had a great weekend. It is really spring now—the cherry, apple, and dogwood trees are all blooming. On Friday night we went on a walk along the lake in Freedom Park to see the cherry trees in full bloom—then went out to dinner. Saturday we drove to Latta Plantation Park and took a wonderful 5 mile walk along Mountain Island Lake—it was perfect and warm and so quiet, with hardly anyone else on the trails with beautiful views of the lake. Yesterday while I walked, Michael took a bike ride with his friend. He came back grinning ear to ear.

And then to cap off a great weekend, we had Chinese take-out with David and then went to the Double Door Inn for blues. And to make it even more special, Scottie and Michele were there and we all had a great time.

Love—Heidi

**BIG NEWS!!**                                        *Apr 13, 2013 12:03pm*

I have been getting chemotherapy weekly and radiation every weekday for 5 weeks now, and the tumor has gotten significantly smaller. Because of where it is and how well it has responded to treatment so far, my doctors feel that this is most likely a thymic carcinoma (starting in the thymus gland). The treatment for this condition is to remove it, if possible, after chemo and radiation have done their job.

Thymic carcinoma is a rare type of cancer, and my physicians and I agreed that we needed to find a thoracic surgeon who specializes in resection of this specific tumor type. Dr. James Huang, at Memorial Sloan Kettering Cancer Center in New York, is such a specialist. Last week we sent my pretreatment CT and PET scans and a more recent CT to him, and he reviewed the images with his colleagues and called Dr. Plunkett to tell him that he would strongly recommend removing the tumor.

This would be major surgery but is great news. It is the treatment that has the best outcomes for my type of cancer. So I am going to have just one more week of treatment (stopping sooner than we had planned), and then go to New York to meet Dr. Huang. If surgery happens I would expect that it would be done in late May, to allow the full effects of the radiation to take effect and to let the inflammation it caused to settle down.

I wanted to let you know where this road seems to be leading.

Michael

# ASSOCIATE WITH PEOPLE YOU RESPECT

THE GROUP THAT I practiced with in Florida had so many problems it became a toxic work environment. In the days before texting and email, whenever I went away for a weekend I walked in on Monday a little queasy, afraid to learn about whatever crisis had erupted while I was gone. The doctors did not get along. It was a multispecialty group, with an eye doctor, orthopedists, cardiologists, pediatricians, family doctors, allergist, and more. Each had a different mix of office and hospital practice. Some did a lot of blood work while others, like me, hardly used the lab at all. Some depended on referrals and others did primary care. But worst of all, many did not respect their partners and were not proud to be associated with them. So inevitably, there were fatal tensions and the group dissolved after I left.

My practice in Charlotte was another multispecialty group, but was much more focused, comprised of only ophthalmologists and otolaryngologists. When the group was founded, in 1923, Eye, Ear, Nose & Throat was a single specialty. These specialties had a historic, in many ways a natural, affiliation, and though there were tensions the group functioned much more amiably than my first.

In both Vero Beach and in Charlotte I tried to be a good partner, to be an asset to the practice and a contributing member of the group. For many years, I helped govern the practices by serving on the Board of Directors, took turns as head of both the Eye Department and the entire group, and helped develop new services, like clinical research and the ambulatory surgery center, to benefit both specialties. And, I usually took call on Christmas along with the only Jewish ENT. It was a nice favor to do for our partners.


## CHRISTMAS CALL


ONE CHRISTMAS DAY at around 4PM, both the Ear, Nose & Throat doctor and I were called into the office to see patients who couldn't wait until morning. We finished our work at about the same time, and as we headed for the door together we ran into the nurse who triaged phone calls and helped with emergencies on nights and weekends. We wished her Merry Christmas, and she said, "I just want to say that I think it's wonderful that you both volunteered to take call again on Christmas and Christmas Eve."

I said, "Happy to do it. Neither of us celebrates Christmas, so why not give our partners a day off to be with their families?"

"Well, I know the other doctors appreciate it. I just think it's really nice of you to be so thoughtful."

"Of course. It's the Christian thing to do."

# CHAPTER 22

## TANGLED WEB

IGHWAY 321 WAS wide open after Lincolnton, the rolling countryside, manicured fields, and pine forest slowly rising toward the Blue Ridge. A great day for driving. 'Should be in Blowing Rock in about 45 minutes', Henry thought. 'It'll be great just to kick back and take it easy at the mountain house for a couple days.' His reverie was interrupted by flashing lights in the rearview mirror. After a reflexive, 'Oh crap' he remembered he was going to be all right. Nothing to worry about. Smiling, he took his foot off the gas and glided to a stop on the shoulder. The state trooper pulled over a few yards behind, sat for a while running the plate, and then got out and strode to the driver's side window.

Henry, one of my partners, rolled it down and said, "Hello Officer. Do I have a tail light out or something?"

"Uh, no," he said. "but I clocked you doing 84 in a 55 zone. What's the rush?"

"Oh, was I driving a little too fast? There's a patient getting ready to go into the operating room at Mission Hospital in Asheville. Needs an emergency cornea transplant. Might go blind if she doesn't have the surgery today."

"Why are you telling me this?" asked the trooper.

Henry gave a thumbs up and pointed over his shoulder to the back seat. There, belted in, was a small Styrofoam cooler with big red letters on the side spelling the words 'Organ Tissue For Transplant —Contains Human Eyes.' He kept it there as insurance. "See that cooler? I'm an eye surgeon, and I'm rushing these human eyes from the Eye Bank to the hospital. I'm so sorry if I was going a little over the limit, but I really need to get there as soon as possible or that poor woman..."

The trooper did not ask him to open the cooler. They never do. That's the beauty of it. Who wants to look at unseeing eyes floating in a jar of cloudy yellow fluid? But instead of the usual, "OK, try to slow down and be safe," this Trooper said, "Wow, that's awful. Tell you what. With the way traffic is on 40, you better follow me. Let's go." He hustled back to his car, turned on the light bar, and pulled out. With Henry following, they took the Black Mountain grade at nearly 90, and reached the Emergency Room in record time.

Henry pulled his car under the overhang, waved to the Trooper and shouted, "Thanks for the escort, Officer." With a toot of his horn, the police car rolled away. As soon as it was out of sight, without going into the hospital, he slinked along back roads for two hours to his mountain house mumbling, "First time I ever drove to Blowing Rock through Asheville."

# YEARNING TO BREATHE FREE

"GET READY. YOUR next patient is Joan," Beth said.

"Did she come alone this time?"

"Hah! What do you think? Fat chance. Her dad is in the chair next to you and her mom is as far away as she can be and still be in the same room. She's already got her hands over her face."

Forewarned, I opened the door and went into the exam room. There was Joan, eighteen years old and ready to graduate high school, with her father and mother looking on nervously. "Hi Joan, how are you doing today? Any problems since your laser treatment last week?"

Her father answered, "I think we are doing fine. No real trouble. What was the name of that procedure again? I know you told us, but what was it for?"

Looking at dad, I said "It is called a laser iridotomy. She needed it because she has something called angle closure. The front part of her eye is very crowded, the natural drainage channels are partly blocked, and the fluid that circulates inside the eye cannot get out. Remember that the eye pressure built up really high last week, so high she had a headache? The laser treatment was to let that fluid drain normally." Again hoping to hear from the patient, I turned to her and asked, "So Joan, how has your eye felt since the laser? Any light sensitivity, pain or redness?"

Her dad blurted out, "Why did you ask that? Should she have stayed in the dark all week? Did we do something wrong? Did she hurt her eye? Joan, I told you that you should have stayed home. Oh, why did we ever let you go to that party?" Her mother began to cry.

"Whoa, whoa, whoa. Hang on, there was no reason for her to stay indoors all week, and if she felt good enough to go to a party with her friends, I'm glad she did." Joan smiled but kept quiet. I looked at the chart and then directly at her. "I see that your vision is better than before the laser. Let's see how the eye looks today."

Everything was fine; the iridotomy was open, the anterior chamber was deeper, there was no inflammation, and the pressure was normal. "Well, that looks just great. The laser worked exactly as I hoped it would. Before, your pressure was almost 50 and now it is down to 12, so you are out of trouble. Probably it never will shoot up so high again. Soon you won't have to take most of these eye drops either. You have done so well, we should plan to take care of the other eye too so it never gets into the same kind of trouble."

Her mother gasped and dad frantically asked, "Did she catch this problem in the other eye too? How did it get from the left eye into the right eye? Wasn't the pressure all right in that one before? What went wrong?"

Speaking directly to Joan, I explained, "The pressure was fine in the right eye and it is still fine. But the right eye is built the same way as the left, and odds are someday the pressure will shoot up in this eye too. If that happens and you are not near an eye doctor, you could get a bad headache and risk losing some vision. Why worry about that? Since you did so well, why not try to prevent this from happening again? It is always better to stay out of trouble than to try to get out of trouble."

Before her father could react, Joan said, "Let's do it." I shepherded them all to Carol to set a date. After they left Scottie and Beth popped out of the middle room, smiling. I could tell they had eavesdropped on the entire conversation.

I said, "I feel bad for that girl. She is a nice kid who wants to make her own decisions, but her parents are just smothering. I bet she ends up going to college far away from here, like in California."

We took bets. A few weeks later Joan was still doing well, and I asked if she had decided where to go to college next year. She smiled and said, "University of Arizona!"

Later that day, I told Scottie, Beth and Carol, "Okay, I lost. She is only going to Arizona." But then after a year in Tucson, she transferred to the University of Hawaii.


# CARE ABOUT PEOPLE


ONE REASON HEIDI is such a good therapist is that she is a great listener. She likes people and is interested in finding out what makes them tick. She says, "Everyone has a story. All you have to do is ask." There is no way to be a good physician or even a good person if you don't care about people, aren't curious about them, and don't enjoy being with them. This is one of the great pleasures of our profession.

As suggested by surgeon and medical writer Atul Gawande, whenever time allows, I try to ask an unnecessary question, one that has nothing to do with the reason for the patient's visit. 'What did you have for breakfast today?' 'Have you read anything good lately?' 'Did you knit that sweater?' Simply by showing interest and a willingness to listen, people become anxious to reveal themselves in wonderful and unexpected ways. Knowing patients is key to providing excellent care, and a good first step is to ask them to talk about what interests and motivates them. It is fun to learn about more than just their eyes.

This conversation rarely happens without an explicit invitation to talk. And often, people who seem to be one thing turn out, with trust and time, to be more complex and fascinating than I could imagine.

# DUCKPINS

GANGLY, HE SHUFFLED into the exam room with short stiff steps, his soles sliding across the carpet as if dancing a soft shoe. His face was blank and tilted toward the floor to avoid falling. With him was his daughter, visibly concerned.

"Daddy just can't see anymore. His glaucoma has gotten bad. He is so discouraged I don't even think he takes his drops the way he should."

"Mr. Dillon, do you feel like your vision has been getting worse lately?"

"Hmph," he grunted. "Maybe a little worse. It's already so bad I'm not sure that anything I do is gonna make a difference anyway."

His eyesight was miserable, with no peripheral vision. And even in his better eye the last remaining island of clarity was so tiny he could pick out only one letter at a time. He couldn't read or drive and had been legally blind for years because of punishing and permanent optic nerve damage. He was resigned to the inevitability of complete blindness.

"Daddy retired from the heating and air business a long time ago, but he sure wishes that he could still see well enough to bowl."

"You like to bowl? Really? Are you in a league? What is your average?"

"Hmph. Duckpins," he reluctantly volunteered.

"Come on Daddy, talk to the doctor," she scolded. "He won't brag about it, but he is in the Duckpin Bowling Hall of Fame. He is famous in that little world; the only duckpin bowling alley in the entire state is at his place in Kings Mountain."

"He has a bowling alley in his house?"

He perked up, "No, I redid the basement of my HVAC business and put in lanes for leagues and tournaments. I still bowl sometimes, but it is hard to see the pins now, so mostly I just hang around with the people who come to play."

We talked for a while about duckpin bowling, which was news to me. He reminisced about places he had traveled for tournaments, setting up his lanes, and bowlers who traveled bowl in his legendary basement. We discussed what might be realistic goals for his treatment.

He never did completely lose vision, and for several years his daughter drove an hour and a half from home, bypassing many other eye doctors, though there was little I could do for her dad's eyes. His daughter said, "If Daddy didn't like you, he sure would let you know." But while there was nothing we could do to improve his eyesight, we must have helped him in some way. Our office was one of the only places he could talk to new people about his passion and where, for a few minutes, a compassionate and curious group of strangers reminded him that he remained a vital, fascinating, necessary person, and not just the disabled, nearly blind, old man he appeared to be.

# CAN'T JUDGE A BOOK

FROM THE START of our hiking vacation in Montana, some in our group were happy to stroll and talk, others cautiously picked their way over rocks and roots, and one couple jackrabbited ahead. All week, these fast walkers ended up way out front on every hike and waited impatiently for the group to catch up. "About time. What took ya'? When you didn't show up I thought maybe we went down the wrong trail or somethin." She was in good shape, but he practically ran up the trail, pulling her along as if by a rope between their waists.

That night at dinner we sat with two other people from our group, an accountant and minister from the Bay Area. Lovely, fascinating people who we met that morning during the walk. And sharing our table was that annoyingly impatient couple. What would an ophthalmologist, a psychologist, an accountant and a minister have to say to these people once we rehashed the day's hike?

Making conversation, I found out he was an auto body repairman and she worked in a lawyer's office. Heidi heard about his job and told him that she had just taken up welding as a hobby and asked if he knew how to weld. He became animated and they talked for a long time about TIG, MIG, brazing, and other kinds of welding that he used to fix cars.

She told him, "I am a psychologist. All day long I sit and talk and listen, so I wanted a hobby that lets me get out of my head a little. I wanted to use a different part of my brain and learn a new physical skill too."

He replied somewhat cryptically, "Hobbies are good. Everybody needs a hobby."

I would have ignored this, but she asked the next question, "Do you have any hobbies?"

"I have two hobbies." Smugly, I thought he would say, "I collect beer cans and watch wrestling." Or, "I play blackjack and steal hubcaps." But instead, he said, "I am a professional skeet shooter. And, I am a piano technician at Carnegie Hall." This was like learning that Mike Tyson relaxes by doing calculus.

"Carnegie Hall? In New York? Really?"

"Been doing it for years."

"Wow. What does a piano technician do? Do you tune the pianos?"

"That's part of it. But the main thing is when a soloist comes to play they always like their pianos set up in a particular way. Maybe they like the keys soft, maybe they like the tuning to be a little different or the bench higher or lower. I make sure the piano is exactly the way they like it. Then I get to watch the performances from the wings. I love it."

He was still annoying on the trail, but this reminded me that first impressions are misleading, and that snobbily jumping to conclusions about people without learning about them is uncharitable and impoverishing. With gentle probing, most people turn out to be interesting and complex. Everybody has a story if you ask and listen.

In the office, when time allows, I like to ask patients about their families, their work, their hobbies, places they've been, and books they've read; whatever gets their juices flowing. But some patients may mistake my interest for something else entirely. I need to draw clear boundaries and keep professional distance so there is no way to misconstrue my human interest as wanting to 'know' the patient in the Biblical sense.

# CHAPERONE

"GIVE THESE DROPS a try and call in a couple weeks to let me know if they are more comfortable than the last ones you used, okay Gail?"

"All right, but what if they bother me too?"

"After a while, if you think you won't be able to take them I will switch you to something else. But I bet they won't give you any trouble. Lots of people take these for years. You're going to do fine with them. And if all is well I'll see you in 6 or 8 weeks so I can be sure they are controlling your pressure."

"Are you sure it's safe to wait that long?" She was a thin woman with long blond hair, thick glasses, and extravagant make-up. Friendly but anxious, bright and broadly educated. We often talked, if there was time, about books, music, and current events.

"Don't worry. The drops you've been taking until now won't completely wear off for a few weeks. Even after you stop taking them, they will stay in your system and will keep your pressure down, so your glaucoma won't actually be untreated for very long. It is impossible to tell how the new drops are working if the old ones are still on board, so there's no way around it; we have to wait at least a month to let them wash out first."

"Okay, that makes sense. Thanks so much for all you do. I always feel better after I see you."

She got up from the exam chair and left the office. As soon as the door closed behind her, Scottie shot out of her room. Beth was right behind her. Carol stood up from her desk and they gathered in the hallway outside her office. They looked at me, silently. Another intervention.

"What?" I asked, turning from one to the others. "What's the matter?"

Scottie turned to Carol and said, "He has no idea, does he?"

"Uh uh," she replied, shaking her head slowly.

"What are you talking about? What's going on?"

"Dr. Rotberg, I'm telling you, that girl is sweet on you."

"Who, Gail? No way!"

"Yes way. It's clear as day. As my Daddy used to say, 'I done seen it a-stickin' out.' Why do you think she's always coming in here and never ends up having anything wrong?"

"Come on."

They all laughed. "Listen, we all can hear how she talks to you. Every time it's, 'Oh, Dr. Rotberg, that is so funny'. Or, 'I really enjoy seeing you, you make me feel so much better'. Or, 'You really listen to me. You are so easy to talk to'. I mean, gag me with a spoon."

Beth added, "We've been talking about this and I think maybe one of us should be in the room when you examine her next time."

"Really?" I asked, incredulous.

Carol said, "Oh yeah. Let me be your scribe for her visits from now on. And it wouldn't be a bad idea if the next time she calls with some big emergency, probably two or three days from now, I tell her that you are overbooked or out of the office and that I will have to work her into somebody else's schedule. I bet she won't come in unless she can see you."

"Wow, I think you're wrong, but...all right, if she calls and wants to be worked in within the next couple weeks put her with another doctor and we'll see what she does. I know what you mean, she makes it sound like she has a major problem and then when she gets here nothing's going on."

A few days later, I walked into the office and Carol said, "I was right!"

"About what?"

"Guess who called all worried and wants to see you right away. But when I told her you were in the OR and she would have to see another doctor she said, 'Oh, it's not that important. Can I see Dr. Rotberg tomorrow?' See, we knew it!"

"Oy vey." I cracked Scottie's door, motioned for her to get Beth and told them all, "Okay, okay, I admit it, you were right. I still kind of don't believe it, but thank you for picking this up. I better be really careful. Obviously, it would be smart for one of you to be in the room during her visits so she and I are never alone behind closed doors."

This was before the invention of email, so at the end of every day I had a big stack of interoffice envelopes, journals, loose papers, and letters to plow through. Much of it went directly into the can. But I always read the greeting cards, because I loved hearing from appreciative patients. A few days after our conversation, I had one card from a woman telling me how happy she was with her cataract surgery, and another from the daughter of a long-time patient who had just passed away, thanking us all for the kindness we had shown her mother over the years. And there was a third card, without a return address. I opened the envelope and blurted out, "Oh no!" They all came running.

"Wait till you hear this," I said. "Let me read you this card I just opened. It says, 'Dear Dr. Rotberg. I really appreciate all that you have done for me and my eyes. I enjoy our time together so much and look forward to seeing you. I think about you when we are not together. I know you are married, and so am I, but I would love to get to know you better. Will you call me? Signed...'"

"Gail?" they all shouted.

"Oh no she dit'n," added Carol, with a smirk and a head waggle.

"You guys saved me. I owe you lunch." I made two calls. First, to Heidi to tell her about my secret admirer. Second, to the head of our Human Resources department to ask her what to do.

"Well, Dr. Rotberg," she said, "I get where she's coming from, I really do, but you can't be her doctor anymore. Boundaries, you know."

"What should I do?"

"Give me the card to put in her file. And write her a letter telling her that you have been honored to be her doctor but that she needs to find a new one in another practice. You will take care of her for the next thirty days if she has an emergency, but that's it. And let me show it to our compliance people before you send it, OK?"

If this had been a movie or soap-opera I would have ignored her advice, but in real life that was the end of the story.

---

**CHEMO WEEK 6**                                        *Apr 15, 2013 8:11am*

Hi—Michael and I are getting ready to go to his 6th and final Chemo treatment—we leave in a few minutes. He's wearing a tee shirt he got in Vancouver with a killer whale on it. The Orcas have lots of meaning for us—one of our best experiences ever was kayaking with the whales in the San Juan Islands. Totally aware of the beauty and magnificence of nature, the ocean, us and the whales. Hope Michael can feel that during Chemo/radiation today.

Those of you who know me know that I like to have a plan. For both of us it has been a strange couple of months—our lives have been turned inside out—and while we want a plan and want to know how this is all going to turn out and want everything to be 'normal' again, we have to just accept the uncertainty and be present. My project has been supporting and helping Michael have the best possible experience and outcome during Chemo/radiation, while taking care of myself and being a mom to Emily, Josh and David. I now have a new project—one that I can make plans for—NYC.

Thank you for all of your support, posts, love, thoughts and prayers. Wish I had the words to express how much that means, how much you mean, and how important you are. Thank you.

Love—Heidi

# CHAPTER 23

## HOLIDAY SPIRIT

S COTTIE HELD THE phone away from her ear, rolled her eyes, and said, "It's Minerva again!"

"We just saw her a couple weeks ago, right after Thanksgiving. What is it now?" I asked.

"Oh, I don't know. Sounds like she woke up with some crust in the corner of her eye and she's all worried about it."

"Well, she's 90 years old; worrying got her where she is, but there's no way I can see her today. I mean, we're swamped, and I've got to get to the OR."

"You go on upstairs, do your case, and I'll see what I can do."

A few hours later, when I came down from the Surgery Center, Kelly, who worked for one of my partners, came over to see me. "We saw one of your patients today. She's so sweet, bless her heart. Like a little bird with her tiny purse and that church lady hat."

"Oh, thanks for seeing her. How is Minerva? What was going on today?"

"Her lids were a little crusty, so we told her to use hot compresses and artificial tears and to call your office if she doesn't get better."

"I'm glad she is all right. She is such a nice lady," I said.

"Yeah, she is. Just before she got up to leave, she said in that little voice of hers, 'Tell Dr. Rotberg I wish him a Merry Christmas.' And when I said, 'Ma'am, I don't think Dr. Rotberg celebrates Christmas,' it threw her for a loop. It kind of confused her. She got flustered, but after a few seconds she smiled and said, 'Oh well, then please tell him I wished him a Happy Kwanzaa.'"

One concrete way to express gratitude and respect is to be polite. I don't celebrate Kwanzaa either, but I appreciated her kindness and welcomed her greeting in the spirit she offered it.

# KINDNESS

ALONG WITH DENIAL, anger, bargaining, and sadness, people who are newly diagnosed with serious medical problems often feel resentful. 'What did I do to deserve this?' 'Whose fault is it that I'm sick?' 'Why me?' But that is not productive or compassionate toward yourself or others. Unless what you really mean by 'why me?' is 'why should this ever happen to anyone?', what you're really saying is that you wish this were happening to someone else instead of to you. Hardly a sentiment likely to open the gates of heaven.

It may seem that negative emotions are the appropriate response to an illness, but in my experience, as both a doctor and a patient, the opposite is true. While facing a medical crisis, gratitude and kindness are infinitely more helpful. An 'attitude of gratitude' is the key to happiness throughout life, and even more so when relying on the help of family members and medical professionals. Feeling and freely expressing thanks for the love they give and the expertise they share is proper and salutary.

Illness presents an opportunity to try to be kind to others. Take stock of relationships that have grown stale, friendships that have faded. What better time to apologize for hurt feelings or to mend fences? Being kind to others makes you feel good about yourself and can restore to your life people who once were important to you but who have drifted, or been pushed, away.

Illness is also a good time to start being kind to yourself. To stop beating yourself up for things you have done wrong or not done at all. For being fat or ugly. For not being a perfect human being. But who is? Accepting yourself, respecting yourself, beginning to like yourself more, doesn't mean deluding yourself that you have no room for improvement. But when you stop fighting internal battles it puts you in a stronger position to tackle the real and pressing external challenges in your life.

And, it is also a good time to give charity, not to adjust your karma, but because it is the right thing to do. I'm pretty sure I didn't do anything to deserve my illness. Maybe the guy standing in the median at the red light, holding a sign asking for money, didn't deserve his hardships either. Maybe he did, but since becoming a patient, I am much more likely to roll down my window and hand over a dollar or two. How do I know he's not going to buy drugs or beer with that money? I don't, and I hope he uses my little gift wisely, but if he doesn't, it's on him. Whenever I have a chance to be charitable, I don't want to judge. I try to opt for generosity and kindness instead.

---

**PHASE 1 OF TREATMENT COMPLETED!**        *Apr 18, 2013 4:54pm*

Michael had his final Radiation treatment today! He has completed the first phase of his treatment. Dr. Plunkett and his staff were so wonderful to Michael—thank you.

The future of Michael's treatment, at this point, is an unknown. Dr. Huang at Memorial Sloan-Kettering will evaluate him on 5/2/13. I will not be posting until then—time to take a break and heal, getting ready for whatever comes next. I will post from NYC—promise!

Thank you for your posts, thoughts, prayers and love.

Love—Heidi

---

**AN IMPORTANT LESSON**        *Apr 26, 2013 11:04pm*

I am reading a book about how to prepare mentally and emotionally for upcoming surgery, and today saw something there that really rings true: "We live immersed in a palpable field of love, yet many don't feel it…. But the love … is always there."

It is not news to me that Heidi and I have good friends, supportive family, and a network of people who care about us. But this Caring Bridge site continues to amaze me. It reminds me daily just how many people our lives have touched and what a deep and wide well of support, care, and prayer we can call upon. With its nearly 9000 visits and 660 Guestbook entries, it is an archive of friendship, love, admiration and concern; a searchable index of the web of

> caring that was always there but was less palpable and less visible when less needed.
>
> I appreciate everyone who cares enough to read this site, who writes in, or who even just thinks of us and wishes us well. The realization that so many people care for us is only one of the many blessings we have to be grateful for and is one of the most powerful lessons that I will take away from this entire experience.
>
> Michael

# METTA

ONE OF THE biggest problems in treating glaucoma is that people have to use eye drops every day, sometimes several times a day, often more than one kind of drop. Glaucoma has no symptoms; vision declines so slowly and painlessly that people can know, intellectually, that their vision is at risk, but never really believe they have a problem serious enough to justify the expense, hassle, and bothersome side effects of their medication. After a few weeks, many people stop taking their drops on schedule or at all. How much better would it be if there was a medicine I could give in the office to control the disease without relying on the patient to do anything at home?

This was the idea behind a study testing a new injectable form of an existing, already approved glaucoma medication. Along with other physicians from around the country, I signed up as an investigator to make sure it was safe and effective. Since this injection was going to be done at many locations, the manufacturer wanted to be sure that everyone used a standard technique to minimize confounding variables from site to site. They flew us to their headquarters to teach us the right way to do these injections using lab animals, dogs living in their lab.

This was troubling to me. It was the first time I ever had to operate on animals. In training, we often used pig eyes from the slaughterhouse to practice new surgical techniques, but never living animals. When I learned that to participate in this study I had to work on living dogs, I asked the study's medical director if it really was necessary. He insisted that it was, and I agreed to take part. But this confused and saddened one of my friends, and after hesitating several days she wrote me a letter.

*Dear Michael,*

*When you mentioned the training you were getting ready to take, it was very difficult for me to understand. I know when people are young and in school or needing to develop their careers, they are often forced to make difficult choices. It seems that when one is well along and well respected in their career, they have the power to take a stance for what is right and humane.*

*For the last week I have struggled what to say as a friend who loves and respects you. There is so much pain and suffering in this world, and it is in my nature to feel things deeply, so it seemed best to write a note and spare you my sadness. When I was in elementary school I read a poem about vivisection, 'They Called Him Rags.' It deeply touched me and was actually the first poem I ever memorized as a child.*

*There is a newsletter I got this week, which addresses acquisition of dogs for research. As you are probably aware, most are taken or bought from shelters. Of course, there are many reasons why dogs end up in shelters. I doubt many people are* aware that their beloved pet might end up as a research animal. Even if a dog is anesthetized during research, it is still confined to life in a small cage before, perhaps euthanized afterward, or repeatedly used. Here are a few thoughts from some famous thinkers, better put than I ever could:

"The question is not, 'Can they reason?' nor, 'Can they talk?' but rather, 'Can they suffer?'" Jeremy Bentham

"I care not much for a man's religion whose dog and cat are not the better for it." Abraham Lincoln

"Animals suffer as much as we do... Until we extend our circle of compassion to all living things, humanity will not find peace." Albert Schweitzer

"The greatness of a nation and its moral progress can be judged by the way its animals are treated." Mahatma Gandhi

Thanks for reading this.

She was right, and I was chastened, so I replied with a letter of my own:

This letter is about the note you left for me after dinner last week. I hope we can talk about this soon.

Most of all, I need to thank you for your letter. I appreciate your taking the time to write it and to share it with me. I feel fortunate that you care enough about me to try to steer me onto the right path, and am humbled that you are so passionate about, and committed to fighting, the evils of using live animals in medical research.

When I read the letter for the first time, I felt the way I would feel if a friend had whispered to me that I had bad breath or some egg on my tie. Not so much chastened as glad that *someone would, in a caring and private way, point out to me a failing that I had not recognized in myself.*

*Why I had a moral blind-spot about doing animal surgery I cannot explain. I have done practice surgery on enucleated pig eyes many times. But in nearly 30 years as an ophthalmologist I have never, not once, performed surgery of any kind on a living animal. I was never placed in a position where I was required or expected to do so. Despite this, most of my human patients seem to have done just fine, so I don't think my surgical skills or training suffered in any way from the lack of prior experience working on animals. I agree that animal surgery is hardly ever appropriate, and why it should be necessary now is a question I should already have asked the company long before your letter arrived.*

*So why didn't I think to question the director of research there a couple months ago when he told me that I would need to go to their dog lab to learn the injection technique that is going to be used in our upcoming study? I cannot explain, but am ashamed I did not.*

*Belatedly, I did call him yesterday to say that I was concerned about having to use living animals to learn this technique, to ask if I could use pig eyes instead, and to be certain that they had not required this of me casually or without good reason.*

*You may feel that this is not an adequate reason or maybe even that there never can be any justification for involving animals in medical research. I now wish I had not agreed to do it, but since I did I think I need to honor this commitment. I am going to go, but regret having agreed to do it, and will never do anything like this again. I am thankful to you for opening my eyes about the ethical issues and am disappointed in myself that I needed your help in this way. I also promise to*

*use my trip to urge the company to find another way to train*
*surgeons in this new technique in the future.*

*I hope this explanation makes sense to you and is one that*
*you can live with. Your love and respect mean a lot to me and*
*I sincerely hope that this aberration will not interfere with*
*our friendship in any way. Thanks again for your guidance.*

# RESPECT

THERE IS A power differential built into all doctor-patient relationships. Usually, the physician knows more about the patient's condition, prognosis, and treatment options than does
the patient. Smart and interested patients do their research,
read pertinent medical literature, and become experts about
their illnesses, but even a patient who is a physician may lose
the objectivity needed to call the shots. For the doctor-patient
relationship to work there has to be trust and respect, authority both freely given and revocable.

The trust and respect flows both ways. To be worthy of the
patient's confidence and to justify the respect that forms the
basis of the working relationship, everything the doctor does
needs to be for the patient's benefit.

I need to respect my patient's intelligence by helping her
understand her illness, the various treatments available, and
the likely impact on her and her family's lives. Much better a
patient asks too many questions than sits silently, too nervous
or fearful to participate in her own care. I am always happy to
answer questions, because it shows that the person sitting in
the exam chair is interested in taking an active role in healing.

I should respect my patient's concerns and try to ferret them out. People believe all kinds of things that can influence their decision making and it is critical for me to identify superstitious, erroneous, and fear-based ideas so people can make decisions free of their crippling effects. Even when the prognosis is dismal it is better to keep facts in mind.

I have to respect my patient's autonomy and privacy, the patient's right to make the wrong decision. One of the most difficult conversations I have with patients is when I tell them that they need to stop driving. For many people, driving means independence. Giving up the license is a sign of preparing to circle the drain, of a future that promises isolation, dependency, and deterioration. The loss of autonomy and freedom is a big deal, especially in a place without good public transportation. But when someone loses so much vision that driving becomes unsafe, we need to have the talk.

People with uncorrectable blurry vision due to macular degeneration, diabetes, or other conditions realize they don't see well. While they hate to admit that the time has come to stop driving, they often recognize that their vision is poor and don't squawk too loudly when push comes to shove. But people who have lost vision to glaucoma are more resistant because of the way glaucoma damages sight. Glaucoma nibbles away at the peripheral vision, and until very late in the disease visual acuity remains clear. People may still see 20/20 while being legally blind because of tunnel vision. They can read road signs, but cannot see people getting out of parked cars, kids riding bicycles in the street, or pedestrians stepping off the curb. They can see, so they remain in denial longer.

In some states, my duty would be to the other people on the road. There, if I learn that a patient is driving with dangerously limited vision, I am obliged to tell the Department of Motor Vehicles. My duty to warn the public overrides the expectation of patient-doctor confidentiality. But where I practice the situation is the reverse. If I tell the state without the patient's permission, I am liable for breaching confidentiality. The onus is on the driver to be responsible enough to know when to stop.

This isn't easy for me, but the patient is a grown, autonomous individual worthy of respect. The patient has the right to make an informed decision and to live with the consequences. The problem is that an irresponsible decision can injure or kill an innocent person. So, after explaining that, in my opinion, the patient needs to stop driving, here is how our conversation usually concludes:

"Oh come on, I can still see fine. I've been driving for more than fifty years and I never had a wreck. I think I'm still a safer driver than a lot of the people out on the road. I mean, have you seen the way some of those kids drive? And anyway, I only ever drive to the market and to church on Sunday. Who's gonna do that for me, huh?"

"Well, I'm glad you haven't had a wreck, but it really isn't safe for you to drive anymore. Your daughter told me she doesn't even like to ride with you. How would you feel if you got in a wreck and hurt somebody?"

"I would feel terrible, but I'm really careful. I only go where I know the roads, and I never drive at night. As long as I'm off the road by dark, I don't think there's a problem. Where I live, I need to be able to drive."

"Well, listen. I'll say it one more time: you really shouldn't be driving, and I'm writing in your medical record that I told you so. But you're the one with the driver's license. You are a responsible adult, and I trust you to do the right thing. I promise I won't report you to the DMV, but I hope you will give up your license before anyone, including you, get hurt." Hopefully, a family member is in the room with us and hears our conversation, but at that point I have to let it go and trust

and respect the patient enough to let her make her own decision.

Part of a respectful doctor-patient relationship is being able
to take it, too. When trust breaks down, there can be no healing. As an expression of admiration and respect, occasionally
patients will criticize something I have done, to point out that
I have fallen short of their expectations and to urge me to do
better next time. Disapproval is never easy to hear, but when
offered, and accepted, in a respectful and loving way, it can be
therapeutic for both of us. For me, because I will not make
the same mistake twice, and for the patient, because the way
I respond demonstrates that I respect her enough to take her
opinion seriously.

Respect for the patient's intelligence, autonomy, privacy,
and fears is a critical foundation of the doctor-patient relationship. For the deepest connection, it is also critical to respect
the patient's opinion, to communicate honestly, and to engage
as equals whenever possible.

---

**SURGICAL CONSULT 5/2/13**                    *May 2, 2013 12:20pm*

Hi from NYC. Michael just had his first meeting with the surgeon
in New York. News is what we expected—big surgery, bad cancer,
still worth doing the surgery. Michael's best prognosis is with
successful surgical resection of the tumor. This cancer is very rare,
and Huang does about 10 Thymic Carcinoma surgeries a year—he
is one of the experts.

We are going on a cruise to Bermuda on Sunday! Be back in
Charlotte on Mothers' Day.

Thanks for being there-

Love—Heidi

# CHAPTER 24

*May 13, 2013 4:46pm*

Hi—We had a WONDERFUL time on the cruise. It was like being in a bubble -a time out of time for us.

Michael is scheduled to have surgery on Wednesday, May 22nd. The surgery will be quite difficult and extensive, and Dr. Huang will not really know what he is dealing with until then. Knowing this, and the potential complications of surgery, Michael is choosing to have the surgery. Successful surgery gives the best prognosis. Michael accepts the risks, and hopefully the reward of a complete resection, with my total support and love.

We are planning on driving to NYC this coming Saturday, so we can spend some time with our kids on Sunday. They and Michael's sister will be there during the surgery.

Your support, caring, prayers, thoughts and posts mean so much to Michael and me. Thank you for being there, part of Team Michael.

I also want to thank you for respecting our need for space and privacy—we know you are there and it really DOES matter.

Love—Heidi

**MONDAY 5/20/13—FROM NY**                    *May 20, 2013 12:00pm*

Hi—The surgery will take at least 5–6 hours and will be quite extensive. While the goal is to remove all of the tumor, Dr. Huang says that based on the scans there is "a better than 50% chance" that he can get it all. We won't know more until he is actually doing the surgery.

Love—Heidi

**FOUR LEAF CLOVER**                    *May 21, 2013 6:17pm*

Surgery is set for tomorrow morning, but today was a free day in New York and we went to the Botanical Garden. Beautiful springtime flowers, etc. While waiting for the bus to come back to Manhattan we were standing on the grass, I looked down, and there was a four-leaf clover!

Michael

**SURGERY IS FINISHED**                          *May 22, 2013 5:02pm*

The surgery is finished and Michael is in the Recovery Room.

They were not able to remove the tumor.

Recovery will be a few days. We are going to stay in NY until
Michael is cleared to go home.

Thank you for giving us the space and time we need right now.

Love—Heidi

**HERE IS WHAT HAPPENED**                    *May 24, 2013 7:39am*

Here is a little more detail. We had three goals for this surgery. The first was to find out if the tumor could be removed, and there was no way to know that for sure without trying. The second was to get more tissue to send to the pathologists so they could test it further to see if any particular treatment options seem likely to be productive. The third, of course, was to actually remove the tumor, but unfortunately that was not possible.

We know that complete resection of the tumor would have been a good thing for my life expectancy, but there is no evidence that removing only part of the tumor would help much. That means that the entire tumor, plus some normal tissue at its edges, would have to be removed to do any good. In fact, if the surgeon had to cut across the tumor there would be a chance that it could spill into the chest and spread more easily, actually making things worse. In the OR, when he entered the chest he discovered that the tumor could not be separated from the ribs or the muscles in the chest wall. This meant that if he continued to try to remove it he would either have to cut across a large part of the tumor, which would be counter-productive, or he would have to remove the sternum (breastbone) and all the ribs on the right side. This would have been a gigantic operation and would have left me very debilitated and we don't even know how much it would have helped. So we decided to just get another biopsy and not to proceed with complete removal.

I think I have had this tumor for a long time before it was discovered and hopefully, by not poking the hornets' nest by being overly aggressive, I will be able to continue to live with it.

Michael

**HEALING CONTINUES**                    *Jun 4, 2013 5:39pm*

Hi—Michael saw his surgeon as well as an oncologist and radiation oncologist. They are very impressed with Michael's healing. Besides being on no pain meds at all, Michael has been walking miles each day (today he walked 8.5 miles). He released Michael from all restrictions and he is free to go!

The radiation oncologist was very complimentary about the Chemo/radiation Michael received in Charlotte. He recommends that Michael complete the originally planned Chemo/radiation now. Michael already has an appointment with Dr. Plunkett for next week!

We are enjoying NYC—especially the time with Emily & Josh—but we are ready to go home.

Love—Heidi

**NEW YORK IS GREAT BUT...**                    *Jun 9, 2013 7:23am*

If we had been there for any other reason, it would have been a real treat to be able to spend three weeks in New York. I have never been in the city for such an extended visit, and we did walk all over the place, go to some museums, a play, and lots of good restaurants. And we also spent a lot of time with Emily and Josh. But we were not in the city as tourists. In spite of not being able to have my tumor removed, we both feel the trip was worthwhile.

Our goal in making this trip was to find out if the tumor could be resected, to try to get more tissue to confirm or refine the diagnosis, and to have another team of experts review my case, make recommendations, and then serve as consultants if we need their help later. We saw not only the surgeon, but a radiation oncologist and a medical oncologist, both of whom have interest and experience in treating this unusual tumor. The timing of my consultations was fortuitous too. The national oncology meeting had been the previous week, and some new information was presented there about my disease. And, I was the subject of the tumor board (where all the doctors get together to discuss complex cases) at Sloan-Kettering on the morning of my last appointment, so I was able to get the consensus opinion of of the entire thoracic oncology and pathology team as well.

In the end, my diagnosis was confirmed as being squamous thymic carcinoma. The doctors in NY agreed that the treatment I have gotten in Charlotte is exactly the treatment that they would have chosen for me themselves. They were pleased with the competence and quality of my treatment here and admitted that they often see patients who come to them having not had appropriate care at home. Thank you Drs. Mahoney and Dr. Plunkett!

Now, since surgery is off the table, they want me to go ahead and complete my previously planned course of chemo and radiation and then to follow it up with two courses of higher dose chemotherapy. This is probably when my hair will finally fall out, but since it will also be the end of treatment I am OK with it, especially because the oncologist in NY feels that this plan of treatment is likely to "take care of it." Then we will just be in observation mode, doing scans every few months to be sure everything remains stable.

It was terrific to have an expert opinion—from someone who has both research and clinical experience with thymic carcinoma—that I have had the "definitive treatment" and that I'm "good to go."

It also is great to again have a plan to follow and to be able to look forward to the prospect, before the end of the summer, of the conclusion of treatment and the gradual return to a 'new normal' that hopefully will resemble the old normal as much as possible.

Michael

## CHEMO/RADIATION UPDATE AND LAST TREATMENT

*June 24, 2013 9:16am*

Hi—we are in the infusion room, waiting for Michael's chemo. Radiation is at 4 today. This is the final combined chemo + radiation treatment. After the last 6 radiation treatments Michael will have 2 cycles of high dose chemo only. Given the treatment schedule, we are going to take a couple of trips! For the long July 4th weekend we are going to drive to Florida! We'll see friends in Vero Beach for the 4th, then go to Boca to see David and my mom. Then in August we are taking all the kids on a family vacation to Bar Harbor, Maine! So there is a plan that includes treatment, travel, friends, family and fun.

Love—Heidi

## HAPPY                                          *June 27, 2013 8:30 AM*

Hi—I was out walking in the neighborhood this morning and despite the hot/humid Charlotte summer weather I realized I felt pretty happy and was enjoying my walk. Being the introvert and therapist I am, I began to question this: how could I feel so happy? Was it denial, or habit, or just me? And then I had an image of a cookie with a burnt edge. I would not throw out a cookie with a burnt edge—I'd eat the cookie and try to avoid the edge. I feel like my life is like that cookie—I know there is a burnt edge to my life right now—but I'm still going to enjoy every crumb of that cookie that I can. I have so much to be thankful for—and so much in my life to look forward to and celebrate. I also am very aware —hyperaware—of that burnt edge of Michael's cancer. But life is still good—and Michael and I are still here together—and I'm happy.

Love—Heidi

# CHAPTER 25

## CURTIS AND LILA

"WELL DOC," HE asked with a devilish grin that slid into a full smile, "you think those Blue Devils will be any good this year?" He was in his early 80s, short and trim with thinning hair, freshly shaven, wearing a pressed flannel shirt, khakis, and scuffed brown shoes.

"Probably not as good as the Big Blue, Mr. Tugwell. Kentucky looks like they are loaded again."

"Please don't get him talking about Kentucky basketball," said his wife, who always sat in on his appointments. "I don't know what I was thinking when I married a Kentucky grad. Once he gets going you'll never get him to stop long enough to do his eye exam."

"She's right Curtis. You have complicated eyes and we better get to it. How have you been doing lately?" He had advanced glaucoma. By the time we met one eye was already blind. The other had uncontrolled pressures that threatened his remaining vision. After I did a second glaucoma operation on the good eye his pressure and his vision stabilized. But whenever he walked in the door I held my breath until my first peek through the slit lamp, because I knew it was just a matter of time before something went wrong. If his pressure rose, his only seeing eye would go blind. And overly low intraocular pressure in a hypertensive, anti-coagulated, one eyed man with tunnel vision and coke bottle glasses would be a slow-motion disaster. Still, against all odds, his eye continued to do well.

"Everything seems to be just fine," he said. "No problems, but I am really worried about the Wildcats this year."

"See Dr. Rotberg," his wife said, "that's why I come to all his appointments. It's not just 'cause I love to see you, though I do, I admit it. But if I weren't here he would never tell you anything. And when he got home he wouldn't tell me what you said, either." She had her own challenges. She too could barely see, thick glasses restricting peripheral vision, so her gait was cautious and tentative. She found her purpose in looking after Curtis. He drove her everywhere and she kept his life in order. "He is always complaining to me that he doesn't see well. He can't drive at night. Thank God, since the operation controlled his pressure at least he doesn't have to remember to put drops in anymore."

He was hard of hearing, but said, "Oh, come on now..."

She added, "His memory is getting pretty bad too. I like to hear what you tell him because I don't think he remembers too much of it by the time he gets home. He just says you two mostly talk about basketball, and if I ask him he won't or can't tell me what else you said."

One day he came in for his appointment without her. "Mr. Tugwell, where's Lila?"

"She wanted to come with me but she doesn't feel too good today, yesterday either. She's kind of tired of hearing about Kentucky basketball, anyway. You know she went to Duke, right?"

"I know it," I said. "She's the smart one in the family." He chuckled. "Please tell her I asked after her, all right?"

"Sure, I've been doing fine with my eyes…"

In fact, his eyes were stable, his vision hadn't changed, his surgery was still working, his pressure was good, and there was no sign of infection or irritation. Although blind, the other eye was comfortable. "Well Curtis, you look all right. Be sure to tell Lila that she can call me if she has any questions about today's exam, OK?"

"Sure, I'm going right home. See you in a few months. The season will be over by then and we can both cry about how our teams did this year." As he walked down the hall he chatted for a minute with Carol, made his next appointment, and headed for the front door at about 12:30. He was the last patient of the morning.

The afternoon was busy, one crisis after another. At 4:30, as I was finishing a note on the computer, I looked up to see Carol standing in the open door with a worried look on her face.

"What time did Mr. Tugwell leave here?" she asked.

"About 12:30, I think. Why?"

"Did he have to go for any tests or did he say he was going anywhere after you finished with him?"

"No, he said he was going straight home. What's up?"

"Well, his wife just called to ask when he was going to be finished here. He still isn't home."

I looked at the time. "Oh no. That's bad. It should have taken him only ten or fifteen minutes. You know, this is the first time in years that she hasn't come to his appointment with him."

"I know. She said she hated that she couldn't. She is worried that his memory is getting worse and worries about him driving by himself. She said, I can't see, but at least I know where I'm going. And he doesn't have a cell phone, either."

"She better call the police. He might be lost."

An hour later, she called back to tell us she knew where he was. The police had called her. When Curtis left our office he didn't go home, but instead somehow got onto the highway and headed west for about an hour and a half. He made it all the way to Saluda, but then lost control, went off the road, and wrapped his car around a tree. He was in critical condition with head injuries and was being flown to a hospital in Asheville, where he died a few weeks later.

His wife came by after the funeral and we had a good cry. She said, "I told you he didn't know where he was going. But thanks to you his eyes were good enough to get him all the way to Saluda."

# NO RESERVATIONS

WE HEARD GREAT things about a new farm to fork restaurant in Midland that was owned by a French chef and his wife. I emailed and then spoke to the owner to book a table for our anniversary dinner.

A few weeks later, when we walked in and gave our name to the hostess, she could not find the reservation. It was a tiny room, they were completely full, and 'very sorry sir, but there is nothing we can do for you.' When I insisted that I had personally confirmed with the owner, they called her to the front.

She said, "I am so sorry. I do remember talking to you about your anniversary and I apologize for this mix-up. If you will wait just a minute I think I will be able to seat you." She led us to a small table in the back room and we had a wonderful dinner, delicious from starter to dessert. As we were finishing, she returned to our table to check on us.

"Is everything OK? I am so embarrassed about the problem with your reservation."

"Oh, no need to apologize. We appreciate that you found us a table. This is our first time here, but it will not be our last. Everything was so good."

"I'm glad you enjoyed your dinner. I'm afraid this kind of thing happens to me every so often since I had my brain tumor."

Heidi looked at me as if to say, here we go. Another stranger revealing her life story. I can sit next to someone on a flight from Charlotte to London and in eight hours say only, "Excuse me, I need to go to the bathroom." She will know everything about her seatmate before buckling in. She asked, "What do you mean you had a brain tumor?"

"Well, a few months ago I had some blurry vision. My optometrist checked me and told me I had stress. I know I have stress, I always have stress; I run a restaurant. That's not news to me, there is always some kind of disaster, but I never had trouble with my eyesight before. It kept getting worse, so I decided to get another opinion and I saw the most wonderful eye doctor. Have you ever heard of Dr. Arthur Butensky?"

"Actually, I'm an eye doctor too, and he is my partner and one of my best friends. His office is right next to mine."

"No way, I don't believe it. What a coincidence. I'm so glad I didn't let you leave. Anyway, he dilated my eyes and right away when he looked in he stopped, pushed back and said, "Hmm. I don't want to scare you, but we need to set you up for an MRI today." He found out that I had a benign brain tumor, and a few days later I had it removed. Now I am fine, but once in a while I still mess up a reservation."

"Listen, we had a wonderful meal, everything worked out fine, so don't worry about it for a minute. But when I see Dr. Butensky on Monday I'll be sure to tell him that I saw you and he will be happy to hear that you are doing so well. Has he ever been here for dinner?"

"No, I keep telling him to come but we're an hour away and I guess he's busy..."

"I'll make sure he comes here, I promise."

A year later we went back, this time with friends. The place was jammed. As we were finishing up the owner stopped by to ask if everything was OK. I said, "Wow, I'm happy for you, you are really busy tonight."

"I am so glad you came in," she replied automatically, looking toward the kitchen.

"You probably don't remember, but the last time we were here we talked about my partner, Dr. Butensky, and how he figured out why you were having trouble seeing."

"He saved my life...", and then she stopped, her hand came up to her mouth and her eyes opened wide. "Oh my God, I am going to cry. I can't believe this. Of course, I remember. You had a problem with your reservation, you were sitting at the table in the corner over there, and you are a psychologist, right?" she asked, pointing at Heidi.

"Wow, you have a good memory," she said, while our friends looked on.

"You won't believe this, and I am freaking out a little too, but I was on the internet last night looking for you. I lost your card and just last night really wanted to find you to talk about therapy for a friend of mine. I am shaking, look at me, my heart is pounding. I can't believe that the day after I looked for you online you are here."

### IF I AM GLOWING IT WILL NOT BE FROM RADIATION

*July 2, 2013 1:08pm*

Yesterday was my last trip to Dr. Plunkett's office for radiation. Over the months I have had a total of 39 sessions to go along with my weekly chemotherapy. Happily, the combination seems to have worked to shrink the tumor and to prevent it from spreading. And I was able to tolerate the treatments without any debilitating side-effects.

A few minor issues, though. For the past few days I have had some discomfort when I swallow, especially hard or sharp foods, like chips or crusty bread. And my energy level and stamina are down compared to before treatment, especially in the afternoon.

Most days now go like this: I get up with Heidi, since I am really trying not to get into the habit of sleeping late. After breakfast I do some sort of exercise every day, usually walking, but sometimes I ride my bike or go to the gym. My exercise tolerance seems to be the same as before treatment. I am still doing limited weight training too but since surgery have reduced the amount of weight I lift.

Every day I also take about an hour to do some mental/spiritual work. If the mind can influence the body's healing and health then I want to do all that I can to enlist it. I do visualization to imagine, in various unrealistic ways, the tumor shrinking and disappearing. For example, sometimes I imagine that I am doing cataract surgery on the tumor to remove it, even though no thoracic surgeon would recognize this as a possible approach. Then I listen to a guided imagery relaxation or meditation on my iPod. This is a great help in keeping me focused on health and not on illness, and gives me an energy boost too. Otherwise I would end up taking a nap almost every afternoon. I also have a list of good affirmations that I say to myself throughout the day.

And, several days each week I try to do something social, while avoiding crowds. I am so lucky to know people who are either retired or who have enough control of their work schedules that they are able to get together with me during the day. We walk, have coffee, or just sit and talk. This opportunity to spend more time with friends has been one of the best things to come out of my having this new routine. Unfortunately, all my friends from work are busy during the day, so it is harder to stay in touch with them.

Now I have a couple weeks to get my energy up and my immunity back before getting my first round of high dose chemo. Right now we are not looking for any exotic adventures, but are content to try to find the joy in everyday living.

Michael

# CHAPTER 26

# HUMOR

**W**ORRY, SADNESS, ANXIETY, consternation, anger, fear, anticipation, suspicion, confusion, envy, shame, suspense, impatience, hope, happiness, appreciation, relief. Almost every emotion shows up during a day at work. Giving good news is gratifying, uplifting, and fun. Sharing bad news is heartbreaking.

By taking classes through summers, I finished medical school a semester early, in December instead of May. Since I could not start my internship until July, I found work with the Pediatric Oncologists at Duke. I rounded on inpatients, helped in their clinic, and learned how to speak honestly and hopefully to people consumed with dread. I just couldn't do it for long; it was emotionally draining.

Happily, in ophthalmology even the most dire diagnoses are rarely fatal. Everyone fears blindness, and it can be devastating, but life goes on, so the emotional stakes are lower than in working with terminally ill children. Still, there are fears and tears. Luckily, the flipside is also true. Some of the funniest things I have ever seen have happened at work. Unexpected moments of "What?? Really??" brighten my dreariest days with laughter.

When I sense patients are amenable, I like to use humor to defuse tense situations, to put them at ease, to chip away at their anxiety, and to deflect their emotional trajectory toward hope and healing.

# CHANDELIER

NEW TO OUR office, she had short, straight, graying hair, formal makeup, and a silk blouse. "I do hope you will be the answer to my prayers."

"I'll try my best. What brings you here today?" I asked.

"All the other doctors that I have seen for my eye problems help me for a while and then, for some reason, our communication breaks down and we stop working well together. My last doctor actually got angry with me."

"What happened?"

"I had a few questions after he examined me. Maybe more than a few. Anyway, all of a sudden, he pushed his stool back from this machine, these binoculars, took a deep breath, and said, 'They are not paying me nearly enough to answer all these questions. Either you have to stop asking so many or you'll need to get yourself another doctor.' Can you believe that? I didn't know what to say. Will you take time to explain things to me?"

Odds were against our working relationship ending any more amicably than her last, but we grew to like each other and worked well together. She was charming, even if at times I understood her last doctor's frustration. At the end of a typical visit, I asked, "Do you have any questions or concerns today that we haven't addressed?"

As patients sometimes do, she said, "Let me see," then reached into her purse and extracted a small spiral notebook. I noticed densely packed writing on every line. "Oh, here it is. I wrote down a few things to ask you. I forgot to tell you about this spot on my lid. Is that anything serious?"

"Lean forward, rest your chin here, and I'll take another look. Uh huh, I see what you mean. That's just a freckle, nothing to worry about. I saw it but didn't even think to mention it." I sat back and rotated the instrument out of the way so we could talk. The particulars she asked about were less important than my giving her time, attention, and respect to calm her understandable anxieties.

"That's a relief," she said. "And can you check, there's a little bump on the white of the other eye."

"Let me see. Oh, that's just something called a pingueculum, sort of a callus on the surface of your eye. Totally normal. Usually from years of sun exposure. Look closely at your friends, and you'll see that most of them have the same thing. Very common, not a problem at all."

"How did I get that? Are there any vitamins I can take to get rid of it?"

The next time she came to the office, I opened the exam room door, stepped in, looked at her, and stopped. I was speechless. She was wearing a necklace made of 25 or 30 large pieces of cut glass. It must have weighed ten pounds, as if she had deconstructed a chandelier and slipped it over her head. Her eyes sparkled, and she gushed, happily clapping her hands, "I knew you would say something. I just knew it!"

"I haven't said anything yet, but that really is quite a necklace."

"I knew you would want to say something clever, so I am ready for you. Okay? Here goes. Here is what I want to say. Ready?" She cleared her throat, grinned, and recited, "Just as Scarlett O'Hara pulled down the drapes in Tara to make a formal gown, I used a chandelier to make a necklace. What do you think about that?"

"Frankly madam, I don't give a damn." She laughed, and we got down to work.


# MUSTACHE


RED CLAY DUSTED his work boots. Spider veins and sun damage scarred his jovial face. Suspenders compressed his belly like rubber bands around a pillow. His gray handlebar mustache was waxed to curl upward at each end, an incongruous theatrical touch on an otherwise unadorned farmer's face.

One day I asked him, "How long have you had that great mustache?"

"Oh, I don't know, maybe 20 or 30 years."

"Does your wife like it? Doesn't she ever bug you to cut it off?"

"Hell, I'm sick of it. I would have cut it a long time ago, but she won't let me. She says it tickles her thighs."

# APPETIZING

HER HAIR WAS thin and stringy. Each finger ended in a long, curved, tobacco stained claw. Scanty white whiskers sprouted from her upper lip and chin. She smiled like an affable wicked witch, with a red neck instead of a green face.

"Nice to meet you," I said, "I understand that you're here because you lost your glasses?"

"No, I didn't lose them, I got them right here, but they broke, so I ain't seeing so good right now."

She picked her purse off the floor, wrenched it open and started digging around inside, stirring the contents. "I know they are in here somewheres. Let me look. Oh, here they are. Whoa!!" Her arms shot out and launched the bag off her lap. When it hit the floor, two large cockroaches skittered out, paused to look around, and then raced toward the darkness under the cabinet.

I squealed, "Carol, help!", and together (mostly Carol) we cornered and squished the bugs. After taking a minute to settle down, I finished the exam. She did need new glasses.

"Here is the prescription for your glasses. Do you have time to get them now?"

"I don't think so. I'm gonna be late for work. Can I have a note for my boss?"

"Sure, what kind of work do you do?"

"I make biscuits at the bakery. Want me to bring you some next time?"

# NOT SO EASY

SHERRY WAS MORE interested in eyes than most internists and called when she realized she had a free afternoon. "Sure," I said, "I'd love you to visit our office today. You won't believe how much easier it is to examine the retina when the pupils are dilated. It's almost like cheating."

She arrived right after lunch, "Thanks for letting me look over your shoulder. I've been wanting to do this for a long time."

The waiting room was already full. "I'm excited to have you here. There's at least one patient with red eyes on the schedule. And I am sure you will see a bunch of diabetics with abnormal retinal vessels and some glaucoma patients with asymmetric discs too. Should be fun. One of the nice things about ophthalmology is that the days usually flow pretty smoothly, not many emergencies, so we should have plenty time for show and tell."

The patient with the red eye had a corneal abrasion from wearing contact lenses too long, and this gave me a chance to explain the various causes of red eyes. Then we saw the usual mix of patients, many with the trifecta of diabetes, hypertension and glaucoma. We reviewed how to check visual fields and pupils, then watched a video of cataract surgery so she could be more informed when talking with her own patients about this common procedure. And she got lots of practice examining the retina and optic nerve.

The office was flowing nicely when we went into the middle room to see Simon Oliver. He was a retired car salesman, talkative and very friendly. A real raconteur. "Hi Simon, how are you doing?" I asked. "I have a visiting doctor today. She is an internist spending the afternoon with us to learn more about eyes. Is it OK if she sits in?"

"Sure, nice to meet you. What group are you with?" She told him and he said, "Ha. I sold a car to your partner. Interesting guy."

"OK, please lean forward so your chin sits on this little shelf and then tip your forehead forward so it touches the white band." She saw his early cataracts and we talked about the difference between a pingueculum and a pterygium. I pulled the slit lamp away. "Everything looks good in the front of your eye. Now I'll check the optic nerve and retina." I put the ophthalmoscope on my head, turned out the lights and said, "Please lean back and...." Bang! He was hanging off the back of the chair.

"Ow!!" he shouted, "My head!" When he leaned back the ancient chair broke and slammed his head against the shelf behind him. I threw the light switch and helped him sit up. He was gently rubbing his neck.

"Mr. Oliver, I am so sorry. Let me look at your head. No blood. Does it hurt when I touch here? No? Good. Oh boy. I don't believe it. What do you think Sherry, should I have him stick around for a while? Think he needs a CT?"

"No," she said, "that was pretty dramatic, but just keep ice on it for the next few hours. Be sure to call here or your own doctor if you get a headache or have any trouble walking or talking clearly."

"You OK with that Simon? You'll never forget this eye exam, will you? Want some free eye drop samples?"

By the time he left he was smiling and jocular, but I was shaken. Sherry and I went into my office. "Nothing like that has ever happened here before. I guess I need to get a new chair. Let's hope the rest of the day goes without a hitch." We talked while Scottie and Beth worked up the next patients. One of them was Marty Allison, a man whose glaucoma made him a frequent visitor to the office. He was retired from the IRS, had a slow Tennessee drawl and a thick snow-white head of hair. An otherwise archetypical grandpa, he loved to travel abroad and had the incongruous habit of mailing us 'wish you were here' postcards of topless women on foreign beaches.

"Doctor, Doctor, come quick!!" shouted Scottie. I looked at Sherry and we jumped up and ran into the room where Simon had his accident. Marty was lying on the floor. "I just brought him in here to check his vision and pressure and to give him his drops, but before I could he got sweaty and pale and said he was going to faint. He wanted to lie down so I helped him slide off the chair."

Sherry took over, "Are you having any chest pain? Let me see the chart." He had a history of coronary disease. She checked his pulse and blood pressure, we raised his feet, put a pillow under his head and kept him comfortable while we waited for an ambulance to take him to the emergency room. Once they hoisted him onto a gurney and wheeled him away, I looked at Sherry and said, "This is incredible. We can go a whole year without calling the EMTs for a patient. You have to believe me, it is never like this. Those patients are so lucky you're here, and so am I."

A few minutes later someone in the waiting room pounded on the office door. I was about to apologize that the emergencies made us run so late, but when I opened the door the person standing there pointed to her left and said, "You better come out and take care of this man."

A legless man was lying on his belly on the waiting room floor in front of an empty wheelchair. Trying to lift his face off the carpet, he seemed unable to sit up or roll over, and appeared to be more annoyed than injured, like an inverted turtle. A worried and embarrassed woman stood over him. Everyone else in the waiting room stared and whispered. "What's going on?" I asked one of them.

"This lady here is his caretaker. She forgot to put his seat-belt on and they both fell asleep."

The aide shook her head, "I shut my eyes for less than a minute. I don't know how he got out of that chair. But he is way too heavy for me to lift."

I got down on my knees, Sherry looking over my shoulder. With my face next to his ear, I asked, "How are you?"

He said, "Doc, this is some kind of rough rug you got here." We lifted him into his chair and secured the belt. Aside from a little road rash he was fine. I checked his eyes, Sherry checked his head, and the rest of the afternoon slid by uneventfully. At the end of the day Sherry said, "I thought ophtho was so cushy, but you guys see way more emergencies than I do!"

---

**TODAY'S CHECK-UP**                          *July 22, 2013 6:52pm*

This morning I saw Dr. Mahoney for a check-up a week after having my first high dose infusion of chemo meds. I was happy to be able to tell him that I got through the week without any nausea or vomiting (TMI?), certainly due to the good drugs he gave me before the chemo. The only problem I did have was some pain in my legs and feet for a few days, which has cleared up, and some mild lingering dullness, but not actually numbness, in my thumbs and a few toes. He said this is a neuropathy from the Taxol and was encouraged that it was improving so quickly. My white cell count was still in the low normal range but had fallen, as expected, and he gave me a shot of a medicine to goose my bone marrow to make it produce more white cells to reduce my risk of infection and bleeding. So, I will continue to avoid the sun, since these meds make it easier to get sunburnt, will stay away from crowds until my counts come up, and otherwise keep on doing what I have been doing for the last few months. By the time we go away in a few weeks I should be less hirsute but otherwise back to new normal and will then be ready for the second and, for now, last round of chemo when we return.

Michael

### Rocking a New Look                    *August 1, 2013 8:50 am*

Today is Day 18 since Michael had his high dose of chemo, and he started losing his hair. At 9am he had it all buzzed off—and is rocking a new look. Someone at work said he looks like a white Denzel Washington. Emily said it was very "George Clooney," David says "Lance Armstrong," and I say Eric Clapton.

Love—Heidi

**SHANA TOVA! HAPPY ROSH HASHANA!**    *September 4, 2013 8:43pm*

We wanted to wish everyone a sweet, happy and healthy New Year. Tonight is the start of Rosh HaShana, the Jewish New Year and the beginning of the 10 Days of Awe culminating in Yom Kippur. The Gates of Heaven are open, and the Book of Life has yet to be written. "On Rosh HaShana it is written, on Yom Kippur it is sealed."

Our prayers and hopes and thoughts should ascend to heaven—a sweet, happy and healthy New Year.

Love—Heidi and Michael

**FIRST SCAN SINCE ENDING TREATMENT**    *September 9, 2013 11:35am*

My last planned chemotherapy treatment was almost a month ago. This past Friday I had my first PET scan since early May. The reason for doing the scan was to check on the size of the tumor, to find out how metabolically active it is (the less active the better), and to see if it has spread from its original location. Really, this scan is going to serve as a new baseline for comparison in the future. And we got good news.

I never considered it possible that the tumor would be completely gone, and of course it is not. But it is smaller than it was in May, it is less active than it was, though still more active than normal, and best of all it has not spread to other parts of the body. So, all good. Now the plan is to let it continue to simmer down from the recent treatment and then to repeat the scan in a few months. No more treatment needed for now.

Michael

YOM KIPPUR                                    *September 12, 2013 6:41pm*

The Yom Kippur holiday begins at sundown tomorrow (Friday). This is the holiest day of the year in the Jewish religion and is commonly called the "Day of Atonement." One of my friends asked what the experience of the day is like. It is a day dedicated to fasting, prayer, and repentance, all designed to let us acknowledge, as individuals and as a community, that we have sinned and that we regret it and hope to be given another chance to do better next year. The fasting is complete, no food or water for 25 hours. The prayers are done at synagogue, where services basically last all day, from about 6–9 PM tomorrow and then from 10AM-8PM on Saturday with only a short break in the late afternoon. The final prayer is called Neila, which means "closing," since the gates of heaven are open particularly wide for our entreaties but soon will be closing, though of course they never fully shut for anyone. The repentance has two parts. First of all, we ask to be forgiven if we have made any vows or promises to God that we have failed to fulfill in the past year. But for things we might have done wrong to other people we are obligated to make it right person to person; prayers will not get the job done. So, since I cannot see too many of you face to face, I want you to know that if in some way I have hurt, offended, or harmed you I sincerely apologize and I hope you will forgive me, just as I forgive you (although don't worry, everyone has been extraordinarily kind and I don't, in fact, have anyone in mind here!). Heidi and I wish everyone a good, happy, and healthy year and thank all of you for your amazing ongoing love, care, concern and support.

Michael

# CHAPTER 27

9/24/13                                    *September 24, 2013 3:22pm*

Hi—Wanted to just let you know where we are with things.
Michael and I are trying to figure out—now what? The first 6
months are past, treatment is over, now what?

Michael wants me to get back into my life—work, friends,
volunteering, blacksmithing, knitting, entertaining—but I want to
be with Michael as much as I can. So for now I am back working,
but on a reduced schedule, and I am doing all of my activities but
in a more limited way.

Michael wants to figure out what next for him too. It's a process.

One thing we both love is travel. We are going on a big trip in
October—we are going to Chile and Peru! Michael got medical
clearance to go and is very involved in planning all the details. Two
new countries, a big adventure.

As we figure stuff out I'll tell you—but we're not posting just to post. We LOVE hearing from you—please keep all those thoughts and prayers coming. Your support means more than we can say. Adios!

Love—Heidi

# COLD FUSION

ANDY AND I rode our bikes across McAlpine Creek and into the woods. It was a glorious October morning, early enough that we didn't have to dodge too many runners or dogs on long leashes. I said, "I'm glad we're out here early. Half the time anymore when I yell, 'On your left,' people can't even hear me, their music is so loud."

"I know," he said, "it's amazing we haven't run anybody over."

Our Sunday morning bike rides were a weekly ritual. For years we pedaled forty miles on country lanes until Charlotte's sprawling growth made them unsafe for cyclists. Now we rode the Greenway, a linear brookside park. On mountain bikes, our ride was both a workout and a rolling conversation. "I'm having a hard time figuring out what to do about work," I said.

"What do you mean? I thought you're not working anymore."

"I'm not, not yet anyway. I stopped because my treatment was five days a week, but that's done. Out here riding the Greenway, I feel pretty good, thank God, but I still don't have the stamina. There's no way I could work a full day, see forty patients, take call, all that. Part time maybe."

"Why would you even want to go back?"

"If I feel good enough to work I probably should. I like it, I miss it, and I'm good at it."

"Yeah, but why bother?"

"I didn't plan to stop so soon. Once I got to be 65 I figured I'd give up surgery but keep working. So it's hard not to go back to work now. I miss seeing my patients and everyone at the office. Being an ophthalmologist is a big part of who I am."

"Well, life happens, plans change. Better you stop too soon than too late. I think you'd have to be crazy to go back to work. You've got it made. You don't have to work. There's money in the bank, your kids are doing well. A lot of guys would say you're living the dream."

"Except for cancer, you mean."

"Yeah, okay, that part's not so good. I'll give you that. But you're a cancer survivor."

"I won't be a cancer survivor until I get run over by a bus," I said. "But in a way you're right; I'm incredibly lucky. A lot of people don't have the option not to work. I'm grateful I can just concentrate on taking care of myself. Probably one reason I've tolerated my treatment so well." At first, not working was a temporary concession to my intensive treatment schedule. I couldn't work, and time off was the silver lining that let me better endure radiation and chemotherapy and to dedicate all my energy to healing. But other cancer patients have told me they feel otherwise, that working during treatment helped them get through their illness. And many people, maybe most, would like to take time off but have no choice.

"So why would you even think about going back to work?"

"I want to get back to the way things were. And I hate to end my career right when Dave is getting ready to start his." My son was in his third year of medical school, and I did not want to abandon my career casually or unnecessarily.

"Does he want you to keep working?"

"No, he just wants me to enjoy every day and to take care of myself. Heidi and Emily too."

"So, who wants you to go back to work?"

"People are always saying things like, 'I'm waiting to have my cataract surgery until you come back,' or 'I was due to have my eyes examined 3 months ago but I want you to do it.' Every week someone says, 'I had to see another eye doctor because you were out, and he was OK, but he wasn't you.'"

"So you might go back to work because people want you to do their next eye exam?"

"Well, yeah. I hate to leave my patients in the lurch. And I feel like if I go back to work it means I'm all better."

"Listen. If you stop working now there will be people upset that they have to go to somebody else for their next eye exam. But so what? If you work until you are 85 there will be other people mad that you quit before they could see you once more. That's no reason." Andy shouted, "Hey, on your left!" He swerved off the path to avoid a runner lost in her music, who looked up, startled, as we bounced by on the grass.

"She never even heard us coming, did she?" I asked and steered back onto the pavement. "Anyway, I'm torn up. I love my staff. They've been with me forever, and they're in limbo waiting to find out what I'm going to do."

"By not telling them, you're the one keeping them in limbo. I bet they just want what is best for you too. When you tell them you're not coming back they'll be sad, but they'll move on. They probably already know."

"Yeah, I really need to decide," I said. "And if I'm not working I can spend a lot more time with Heidi, Emily, and Dave."

"That's the thing," he continued, "you've had a great career. Your patients love you, you've helped thousands of people, your partners respect you, but you have already done everything you can do as an eye doctor. You have nothing left to prove. If you go back it won't be anything new. Been there, done that. So why go back at all? It's not as if you've been working your whole life on some gigantic, long-term project. If you could only work 6 more months you'd finally figure out cold fusion? I don't think so. Just more of the same until you decide to quit for good. So why not go out on top and use this time to do something else. Why go back, why go backwards? Go forward in some new direction."

"Huh, wow." I pedaled silently for a minute as we crossed under Monroe Road. "That cold fusion example might be the wisest thing I ever heard you say. Like a bolt of lightning from blue sky."

"You're welcome. I'm happy I can still surprise you sometimes."

When I got home, I told Heidi about the ride and she said, "I'm sorry this is such a struggle for you. What else is going on?" As we talked, I realized the main stumbling block was not my feeling that I had to work to be okay, but my fear that leaving work meant I was about to die. "Doesn't make much sense when I say it out loud, does it?"

"That's magical thinking," she said. "Whether you choose to do eye exams won't be what determines if you live or die."

If I had a crystal ball and knew I would live another twenty years I might have decided otherwise. With a curable disease like lymphoma, breast cancer, or pneumonia, my time away from work during treatment would have been like a train pulling onto a siding and then, when the signal turns green, proceeding to the scheduled destination. But did my track even reach the next station? My prognosis was hazy; no one could tell me what lay ahead, but the odds were against me. My doctors had given me aggressive treatment and suggested I retire, so I was hesitant to continue as planned. In my altered circumstances, unable to return to full time practice and with a short time horizon, it seemed smarter to head in a new direction.

Talking with Andy and Heidi freed me to move ahead and to stop pining for the past. I was finally able to see that, like a flooding river forces a new channel, illness also provided me opportunities that the flow of life would otherwise have carried me by unaware. Seeing my dilemma as a positive choice flipped a switch, so when I finally decided to leave my practice it was not because I feared I was about to die, but because I hoped I was going to live and preferred to use my remaining time differently.

**NEWS ABOUT WORK**                              *Nov 22, 2013 7:58am*

For several months I have struggled with the knowledge that my prolonged 'medical leave' could not go on indefinitely and that I would have to concede that I had officially stopped working, but was never able to get to the point where I was ready to pull the trigger, hit the send button, and make it real. As the end of the year approaches I finally have gotten comfortable enough with this new reality to send the following email to my partners yesterday. Some were concerned that I suddenly made this decision because of new bad medical news, but it was not a sudden decision and happily I still feel fine. So now it is time to move on to the next chapter....

To: Board of Directors
Re: My work status

As you know, since early in March I have been out of work due to my illness and treatments. I always planned to come back to work as soon as my health returned to normal but I now realize that will be impossible. This has not been an easy, a welcome, or really even a voluntary decision but I have already resisted making it for too long.

It has been a real honor and privilege to be associated with our practice and I am grateful beyond words for having had the opportunity to work with such an outstanding group of people. My affiliation with the group has enhanced me in every way.

# GOODNESS

The Rogers family is proof that goodness has little to do with being rich, happy, or bright.

The son is married, has a job and children and navigates the world independently. He lives nearby and has a life of his own. The daughter is also grown but is intellectually limited. She is in her forties, lives with her parents, helps with household chores, and works in a sheltered workshop. She is friendly, grateful, pleasant and courteous, and never doubts that she is valued and loved.

The father is completely demented. He mumbles and argues. Unaware of his own suffering, he needs constant attention. He wanders. He falls. He never sleeps through the night.

Mom graduated high school and worked in a clothing store until caring for her family became a full-time occupation. She has no money but rarely complains. She hates what has happened to her husband but remains grateful for every day they have together. She bears this burden willingly and cares for him because it is the right thing to do, part of the package you sign up for when you love someone. She is the glue that holds the family together and only wishes she could do more.

During dad's eye exam, he squeezes his eyes closed, jerks his head to the side, and tries to stand, "Gotta go now. Let's go. Gotta go."

Mother and daughter jump up, support his head in the slit lamp and gently calm him by massaging his shoulders. She says, "Now daddy, don't you want to get your eyes checked? Dr. Rotberg is almost done."

"No! Let's go, let's go now!"

"We love you, daddy," says mom.

"Yeah, we love you daddy," echoes daughter. "Let Dr. Rotberg finish looking at your eyes and we'll take you right home."

"We love daddy, don't we Rhonda?"

"Yes we do, Mama."

This is twenty-four hours a day. They don't understand why their lives turned out this way, so much more difficult than others'. They humble me, and by their example remind me that anyone can choose to be good, kind, and selfless, to serve others with love, and be a light to the world. Becoming a blessing to others requires no special training and is an option open to all of us.

# EMPATHETIC AND COMPASSIONATE

THE BEST DOCTOR is not the one who can quote esoteric medical literature or do a cataract operation in three minutes, but the one who engages as much as possible with the people who honor him with their trust. Good patient care demands the heart as well as the head. The point is not to join in the patient's suffering, but to be sensitive to the impact the disease has on his or her life.

How would I feel if I had to take all these medicines every day? How would my life change if my vision was so badly damaged? How would I negotiate my day if I was wheelchair bound, blind, living alone, uninsured, or without enough money to afford both my medicine and my rent? Now, having lived as a cancer patient, I thank my lucky stars that I was fortunate enough never to be in this position. How much more difficult would it have been for me to undergo radiation and chemotherapy if I had to force myself to work while sick, if I did not have the luxury of devoting all my energy to taking care of myself, or if I was facing my illness alone? I don't know how some of my patients do it. Most of them have it much harder than I do, and I am in awe of how they face and overcome so many obstacles.

People usually rise to the occasion, tackle their challenges, and do what needs to be done. But others, because they have suffered so long or are less resilient, become hopeless, anxious, and resentful. Caring for them can be emotionally draining. There is a reason I didn't go into psychiatry. I want to help and do my best to empathize, but as they suck the energy out of the room I have to fight the unprofessional urge to be abrupt or run away. Something that helps me stay positive with such patients is to imagine them as children, not to infantilize them or their concerns or to take them less seriously, but to try to see them as their parents once did. Who can help feeling for a sick baby, to forgive crabbiness in a child with a fever? Otherwise delightful kids can be insufferable when they are suffering. Stepping back to see the patient as if he were a crying child with a skinned knee or chicken pox gives me a boost of empathy, caring, and compassion that lets me refocus on trying to help. And when miserable people feel better again, they often turn out to be lovely.

Interpersonal distance prevents connection, but letting empathy draw me too close to a patient is a barrier to healthy healing relationships too. Being compassionate does not mean being indulgent to the patient's detriment. Becoming enmeshed is as bad as remaining too distant. It is important to keep some professional distance and to remember that the patient is the one with the problem. I'll do my best to help, but in the end my eyes are not the ones at risk. Sometimes, to get their attention, I ask patients whose health is compromised by their failure to keep appointments or to take their medicines, "Why should I care more than you do?" This sounds harsh but is not meant to be cruel. I say it as a wakeup call to trigger honest conversation about the risks of ignoring their serious eye disease.

Missing appointments or failing to take drops can be a sign that the patient is too casual about his care. But just as likely, this behavior can also stem from stressors outside his control such as poverty, misunderstanding the disease, lack of transportation, or social isolation. For each patient, I need to figure out why the treatment plan isn't tolerable and come up with a new approach after recalibrating my understanding of our practical options.

**GOODBYE 2013!**                                    *Dec 30, 2013 12:30pm*

Hi—I can't believe that 2013 is almost over. Goodbye!

What a crazy year this has been for us. Last New Year's Day Michael and I were busy with our lives and had no idea that everything was going to change. It really does feel like our lives were one way before 2/25/13 and then the new reality of after that day.

Michael and I were walking last week and we were talking about the year and the journey. Michael said he never would have believed it, but it ended up being "a great year." I was so surprised to hear that; I stopped and turned to him and asked how was it a great year?

His answer was that he was treated and the treatment worked (cancer is smaller, not spreading or growing), he was able to go through treatment with quality of life, he is not in pain and feels good, his staff and partners have moved on—they still wish he was working but they are doing well and taking care of his patients, and our family and friends all embraced him (and me) with love and support. Michael is amazing!

Michael has had only 2 jobs since finishing his residency in 1984—in Vero Beach, Florida and here. We left Vero Beach to move to Charlotte for this opportunity and for more options for us and the kids. Michael's last day at his practice in Vero was 12/31/1991.

Now this year, 12/31/13 is also his last day at his Charlotte practice. Michael loved every day he worked there. Michael has had the most incredible staff (thank you Carol, Scottie, Beth and Michele), the best partners, and the most amazing patients. Michael tried to learn something about each patient—books they liked, things they had done in life, travel, family—they were not just a patient but a person.

I'm writing this—not Michael—because I think it important to acknowledge the 21 years as Michael closes that chapter. Time to move on—the adventure continues!

As you read this we will be with our kids. The BEST way to celebrate the New Year. Thank you for being here with us, thank you for your love and support, thank you for everything you have given us and shared with us this past year. Wishing you and your loved ones health, happiness and joy in 2014.

Love—Heidi

# CHAPTER 28

## TAXI LINE

E QUAL PARTS CLASSROOM, trade show, reunion, and circus, the annual meeting of the American Academy of Ophthalmology is the largest gathering of eye doctors. Attended by thousands of ophthalmologists and vendors, it is exhilarating and disorienting, crowded, hectic, raucous as rush hour in a subway station.

After four days of learning, schmoozing with friends, and being accosted by sales people, I was anxious to get back home. My friend Bill and I grabbed our luggage and joined the taxi line outside the convention center. As we inched forward, someone tapped me on the shoulder. I turned to see a middle-aged man in a sport-coat, dress shirt and tie, with a convention badge hanging from a lanyard around his neck. "I wasn't eavesdropping or anything, but did I hear you guys say you're going to the airport?"

"Yeah, we are. Want to share a cab?"

"Love to." He put out his hand and said, "I'm Dan, nice to meet you. Where are you guys headed?"

We introduced ourselves and I said, "I'm going to Charlotte, and Bill here is flying home to Tampa. How about you?" He mentioned a city in the Midwest, and I said, "I know it's a big town, but one of my best friends from med school is an anesthesiologist there. Do you ever scrub with Paul Leifer?"

"That's crazy! His group staffs most of my cases. We work together all the time."

"No kidding. He's a great guy. Be sure to say hi for me." Once in the cab, we realized that Dan and I were both glaucoma specialists. He asked, "One thing that bugged me at this meeting was, did you guys notice that with all the talks we heard about glaucoma surgery, none of the speakers mentioned how they do anesthesia for their cases?"

"No, what do you mean?" I asked.

He leaned in, "Well, they showed lots of surgical videos but each one started after they were already underway. No one said anything about how they numbed the eye. Do you give blocks anymore?" He wondered if we numbed eyes for surgery by injecting local anesthetic into the orbit, behind the eye. For years, this was the standard approach.

I said, "For cataracts I just use drops. What do you do?"

"Well sure, nobody blocks cataracts anymore," said Dan. "Haven't done that for years. But I can't remember the last time I gave a block for glaucoma surgery either."

"Not for trabs or tubes either?" Glaucoma procedures, like trabeculectomies and implant tubes, take longer than cataracts, and I wasn't sure that patients would be comfortable his way.

"Nope. There's no reason to," he said, "Just some lidocaine jelly before the case and sub-conjunctival lidocaine when I start. For tubes, I might give some sub-tenons too." He used numbing ointment on the surface of the eye and a tiny injection where he made his incision. No shots behind the eye.

"And that keeps people comfortable?"

"Every time. I think it's almost malpractice to stick a needle blindly behind somebody's eye. With all the risks, all the trouble it can cause, you just don't need to do it. How would you defend yourself in court if somebody had a complication from an outmoded injection that you shouldn't have given in the first place?"

We rode in silence for a few minutes. At that time, I did use injections for glaucoma surgery, and here was Dan telling me he thought it was malpractice. Strained small talk filled the car until we finally reached the airport.

The next day, I was in the OR getting ready to do a glaucoma case. The patient was supine and relaxed. The anesthetist placed the oxygen cannula and an IV. I nodded to her and she pushed some Propofol; a minute later the patient was snoring. I took the syringe in my right hand, aimed the needle at the ceiling and expelled some air, felt the inferotemporal orbital rim with my left hand, ballotted the eye up and in and then slipped the needle below the eye, advancing slowly until I felt a subtle pop as the tip entered the muscle cone. I injected lidocaine, removed the needle, gently pressed on the closed eye for a minute, and left the room to wash my hands.

That evening I called my friend Paul. "In Dallas yesterday I ran into someone you know—Dan Juggson."

"How is Dan?" he asked.

"He seems to be a guy with strong opinions," I said. "He kept going on about how it was malpractice to give retrobulbar blocks."

He chuckled. "He said that? Remember the time I spent a day in the OR with you? The way you gave a block was very slick."

"There's nothing special about the way I do a block, is there?"

"I don't know about that, but back home I staff lots of eye surgery cases and they don't all go as smoothly as yours did that day."

"That's nice of you to say, but you better knock on wood."

"Oh yeah, sorry." I heard him knocking on a table. "But last week I worked with your buddy Dan, and you should have seen what happened after he gave a block. He sort of jammed the needle in, almost like he was throwing a dart at the poor guy's face, and the patient got a horrible retrobulbar hemorrhage. There was so much bleeding behind the eye that it bulged out and the lids got bruised and swollen. He must have hit an artery or something. It was so bad that he had to cut the eyelids to control the pressure, and of course he had to cancel the case. What a mess."

"Hold on. Dan gave a block? I didn't think he gives blocks anymore."

"I don't know where you heard that. He blocks all his glaucoma cases, just like you do."

Most doctors understand the importance of honesty and humility. As the surgeon's adage says, 'God heals. I just put the tissues together.' This doctor lied to glorify himself to a stranger, but his pointless dishonesty diminished him instead.

# WONDERFUL LIFE

"You are going to have to calm this one down. She is on a rampage," warned Beth.

"Who is the next patient?" I asked.

"A woman you've never seen before. That emergency put us way behind schedule this morning, and she sat in the waiting room for about 45 minutes before I called her in."

Not a very good first impression. I took a deep breath, put on my most charming smile, and opened the door. Before I even had the chance to say hello she was all over me like an angry cat. Stepping into the surf, I was toppled by the first wave.

"Oh my, I am old and I am sick. I am suffering so much. I had to wait an hour and a half already, and my eye is killing me, I can hardly stand it."

Not arguing the precise length of her delay, I said, "I am so sorry we kept you waiting so long. We usually stay more on schedule, but we have had some emergencies and I do apologize."

"But I am an emergency too! What about me?"

"What seems to be the problem?"

"I have this incredible pain. And there is a lump on my eyelid. It has been there for more than a day and it hurts when I touch it."

"Is your vision all right?"

"Yes, thank God. Just the pain, so much pain." From where I sat, I could see that she had a small chalazion or stye, a zit on the edge of her lower lid. Her lid was a little puffy, in one place red, and probably would have been tender if I pressed on it. "I tell you," she continued, "in all my 92 years, between having to wait two hours and suffering such agonizing pain, I think this might be the worst day of my life."

What could I say? I looked her in the eyes, smiled, and said, "You really must have had a wonderful life." She grunted, grudgingly grinned, and settled down for the exam.

# AVOID BEING RESENTFUL

IT MIGHT SEEM natural that the more dismal your diagnosis, the more likely it is to get you down. But, in fact, the severity of a person's illness poorly predicts her attitude toward it. I have seen plenty of patients keep their chins up in the face of irreversible blindness and dependency because of a hopeful demeanor and good social support. Though nearly blind and grieving their lost vision, each knew there were still reasons to be grateful for all that remained and for their overall good fortune.

But other people with minor or even trivial medical problems wallow in misery. Some are 'glass half empty' kind of people, and the negative outlook that frames the rest of their lives extends to the way they approach their illness. Why should it be otherwise? If the way they navigate the world has always been resentful and pessimistic, it would be surprising if they became hopeful and grateful when confronting a health challenge.

But what a shame. To a certain degree, it remains a choice. Their lives could be so much more pleasant, their recovery so much more likely, if they could take a new approach. Easier said than done, and often impossible for someone with years of experience facing the world in a certain way.

# MOM'S MONEY

HE SEEMED DISTRACTED, so at the end of the exam I asked, "I'm happy to tell you your eyes are doing fine, but you seem kind of tense today. Is something else bothering you?"

"It shows, huh? It's my mother. She's making me crazy."

"What's going on?"

"She's driving me nuts. She's convinced she's going to run out of money. It's all we ever talk about anymore."

"I know what you mean. My mother feels the same way."

"Right, I asked her why she didn't get tickets this year for the theater series she always goes to. All her friends go, and she loves it. But she said, 'I can't afford it anymore.' I told her, 'Mom, I get your bank statements every month. You have plenty of money,' but she doesn't believe me. So I said, 'OK, let's figure this out.' And I went over to her place, brought all her statements, sat down at the kitchen table with her, and she watched me as I went through them line by line with a calculator. Finally, I said, 'Listen mom. You're fine. I am 100% sure about this. You have absolutely nothing to worry about. With the amount of money you have and the way you have been living, you have enough to last until you are 140 years old.'"

I said, "That's great, right?"

"I thought so, but she just looked at me and cried, 'Then what!?!?'"

# CHAPTER 29

## POSITIVE AND HOPEFUL

You've heard the saying, 'It's just data.' Facts are different than truth. We can agree on the facts and disagree about their implications or their meaning. A sale that lowers the price of a $20 bottle of wine by $5.00 seems to be a great deal. If a car dealer reduces the price of a Chevy by the same amount it is a rounding error. Both save me five dollars, but one feels like a bargain, the other an insult.

When the doctor calls and says, "I'm sorry to tell you that you finally have become diabetic," or "The tests show your cancer has spread," there is no way to sugarcoat the fact that the news is not good. Certain aspects of your life are going to change in ways you wish they wouldn't. Some parts of your daily routine will fall away to be replaced by others you'd never freely choose. No more chocolate. Stick your finger and give yourself a shot each day. Or travel to a cancer center several hours away to meet a doctor you don't know to talk about the next invasive or disruptive treatment, or worse, to find out that there really is nothing they can do. The bad news means you are about to lose the illusion of control. The facts are indisputable.

But still, it's just data. The information may be true, and may have an unavoidable impact on your life, but just as important, maybe even more important than the actual news, is what you do with it, how you interpret it, how you internalize it and hold it in your consciousness. This is not a new insight. Every wisdom tradition agrees that the way to minimize suffering is to shed desires. To be content with what you have. To be grateful for the way things are. When trouble intrudes, to try to live gratefully and happily within the parameters of your new reality.

Gratitude is certainly the key to happiness. 'It could always be worse' sounds like a platitude, but as long as you are breathing it happens to be true. Someone, somewhere, wishes they could trade places with you, even though you have diabetes or cancer or glaucoma or a broken leg. Or thymic carcinoma.

Before starting treatment, I wondered, 'Is the chemotherapy that starts tomorrow going to make my hair fall out, drain my energy, and make me vomit?' It can and did. But it was also, and mainly, the first step on my journey toward healing. A speed bump on my latest road trip. More like gutting my kitchen for renovation than demolishing my house. The facts may mean I have to face some things I would rather avoid, but the way I contextualize the news is half the battle.

# MEATBALLS, DONUTS, AND MORE

BY MID-MAY OF 2013, Spring had already come and gone in Charlotte. Our tulip magnolia blossomed, as always, just before a frost. The pear trees looked lovely and smelled awful. My cancer made the ephemeral beauty of the cherries in Freedom Park even more poignant than usual because they bloomed and fell so soon after I was diagnosed. Only the dogwoods had yet to flower. But as we drove over the mountains and then north through the Shenandoah Valley the color palette was leaden, the trees were bare; we entered a world of endless winter. After eight weeks of treatment at home, were traveling to New York for my surgery at Sloan-Kettering.

That morning Heidi woke up at 4:30 AM and we were on our way by 5:00. It was a perfect driving day, dry, sunny and with almost no traffic. We made record time: breakfast in Virginia, lunch in Carlisle, and when we crossed the Delaware River into Jersey we realized that it was still only 2 o'clock.

"Hey, let's call Emily. She won't believe where we are. Maybe we will even get to the city in time to see her and Josh tonight," I said.

"We still have to get over to the East Side and move into Jodi's apartment, but how long can that take?" Heidi wondered. Her sister loaned us an apartment near the hospital for a few weeks.

"I know. At this rate we should be in the city by about 3:30, so by 4:30 we can be unloaded, put the car in the garage, and walk across the park to see them."

She dialed, and I heard Emily's voice on the Bluetooth speaker. "That's great!! I can't believe you are already in Jersey," she exclaimed. "Josh's parents are coming for an early dinner. I made meatballs, and then the four of us are going to the theater. Come over before we go. I made lots of extra meatballs."

"OK, we'll try, but no promises. We woke up early this morning and we've been in the car almost ten hours, but we would love to see you today if we can. I'll call when we get into the city."

But then, as we approached Newark Airport, traffic stopped. Nothing moved, and all I could see were tail lights to the horizon. Emily called, "How's it going? Are you in the city yet?"

"We are stuck in traffic Em. Not even to Newark Airport yet. Hopefully it won't last too long and we will still be able to make it before you have to leave."

"You have to get here for dinner. I have so many meatballs!" she exclaimed.

A half hour and less than a mile later, I got off I-78 onto Elizabeth Avenue. "Where the hell are you taking us?" asked Heidi.

"Who knows where this traffic jam ends? Could go all the way to the tunnel. But I know how to get from here to 280, and from there it is a straight shot to the Turnpike, so we'll still be all right."

Up Elizabeth Avenue, across to McCarter Highway, in just a few miles we should have been through Newark and merging onto I-280 in Harrison. But halfway to downtown the traffic froze again. We watched the light cycle three times. I made a frustrated U-turn and squealed down a side street. "Don't worry. This will take us to Broad Street. It goes to the highway too."

But barricades blocked Broad Street a few blocks before downtown, and a detour sent us back to McCarter Highway. "What's going on here?" I whined.

A cop at the next intersection came over when I rolled the window down. "You are S.O.L., Buddy. It's Rutgers graduation at the Arena today, so all the streets around here are closed."

Emily called twice more before we finally reached the highway and was disappointed that we were no closer than we had been an hour earlier. By the time we got to our apartment at 76th and York Avenue it was after 6:00 and we were both exhausted. We called and said, "Listen Em, we really wanted to come see you but you are leaving for the theater soon, we are totally drained, and we won't be able to make it in time. We'll see you tomorrow morning for breakfast."

"No, you have to come over now. What am I going to do with all these meatballs?"

"So eat the extras tomorrow. What's the big deal with the meatballs? Finish dinner, have a good time at the show, and we will see you in the morning. What time should be come over?"

"Come over now!"

We showered, had an early dinner, and were in bed before 9:00. We slept late, dressed, and strolled across the Park to their apartment overlooking the Museum of Natural History. Along the way two more phone calls prodded us to walk faster, and we rang her bell a few minutes later.

Josh opened the door, Emily ran over to give us a hug, and we said hello to Josh's parents. On the table, bagels, lox, cream cheese and sliced tomatoes, along with champagne. "Wow, champagne!" said Heidi.

Josh had his arm over Emily's shoulder. "We are hardly ever all in the same place at the same time, so Josh and I want to tell you that...WE'RE PREGNANT!!!!" They both smiled, laughed, and cried. We shrieked, jumped up and down, and had a giddy group hug.

"That's so great! Mazel tov! What's the story?" An ecstatic cacophony.

"Well," Emily said, "we decided a few months ago that we wanted to get pregnant, and I just found out this week. I couldn't wait to tell you. We wanted to tell you last night; what took you so long to get here this morning?"

"Oh, so that's what was behind all that business with the meatballs. Now I get it. When are you due?"

"In January. My first OB appointment is going to be in a couple weeks." Emily and Josh swore us to secrecy; they didn't want anyone else to know she was pregnant until the end of her first trimester.

For several weeks after I was discharged from the hospital we stayed in the city. While I recovered from surgery, Heidi gave me a daily project, so each day I tried to do just a little bit more than the day before. We walked all over Manhattan, farther each day, and explored new parts of the city. We went to the theater, took the bus to Philadelphia to the new Barnes Foundation, and most days also saw Emily and Josh. When Jodi and Charlie, Heidi's sister and brother in law, came to town we moved from their apartment to a hotel.

"Hey Charlie," I said, "I've been looking at Roosevelt Island from your balcony. Have you ever been over there?"

"No, we should go." After lunch, we walked down to the cable car station, flew over to Roosevelt Island, and hiked its entire circumference. The skyline views were impressive, but it was a hot day for a long walk. We talked about the hospital, our kids, shows we had seen, and restaurants we had tried. "Dave was here for my surgery," I said. "He found a place online that's supposed to have the best jelly donuts in New York. I don't know why he was even looking, but he told me, 'Dad, when you get out of the hospital you really have to check this place out. It's amazing.'"

"What could be so special about a jelly donut?" Charlie asked.

"That's what I wondered too, but I went there with him, and all I can say is wait and see for yourself. It's only a few blocks from your apartment."

Later, on the tram ride back to Manhattan, Charlie said, "We probably walked 7 or 8 miles today and I'm starving. Don't you think we've earned some of those jelly donuts? Want to go now?"

So, sweaty and drained, spurred on by the promise of a sweet reward, we trudged up to 78th to Orwasher's, the tiny bakery that Dave had discovered. On the counter was a tray of what appeared to be jelly donuts. Charlie asked the clerk, "What flavor are these donuts?" and he replied, "What flavor do you want them to be?" and pointed at the wall behind him. There, hanging from a pegboard, were four transparent caulk guns, each filled with a different type of preserves.

"I had blueberry last time and it was so good," I said. "Today I think I'll go for sour cherry." Charlie asked for blueberry, and we watched the counterman choose a donut, pierce it with a closed scissors, and then jam the caulk gun into the hole he had just made. Like a deflated basketball, as fruity goodness pumped into the donut it expanded until any more would have caused a gooey explosion. Outside, on the sidewalk, Charlie reached into the paper bag, gingerly lifted out his donut, took a bite, and stopped walking. He said, "This is a work of art."

When I finally got back to the hotel all wanted to do was to sit down, cool off, drink some ice water, and tell Heidi about our adventures. I opened the door and said, "Charlie and I had such a great day. First we walked..."

"Sit down," she interrupted.

"Wait, I want to tell you about all we did today. First..."

"Sit down. Now!"

"OK, fine," I said. "I need to sit down anyway to take off my shoes. What's the big deal? You wouldn't believe..."

"Just sit down!" So I did. She looked at me and laughed, "Emily is having twins!"

"What? Twins!?!" I jumped up and, clammy as I was, we hugged, giggled, and bounced. "Really?"

"I just got off the phone with Josh. It is killing me that I haven't been able to tell Jodi that Emily is pregnant, right? I was with Jodi and I got a phone call and saw that it was from Josh. I knew that they had their OB appointment today and I was dying to talk to them to find out how it went, but if I took his call Jodi would figure out that Em is pregnant, so I didn't pick it up. Then he called back a few minutes later and I told her she had to leave so I could take the call. Maybe she thought it was one of my patients. And as soon as the door closed behind her I called him back and he told me that while the OB was doing the ultrasound she said, very casually, 'Well, there is the baby, there is the heart, you can see it beating, there is the spine, everything looks good. There is the other baby, you are having twins, there is…' And they both shouted, 'Wait, what did you say?' And she says, 'Oh, right, you are having twins. Everything really looks great.' But when Emily started crying the OB left the room and then the crying turned to laughing and to 'I can't believe this.' All Josh keeps saying is 'Oh my God, Oh my God.'"

"Oh my God!" I echoed.

"They are totally stunned. Emily had to go back to work because she took time out to go to the appointment and Josh said he doesn't want to be alone. Let's take him along when we go out for dinner with Jodi and Charlie. He has to let us tell them now. I can't keep it secret anymore."

A little later Josh knocked on our door for yet more incredulous joyful hugs. As promised, he kept saying, "Oh my God, I can't believe it." He told the bartender, he told Jodi and Charlie, and over and over told himself until he believed it might really be true. At dinner, I looked across at him. He had his

elbow on the edge of the table and his right hand on his forehead. He was looking down at his lap. He slowly shook his
head from side to side, looked up, smiled, and said, "Oh my
God." It was nearly a week before I told Heidi about my most
excellent day, but the hike and donuts turned out to be just
footnotes.

**HELLO 2014!!**                               *Jan 2, 2014 2:43pm*

Michael and I want to wish everyone a WONDERFUL New
Year—and we would like to announce the birth of our
grandchildren! Emily and Josh had twins this morning—a boy and
a girl. Mom, babies, Dad and all grandparents are FANTASTIC!

Love—Heidi

**WONDERFUL**                                  *Feb 8, 2014 9:39am*

Hi—It's been a while since I posted. The biggest event in our lives
this New Year is not cancer (YAY!) —it's the twins. They are
AMAZING. We spent the whole month of January in NYC helping
Emily and Josh—it was great. Nothing like seeing your daughter
and son-in-law being fantastic parents and watching the babies
change and grow before your eyes. Michael said to me, "I can't
describe the happiness and joy I feel." It was WONDERFUL.

Now we are back home (another YAY!)—and it has been an eventful week. Monday was the retirement party for all staff. It was a way for any employee to see Michael and say goodbye and good luck. Some tears, many hugs, and lots of baby pictures.

Last night was the retirement dinner for the physicians. Everyone was there to tell Michael how much they valued and respected him as a physician, leader, and friend. Everyone was there to tell Michael they love him. That was the evening. Just filled with love. I smiled the whole time—watching Michael talk to every person there, watching them hug him and talk to him, hearing their stories and love for Michael, listening to the speeches. Michael said a few words too—he just wanted to tell everyone how filled with gratitude he is for his 22 years there, and how much he loved being an Ophthalmologist for his 30 year career. Still loves it.

So that's the theme of today's post. Michael is WONDERFUL—and we feel so blessed and thankful and happy to be here.

Love—Heidi

---

**CELEBRATION**

*Feb 8, 2014 10:44am (the morning after my retirement dinner)*

Someone said last night that it was sad that I was no longer working. But in fact, I felt no sadness in that room. It was an emotional and heartfelt celebration and a mutual thank you between me and my partners. How fortunate I am to have had the chance to do work that I love with people I respect and, when it is time to move on, to be so genuinely appreciated. Here is some of what I said at the dinner:

First of all, I want to thank all of you for coming here tonight. The last retirement dinner I went to was more than ten years ago. I never would have guessed that I would be next one in line, but here we are. This has been a year of amazing highs and lows, from the lows of illness and treatment and no longer working to the counter-balancing heights a few weeks ago of the birth of our twin grandchildren. Not in spite of, but because of, these changes I realize that I have so much to be grateful for.

I am proud to have been a part of this practice. Since I joined in 1992 the group has gotten a lot bigger, but I have always been proud to tell people that I work here. I would be happy to see or to refer a friend or family member to any the partners. How many people have the privilege to work in a place where they can respect every one of their colleagues? I am grateful for this.

Most people have no choice, they work because that's what they have to do to get by, but I have always been happy to come to work in the morning and I realize how lucky that is. I am grateful to have found work that I enjoy and a career that makes me think, makes me keep learning, and allows me to do some good.

Finally, I am grateful that I have a wonderful family behind me and the support of so many other people. Everyone here has been great to me throughout this whole process, with constant support and understanding. All the doctors have also been there for me too, stepping up to handle hundreds of my patients when their schedules were already full. These past months I have also been showered with an outpouring of concern, love, and respect that has been unexpected, overwhelming and humbling. If you ever wonder whether you make a difference in people's lives with what you do every day, read some of the cards I have received or what patients have written on my Caring Bridge site. It is so touching to think that simply by treating people with respect and by doing work I enjoy anyway I have managed to have an impact on so many people; the fact is that you have too, and I hope it does not take something like this to make you realize it.

So, thanks to everyone for coming tonight, but thanks much more for being my partners and my friends.

# THANK YOU

DRESSED IN A flowing black chador, the elderly woman scuffled into the exam room, guided by her two girls, one at each elbow. Only her face was visible, and it leaned toward the floor, her steps cautious and hesitant. I lifted the foot rest to let her reach the exam chair without stumbling. Once settled, she scanned the room with a blank stare and a fixed smile. Her daughter said, "This is our mother. She has had glaucoma for many years. Her vision is very bad and seems to be getting worse."

The patient said something in another language, and I realized she was not speaking Arabic. "Is that Farsi? Is she from Iran?" I asked.

"Yes," her daughter answered, "but she likes to say she is from Persia. How did you know?"

"Just a lucky guess. She is dressed as if she is from the Middle East. I don't know how to speak Farsi and I don't know how to speak Arabic, but I do know that they sound very different."

"What do you mean?"

"To me, Arabic is all la la la la, wa wa wa, Hebrew is chhhh chhhh chhhh and Farsi is somewhere in between. Right?"

Laughing, she said, "You are right. You are very smart doctor."

They were delightful people. Several times a year she came to see me, but her vision, poor at first, continued to deteriorate despite aggressive treatment. By the time we met it was too late; glaucoma had stolen most of her sight. Though her vision was irreversibly damaged, she appreciated our care. The only English she ever picked up was 'Thank you'.

"Hello, how are you today?"
Her daughter translated, "She said thank you."
"Please try to take your drops on schedule every day."
"Thank you."
"Are you going to go anywhere this summer?"
"Thank you."
Teetering on the edge of blindness for years, she saw her sight slipping away. But she also knew we were trying to help and that her family wanted the best for her. Appreciative and resilient, poor vision never broke her spirit. Faced with an unfamiliar language, what could be healthier than first learning to express gratitude?

**ANNIVERSARY**                                    *Feb 25, 2014 5:32am*

One year ago today I had the chest X-ray that first found my tumor. It was a Monday morning and on the way to work I went to get the X-ray just to be sure everything was all right. But it certainly was not, so over the following 2 weeks I had, in quick succession, several more tests, a preliminary diagnosis, and started chemotherapy and radiation treatments. It all happened so fast that there was no time then to think about odds, prognosis, or what-ifs.

But I am sure that if you had told me then that a year later I would feel that the year had been a net plus for me I would have been incredulous. Of course, the main thing is that I am still here to even think about this. True, I had to stop working, I had to undergo months of treatment and may someday need more. But in exchange I now feel better than I did then, I have had the chance to form some new friendships and deepen others, I have been able to spend intensive and extensive time with Heidi and the kids, and I have met and begun to know my twin grandchildren. And through this Caring Bridge site I have been constantly reminded how many people care about me. On balance, there is no way to consider this past year to have been anything but a good one, and I am pleasantly surprised and extraordinarily grateful that this is so. Michael

# CHAPTER 30

P EOPLE JUST DON'T know what to say. They want to let you know they care, but sometimes what comes out of their mouths can be stunningly clueless, even hurtful.

So many people have told me, happy to reveal a silver lining I must have overlooked, "It must be great to get some time off work!" Or, "You are so lucky that now you can be with your grandchildren more often." Thanks, but I am pretty sure I would have squeezed them into my busy schedule even if I didn't have cancer. Another wondered, out loud, what I might have done to bring this illness on myself. Hint to those who don't know what to say: it might be best to keep your mouth shut. Blaming the patient does no one any good, except to let the healthy speaker falsely reassure himself that bad things only happen to others.

Negative thoughts don't cause cancer, but I am convinced that harnessing the positive powers of mind and spirit is invaluable in making healing more likely and treatment more tolerable. It is important to believe in your own capacity to heal, and to devote as much of your mental and physical energy as you can to that goal; to enlist your entire being in the service of recovery.

Of course, this starts by eliminating actual risky behaviors. No one, especially when facing a serious illness, should smoke. Other components of a healthy lifestyle, like getting enough sleep and avoiding excessive alcohol consumption, fall under the same category, making it impossible for anyone to blame the patient for being reckless with his health.

A few days after I began treatment, Heidi said, "Listen. There are some other things I want you to do for yourself."

"Like what?"

"You need to exercise every day."

"I don't know. I really don't think it's a good idea for me to go to the gym or a hot, sweaty cycle class while my immunity is down."

"Of course not, but you can take a walk every day. Get out in the sunlight. Exercise is important. It helps keep you strong and fit, it's great for your mood and your attitude too." One recent study found that exercise has benefits comparable to taking anti-depressant medications.

Exercise also combats stress and anxiety. It is hard to discharge pent-up psychic energy while expending physical energy. A good sweat has lingering effects on mood, by boosting endorphins, improving self-confidence, and making it easier to sleep through the night. I try to exercise every day, mixing my routine so I never get bored. One day I might do a cycle class, another day swim for 45 minutes, use the elliptical trainer, or just take a walk. This always leaves me feeling better and reassures me that I am doing all I can for both my physical and mental fitness.

Heidi also encouraged, or more accurately, demanded, that I get into the habit of practicing other mind/body interventions as part of my daily self-care routine. First, she guided me as I developed a list of affirmations to repeat to myself. She said, "Saying these words won't make them true. But saying them as if they are true is a good way to remain optimistic and focused." Eventually, I came up with ten phrases that I say silently to myself throughout the day, and always just as I fall asleep at night.

1. I am healthy and strong

2. I am living a long and active life

3. My treatment is working

4. My tumor is shrinking and dying

5. My doctors are helping me

6. So many people are helping me

7. I am grateful for everyone who cares about me

8. I am surrounded by caring and love

9. Regular people can do remarkable things

10. My worst fears will not come true

These affirmations remind me to be hopeful, to be grateful, and to believe that I can tackle whatever comes at me. They are aspirational; may each line be and remain true. Nonspecific and yet intensely personal, these stay fresh and encouraging no matter when I say them, sort of a mantra, the act of repetition as therapeutic as the hopes they express.

Dick Blackwell, a friend of ours, is not only a skillful psychologist but also an ordained minister who used to work in our local hospice. He came to the house and sat down with me to talk about the importance of visualization and guided imagery, relaxation, and meditation. He told me that some people like to envision their chemotherapy medicine as little Pac Man-type creatures flowing throughout the body, chomping up cancer wherever they find it. He said, "I had one patient who loved reading fantasy novels. She imagined that she had a magic sword that could focus the power of lightning bolts from the sky right into her tumor."

"Yeah, that one's not going to work for me."

"Okay, come up with an image that works for you. Let's brainstorm." And I found three images that I used throughout my treatment. As chemo drugs flowed into my arm, I envisioned them as sunbeams changing a juicy grape into a shriveled raisin, and at home, often watched a time-lapse video online to reinforce this image. During radiation, whenever the machine above me started buzzing, I visualized my tumor boiling away in a focused torrent of furiously boiling champagne bubbles.

And at home, every day during my treatment, I spent about ten minutes of mental work removing the tumor as if it was a cataract. Over the course of my career I did several thousand cataract operations and know every step of the procedure, which is a controlled and reproducible way of extracting something unwanted from the body. Never mind that my tumor was not, and bore no resemblance to, a cataract. In my mind's eye I excised a large cataract from my chest every day, without any surgical complications.

Later, after treatment started working, I came up with another powerful healing image. An oncologist friend told me, "When patients' tumors shrink but don't completely go away, I tell them it is like a stump that's left after you cut down a tree. It might last for years, but over time it gradually crumbles and never grows back." Soon after this conversation, while walking in the woods I passed a charred tree, burnt in a forest fire. It was standing but dead, present but inert. What a perfect metaphor. Its photo sits on my desk to remind me that although I still have a mass in my chest, it may be charcoal too.

Dick and Heidi also helped me to start doing formal re-laxation training and to learn about meditation. At first, it seemed kind of ridiculous that I should need to learn how to relax. I have always been good, maybe too good, at relaxing. My favorite place in the world is the hammock in a shady corner of my backyard. Though engrossed in reading a tense thriller, after a few minutes there my lids drift shut and the book falls to the ground. But relaxation training is about more than improving my already well-developed napping skills. It is a systematic way to reduce stress and anxiety. Dick gave me a recording of a guided relaxation session and I found others online. Whenever tension or anxiety percolated too close to the surface I put on headphones, tipped back in the recliner or hammock, and sat up 25 minutes later relaxed and refreshed in body and spirit.

Another friend tipped me off to a remarkable, possibly magical, tool called binaural beats. When a steady tone plays through headphones into one ear while a nearly identical tone plays in the other, you hear the disparate pitches as a quickly pulsing sound. The frequency of this sound can be adjusted, and the theory is that these tones can drive the brain to generate matching brain waves. Scientists know which brain wave frequencies are associated with relaxation, with meditation, with sleep, and with a variety of other mental states. Listening to binaural beats for 20–30 minutes has an astonishing ability to induce calm and sleep. The first time I used this app I was skeptical. Wide awake, I put headphones on and thought,

'What a ridiculous idea, this is so bizarre, who knows if the science behind it is even true, brain waves, how crazy is this, nothing's happening,' and then 20 minutes later woke up, converted.

Heidi and Dick also urged me to study, and to begin doing, meditation. Though it can be relaxing as well, the point of meditation is to learn to focus with relaxed attention. I took a class at the Insight Meditation Community of Charlotte and began meditating at home and at their weekly group meetings. During meditation, while trying to concentrate only on the sensation of breathing in and out, other thoughts constantly pop up. 'My nose itches. A motorcycle just drove by. Remember to get gas on the way home. I forgot to focus on my breath...' But that is why they call it practice.

The skill to nurture is the ability to recognize extraneous thoughts and then to set them aside as if they were leaves floating by in a quiet stream. To learn to concentrate on what is, right now, not on what might or might not happen, not on what it might mean. To respond thoughtfully rather than to react urgently. To overcome the inclination of the imagination to catastrophize. Mindfulness meditation has deep roots in Buddhism, but as a strictly secular practice has given me great peace of mind, reminding me that my response to illness and to life is always, to some degree, a choice that I can make either wisely or not.

I have a complicated attitude toward religion. I believe there is more to existence than the material world and more to life than life. It seems to me that throughout history, people around the world have developed their own ways of understanding ultimate reality, just as people in different areas developed disparate languages to express similar thoughts. A friend once told me a story about his Christian summer camp. The counselor told the campers to stand in a circle around a campfire and had them point at the fire. He asked, "Where are you pointing?" They said, "At the fire, of course." "Right," he said, "you are all pointing at the fire, but look. Sally is pointing north, Bill is pointing east, Jeremy is pointing south, everyone is pointing in a different direction, but you are all pointing at the same thing." Most religions point to the same unknowable truths in their own way, and which one people follow has more to do with where they were raised than with the tenets of their particular faith.

I wonder sometimes if the famous story of the Tower of Babel was meant not to explain the origin of languages and nations, but rather to warn people against believing that any one religion has all the answers. The people, full of themselves, and sharing not only a language but a belief system, said, 'Come, let us build ourselves...a tower with its top in the heavens.' For the affront of thinking that humans could ever, by their efforts, reach parity with the divine, they were dispersed and caused to speak a multitude of spiritual languages. Then, no one group could say it had the full picture. We can build towers of elaborate belief systems to express our innate spiritual longings and insights but are inherently too limited ever to fully understand the divine. People can express themselves just as well in Spanish as in English, Chinese, or Tagalog. It seems prideful and tribal to deny that people around the world have also developed a variety of equally valid spiritual languages.

My upbringing was Jewish and it is the spiritual language that I speak most fluently, the tradition that fits me best. It is a fundamental part of my identity and the basis of how I see and experience the world. But illness brings a whole new dimension to belief and an entirely new urgency to prayer. It is comforting to attend religious services to recite the same old words and sing the same old songs along with my community. The rituals are as familiar as a newspaper at breakfast, but once I became a patient I found new meaning in the prayer book. I belatedly realized that these prayers, written centuries ago by spiritual experts, were constructed to offer hope and solace to people just like me. I was newly sensitized, as touching a bruise even gently can be painful.

Standing among other congregants all racing silently through their prayers, things that I read and recited rote hundreds of times jumped out at me as if new. One was, *'You sustain the living with loving-kindness. You revive the dead with great compassion. You support the fallen and heal the ill...'* Until I was sick I used to blow right by this prayer. Now it and others speak eloquently to and for me. They ensnare me, compel me to stop and ruminate while everyone else keeps flipping pages.

A few months after the end of my treatment we were invited to a wedding in Israel. I was anxious to go, not just to celebrate the wedding or to visit Israel again, but to have another chance to pray at the Western Wall. The Wall is a remnant of the retaining wall built in Roman times by King Herod to shore up the Temple Mount. It is the holiest place in the world for Jews. The ancient Temple was destroyed 2000 years ago, no one knows exactly where it stood, and it will not be rebuilt anytime soon, so praying at the Wall is as close to praying in the Temple as is now possible. Typically, the plaza in front of the Wall is crowded with people dancing with the Torah, praying on their own or in small clusters. People write private prayers on little scraps of paper that they wedge into the narrow spaces between the huge, hand-hewn, stone blocks.

I wanted to be sure not to waste my precious time at the Wall, so I asked one of my Rabbis to help me figure out how best to express myself there. He talked about personal prayer and reassured me that there is a selfless way to petition for help from above. Certain Psalms are particularly concerned with healing and others are traditionally linked to the ages of the people in my prayers; he suggested I recite these to supplement my own words. And he reminded me to ignore the hubbub, to take my time, and to linger in that special and sacred space as long as I could.

Men and women pray at adjacent parts of the Wall. Before Heidi went to the women's side, we agreed when and where to meet. The Wall Plaza was crowded with several groups singing loudly, their chants echoing off the stones. Black-hatted Hasids ecstatically prayed and swayed, infused with the spiritual energy of the place. Seeking quiet, I meandered through the arches to the left and found an empty alcove, dark and peaceful. I pulled a folding chair right up to the Wall, draped a prayer shawl over my head, and took out my phone, which I had loaded with the Psalms. Then, with my hand, and sometimes my forehead, pressed to the cold stone, I read the Psalms and recited my prayer quietly, inaudible to others. As I prayed almost silently I heard people gathering behind me. A service started and ended, but while activity swirled around me, I never looked up and no one disturbed or interrupted me. None of them knew what led me to that folding chair in my dark corner of the Wall plaza, but they must have recognized a fellow supplicant who needed and deserved privacy. Finally, after being lost in the peace and power of the moment, I realized that everyone had gone and that more than an hour had passed. Reluctantly, I slid my chair back and scurried out into the dazzling sunlight, where Heidi was waiting patiently. Here is the prayer I wrote to say at the Wall:

אלוקים בבקשה לשמוע אותי, יעזור לי, ולענות על התפילות שלי

God please hear me, help me, and answer my prayers

Next, I recited Psalms 1, 28, 31, 58, 60, and 88, the ages of my grandchildren, my children, Heidi and me, and my mother. Then I chose Psalms 20, 121, and 130, which ask for help from above.

ברוך אתה יהוה אלהינו מלך העולם שהחיינו וקיימנו והגיענו
לזמן הזה

Blessed are You, Lord our God, King of the Universe, who has granted us life, sustained us, and enabled us to reach this day.

Thank you for all the blessings you have given to me and for the wonderful life you have allowed me to live so far. I have so much to be thankful and grateful for. My wife, my parents, my children, my grandchildren, my profession, my country, my religion, my friends, and my vigor. I want you to know that I try to remain aware of these many blessings in my life and the blessing of my life, and that I do my best to take none of them for granted. In addition to all the blessings of my first 60 years, I have been further blessed in the past year by some new and wonderful things: our first grandchildren. They are perfect, beautiful, happy babies, thank you; they bring joy to their parents and grandparents, and they have allowed us the further very great pleasure of seeing their parents grow into their new responsibilities in ways that are both beautiful and heartwarming to witness. They have also brought untold joy to Heidi, who needed and deserved some future focused causes for optimism and joy. She and I both are consumed and diverted by our love for the twins and for their mother. Our son is doing well in medical school, is happy with his life and his prospects, and is getting closer to deciding on the specialty he wants to pursue in his career. May our children and grandchildren continue to be a source of only pride and happiness and may they all enjoy continued good health. My mother still lives and thankfully no longer seems to be subject to the suffering that accompanied awareness of her disabilities. Thank you for preserving her to meet her great-grandchildren.

You know me better than I know myself; you knew me before and will know me afterwards. My Hebrew name is מנשה הרש בן בערל ו'אליהו הכהן. You know that I am facing illness. I pray for healing, for health, and for a long, loving, worthy and peaceful life. I love my life and do want to live a long and healthy life for myself, but also to avoid bringing pain, sadness, and suffering to my wife and children. Some will be unavoidable in each of their lives, but I would like to be one of the people who helps ease their burdens and does not add to them. I know what I want for my future but you know what I need. I pray that what I hope for myself and my family is the same as what you have planned for me.

רפאנו יהוה ונרפא, הושיענו ונושעה, כי תהלתנו אתה, והעלה רפואה שלמה לכל מכותינו, כי אל מלך רופא נאמן ורחמן אתה. ברוך אתה יהוה רופא חולי עמו ישראל.

Heal us, O Lord, and we will be healed; help us and we will be saved; for You are our praise. Grant complete cure and healing to all our wounds; for You, Almighty King, are a faithful and merciful healer. Blessed are You Lord, who heals the sick of His people Israel.

May it be your will... יהי רצון מלפניך

Even if a person is not religious, there is benefit in asking for help from other people and from a higher power not only to regain a healthy body, but also to nurture a hopeful mind and peaceful spirit. It is important to remember that wherever this journey leads, I am not traveling alone.

The mind can constructively influence healing in other ways too. In the bleakest days of chemotherapy and radiation it is hard to remember that these are just necessary, time limited, steps on the road to recovery. A mind that can maintain an optimistic attitude fosters healing and makes it possible to live fully with and through an illness. While consumed by your struggles and worries, life goes on around you. And if you are lucky, unexpected joyful events in your life, even better than jelly donuts, can suddenly jolt your attention from its focus on dread of what lies ahead into the state of grace that comes from anticipation of a happier tomorrow.

# CHAPTER 31

## TAXI CONFIDENTIAL

**"I** DON'T WANT to be late," said Emily as we left her apartment to go to our infant CPR class downtown. Josh ran to the corner of 90TH and Columbus, raised his hand, and hailed a cab. The three of us piled into the back and Heidi took the front passenger seat.

"Where are you going?" asked the driver, a middle-aged man who appeared to be from India or Pakistan.

"33RD and 7TH Avenue," Emily answered.

"It is very busy in midtown today. Lots of shopping," he said. It was late November, the day after Black Friday, and we had an appointment next door to Macy's. Traffic built as we headed South and Emily began to check her watch every few blocks. At about 60TH Street, while stopped at a red light, the driver turned to Heidi and said, "Can I ask you a question?"

Before she could answer, I turned to Emily and Josh and whispered, "Guess what's coming."

They leaned in, "What do you mean?"

"This happens to her all the time. Just sit back and watch."

Up front, Heidi answered, "Sure, what do you want to know?"

The driver said, "My wife and I are from Bangladesh. She has only been in this country for a few months. She is forty years old and we want to have a baby, so she went to the doctor and for some reason he made her get a test, a mammo something."

"A mammogram?"

"Yes, that is it. Then they did a biopsy and told her that she has breast cancer. They said it is very early, but we don't know what to do. Can we believe what the doctors are telling us?" He started to cry. We eavesdropped, silent and still in the back seat.

"Of course, you can believe the doctors. Where is she going for her care?"

"Bellevue Hospital. We don't have any insurance."

Heidi said, "That doesn't matter. They will take care of her anyway."

"That is what they told us. But what do we do now? They want her to see a specialist and maybe have some kind of surgery. I am afraid she might die. We are worried this could mean we will not be able to have a baby. This all happened yesterday." As he drove, he sniffled and wiped his eyes with his sleeve.

"It sounds like your wife is going to be fine, but she does need to see the specialist and to do what the doctors tell her to do," Heidi answered. "Breast cancer treatment is pretty well settled, so it doesn't matter so much where she gets treated. Wherever she goes they will probably take a similar approach, and I am sure the doctors at Bellevue are great. But do you know about second opinions?"

"Somebody told me to get a second opinion, but won't her doctors get mad if we do?"

"No, any good doctors would be happy for you to get another opinion because then you will have confidence in them and be more likely to follow their advice. You are lucky that in New York there are so many hospitals that are good for this problem. There is Sloan Kettering, Columbia Presbyterian, Mount Sinai; any would be fine for another opinion. If she likes her doctors, Bellevue would be great too."

"But what do we do? My wife, she is very smart. In Bangladesh she got two Masters degrees, but here we don't know what to do." Meaning, she is very smart, but so is he; no educated woman from Bangladesh would marry a subsistence farmer. He might be an engineer or a doctor who cannot be licensed in this country. So here he is in New York, in a strange place, working at a job beneath his ability, his training, and his accustomed station, in a scary situation, adrift with his wife.

"Here is my daughter's email address." She asked Emily to write it down and give it to him. "Tell your wife to email us and I will try to help her out."

He turned the meter off a few blocks before the end of our ride. Traffic was gridlocked and Emily finally said, "Just pull over here and we'll walk the rest of the way." He stopped, and the back seat emptied, but Heidi stayed in the taxi as Emily and Josh hurried down the sidewalk.

"Your wife is going to be fine. I am so glad we got into your cab. But I have to ask you, we never met before. What made you decide to talk to me?"

"You looked like an Auntie, and we are alone here in America. I needed an Auntie to talk to." They shook hands and we went to our CPR class so we could become certified as competent baby sitters and responsible grandparents.

The next day we got an email from the driver's wife. Heidi wrote back telling her how to get in touch with the Breast Cancer center at Sloan Kettering, reminding her that the hospital would provide an interpreter if she asks, and reassuring her that she was going to be fine. Then she found a local program for breast cancer patients from Bangladesh, coordinated by a social worker fluent in Bengali. She told her about the cab ride and shared the email she had sent to the driver's wife. And the next day the social worker responded, saying "They are so lucky that you got into that cab. I will contact her today and do what I can for this poor woman."

If you broadcast that you are receptive and interested, miraculous things can happen. Heidi is a trained psychologist, but I think she was born this way. When people meet her, she puts them at ease, looks into their eyes, soothes them with her voice, welcomes them into relationship. I've seen it countless times, and marvel and feel grateful that she's my partner. It takes so little to be kind to strangers and to become a blessing in their lives.

# LISTENING

SOME PEOPLE EXUDE a pheromone that signals strangers that they welcome conversation. Heidi has this preternatural ability, which is one reason she is such a good therapist. It doesn't come naturally to me, so I stand in awe of the way strangers approach her and, with no apparent prompting, reveal their deepest secrets.

To communicate well in the office, I need to draw people out. For sure, I need to explain complicated and emotionally charged information to patients in an understandable way. But that is only part of the challenge. Every conversation has two sides; I also need to be a good listener. This doesn't mean that I force myself to sit there fidgeting while the patient drones on about something irrelevant, oblivious to my being an hour behind schedule with a full waiting room. It means I should eagerly attend to what the patient says, try to unearth the nuggets of meaning buried beneath extraneous words, and attempt to distill the essence of his concerns.

I cannot be a good listener if I interrupt the patient after only a few seconds or if, while he is talking, I am preoccupied with trying to figure out what to say next to move things along. To serve best, I must really hear, understand, and empathize.

Deep listening isn't easy, especially when patients are scheduled every 15 minutes. All doctors know how frustrating it can be to finish an office visit, having addressed every issue a patient mentioned at the beginning of the appointment, only to have him say, as I stand to shake hands and walk out the door, "There's one more thing that's bothering me."

So what can I do to reduce the likelihood of hearing, "Hold on, just one more question," when my hand is already on the door knob? Usually, the way the appointment ends depends upon how it begins.

How can I learn what a patient is worried about except by listening? How would I know that he has had magical thinking or has been catastrophizing a minor medical problem that I assume he realizes is no big deal? How many people will volunteer that they are afraid an eyelid stye might be cancerous? Or that I will remove their eyes during cataract surgery and might run into a complication that keeps me from putting them back in. But people have all kinds of unexpected and unexpressed assumptions that hinder good communication.

Erroneous and deeply held beliefs can also make it hard for people to accept medical advice. Once, when I told a patient that he had glaucoma, he said, "No, that's impossible. I smoke way too much weed." But unspoken beliefs, even misguided ones, can make it impossible for me to set a patient's mind at ease unless identified and addressed head on.

The only way to ferret these out is to explicitly invite the patient to speak and then to sit back and listen. I admit that in the time-pressured environment of the office, as unexpected emergencies and cascading delays threaten to ruin the day, my instinct sometimes is just to 'git 'er done,' and focus on the obvious reason for the visit. A glaucoma patient back for a scheduled four month recheck; that's a pressure check, visual field, optic nerve exam, prescription refill, check, check, check, check. Like scheduled maintenance for a car. Thank you very much, see you next time. But that strategy may leave the patient feeling that I never addressed or even wanted to hear about what was really concerning him when he walked in the door and makes it more likely that these issues will arise later at an awkward time. Just when I'm ready to wrap up the visit I might have to repeat part of the exam, pursue another line of questioning, or take time to explain things all over again. To avoid this, I found ways to get all the issues on the table right up front, so the visit ends up being both what the patient needs and wants it to be.

I start with an open-ended question, one that cannot be answered with a yes or no. "I know you are here to be sure your glaucoma is still in good control, but what else is bothering you or concerning you about your eyes today?" And I might follow up by asking something like, "No redness, or discomfort? No changes in your vision? Are your drops getting expensive? How often do you think you missed taking them last week?" This minute at the start of the visit often saves more time at the end. And, as soon as we start talking, the patient knows that I am interested in what he has to say and am not preoccupied with the full waiting room or my lunch date.

Usually I wrap the visit up with another invitation to talk. After explaining my findings and answering whatever questions the patient asked, I always end with, "I wonder if you have any other questions that we didn't talk about yet?" And if I did my job right, the answer is usually, "Nope, thanks so much. I was worried but now that you checked me and explained it all I feel much better."

Some patients ramble, and my challenge is to coax them to focus on their eye problems. But most are reluctant to reveal themselves until I explicitly welcome them to disclose their concerns and fears. Getting it all out on the table right up front insures that our time together becomes the visit they wanted, and not just the one I expected it to be when I walked into the exam room.

---

**GOOD NEWS ABOUT TODAY'S SCAN**                    *Jun 30, 2014 1:29pm*

It has been several months since I last wrote a Journal entry because while my illness remains on our minds, recently we have been able to live our lives with it in the background and not dominating or directing our days. We realize how fortunate we are and are so grateful that this is how it has been for us lately. Today we got some very good news—my follow-up CT scan, the first since March, shows that there has been no change in the tumor, no growth, no spread, no nothing! And this is without any treatment at all since last August. I have been feeling well, but I have learned the hard way that you never really know, so this comes as a big relief.

Meanwhile, we just got home from two weeks in Israel. We love being there; somehow it feels at once so comfortable yet so exotic, mundane yet so spiritual. We spent 4 days in Jerusalem and 9 in Tel Aviv, and did some of the usual things you do when in Israel, including private time at the Western Wall. But of course this time there was more urgency in my prayers than in the past. And since we were there for the wedding of Josh's sister, it was a beautiful celebration of family and love.

So, I expect it will be a while before I post again, and hopefully the next time it will also be to share good news with you. Thanks as always for your continued caring, support, and love.

Michael

**ALMOST TWO YEARS**                      *Jan 9, 2015 9:37am*

Here is a sentence that I am thrilled to be able to write: It is now nearly two years since I discovered that I have cancer. The chest x-ray that first revealed the tumor was in February 2013, and since then a lot has happened. But thankfully, two years later, here we are, still feeling well and enjoying friends, family, and life in general. Yesterday I had my regularly scheduled quarterly CT scan and again it showed no changes. No growth, no new areas of disease, just stable. And stable is great!

I am not really sorry at all that my Caring Bridge posts have been so few and far between, and don't mind either that they have been so boring lately (no change, no news, etc.). I will be very happy and endlessly grateful if it stays that way for a long time. Meanwhile, thanks as always for your love, support, and concern. I hope we all share a happy and healthy new year.

Michael

# NOT JUST DATA

STEVE PLUNKETT AND I have been friends for years, but the first time I saw him as a patient he said, "We're going for a cure with this thing. That's my goal, and I think we can do it." He warned that he was about to give me so much radiation that I was going to get sick from it, would soon have trouble swallowing, and in five years would almost certainly get pericarditis, inflammation around the heart. "But you'll be happy if you get the chance to deal with that, won't you?" He was never Pollyanna, didn't sugar coat the fact that I had a bad tumor, but always found and focused on the bright side. He knew that while radiation is a powerful tool to fight cancer, an optimistic attitude is just as potent. After two months of treatment he told me, "Your tumor has shrunk so much, it's nothing short of miraculous!" A few days later, my oncologist looked at the same scan and said, "Hmm, looks pretty good. Maybe even a little smaller than last time. Are you really still feeling all right?"

Both my doctors were skilled, bright, compassionate, and fully devoted to my recovery. I could not have been in better hands. But they had dissimilar personalities and practice styles. After a few months we knew what to expect; whatever the facts, one was going to see the bright side and the other would be honest and hopeful, but less effusive.

Nearly two years after my last doses of chemo and radiation I had a scan of my chest and belly and, for the first time, of my neck as well, because the area treated with radiation was near my thyroid. Although I was feeling fine, my energy was good, and my cough was unchanged, my stress level rose approaching the day of the scan. Seeing my oncologists twice a year, I usually live with my illness in the background. But during the weeks before the scan every cough implied something ominous. Did it sound different? Did I feel this way when I had my stable scan six months ago? I felt the same, the data didn't change, but fueled by worry, my concern about it did.

After the scan, my anxiety reached a crescendo while waiting to hear the results. I can't stand to wait. At 10:30, when I got home from the scan, I emailed my radiation oncologist. "Hi Steve, I hope your summer is going well so far. FYI, I just had my regularly scheduled scan this morning." That is code for, "Please take a look so I don't have to wait and worry until Friday when I see my other doctor."

By 4:30 we still hadn't heard from him. I must have been getting fidgety, because Heidi made me a gin and tonic. Just as it started to work I looked at my phone and saw a text from him. In the preview panel I could see, "Scan looks good…" So I made another drink and read the rest of the email. It said, "Scan looks good. Tumor is even smaller than last time. No new areas of disease. Just stable changes related to treatment. YIPPEE!" I loved the YIPPEE.

We hugged and then I said to Heidi, "So what do you think Mahoney is going to say about this?"

She smiled and said, "You know, I love John, he's been great to you. He and Steve saved your life, so I'll always be grateful. But he'll probably just say something very matter of fact like, 'Oh, your scan looks pretty much OK.' Definitely no YIPPEE."

Three days later as we drove to the office, Heidi said, "Well, what a relief. Can you imagine if we didn't already know the scan is good? At least we're not expecting any surprises today." Injecting some negativity, I said, "That's why they call them surprises. You never expect them." Soon we were sitting in an exam room at his office. He opened the door and walked in. After a minute or two of small talk, he scanned back and forth between us and with a serious face asked, "Have you already heard about the scan?"

I thought, "Oh no, here comes the surprise."

But he said, "The scan looks pretty good. I mean, the cancer part. The tumor is actually a little smaller than last time, which is nice, because you haven't had any treatment in so long. And it hasn't spread. So the cancer part is pretty good. But this is the first time we scanned your neck, and you have an awful lot of degenerative arthritis there. Do you have any neck pain, numbness in your hands, that sort of thing?"

I said, "I don't. Not at all.

"Well, here, take a look at this report…"

I interrupted, "John, Hold on. Let me make sure I understand. My tumor is stable, maybe even improving, right?"

"It is. But your neck…"

"Well, it was the cancer part that I was most concerned about, so if that's doing OK, I'm happy. You can copy this report and give it to me every six months from now on for the rest of my life and I promise I'll never complain. And if my neck starts to hurt I'll let you know."

Conversations with patients need to be truthful, but the facts are simply data points. Since neither doctor nor patient know for sure what course the disease will follow, an optimistic take on the patient's situation is always best. This doesn't mean it is helpful to indulge unrealistic fantasies, but even in the most serious predicaments there is usually room for hope.

61ST BIRTHDAY—9/2/2015          Sept 2, 2015 12:17pm

I haven't posted anything on my Caring Bridge site for several months, so some people might be wondering how I am doing, or whether no news means there is bad news that I am not sharing.

But, I am thrilled to say that I have not written in lately because, happily, there hasn't been much medical news to report. I had a scan in July, and everything was stable —no growth, no spread, no new trouble. I don't even need to see the oncologist or to have another scan for six months. So for now, I'm just enjoying being able to live the new normal. Also, today is my birthday, and though every day is precious and none are guaranteed, this one stands out. I thank all of you for your gifts of concern, caring, and love that have been in the forefront for me over these past many months. I don't take any of it for granted and appreciate every one of you, and every kind gesture you have made.

Michael

**HAPPY 2016**                                    *Jan 17, 2016 12:57pm*

Hi—Michael and I want to wish everyone a wonderful, happy and healthy 2016. Just a brief update:

Michael had a scan this week and everything looks the same as the last scan. That's great news—the mass is **stable** with no new progression. This is really fantastic—and life goes on. Yes—LIFE GOES ON. We are both **very grateful** for our lives together. These last few years have not been exactly what we expected, but as Michael says they have also been wonderful. Our time has been spent together, with family and friends. Our family has grown—Emily & Josh had an eventful 3 years in NYC, and now our grandchildren are 2 years old. David graduated medical school and is doing his residency. Michael's mom passed away in 2015, but he has been able to spend more time with his sister and her family. We have shared our holidays in Charlotte with family, and this past Thanksgiving also welcomed Josh's parents from London.

Sharing joyous occasions is so important - we danced at weddings and had visits with friends and family.

Thank you for all your thoughts, prayers and support. This means more than we can ever express. I'm keeping this Caring Bridge site active, but will only post as needed.

Later—Love,
Heidi

# CHAPTER 32

F OR SURE, BEING alone is not the same as being lonely, but both are bad for people fighting illness. Lonely people have impaired immune systems and an exaggerated reaction to physiologic stress. And the consequences of isolation are even more dramatic. Research has found that social relationships have a profound influence upon a person's risk of mortality. People with stronger social ties have better chances of survival than do those who are less engaged with others. Low levels of social support and high levels of social isolation effect mortality more than recognized risk factors like smoking, obesity, alcohol consumption and lack of exercise.

But many people just want to hunker down and keep to themselves when they have a serious health issue. They don't want to talk about it, don't want to be around other people, don't want to ask for, or admit that they need, help. Can't stomach one more sad-faced person asking, with grave drama and breathy concern, "So how *aaaare* you doing, really?" This approach makes some sense; when life springs a big unpleasant surprise, it is natural to want to take some time to figure out what it means and to try to discern the contours of the new normal. Unfortunately though, just as healthy grieving can evolve into depression, the normal wish for time alone can lead down a dead end to denial and detachment.

There is a chance I might have fallen into this trap if I wasn't married to Heidi. Not only is she a psychologist who understands these issues, she has a personality that responds to crises in a proactive way. She makes phone calls, reaches out, starts reading up on the problem, and permits herself no time for self-pity. Almost immediately, she set up our Caring Bridge site to widen and deepen her, and our, circle of support. And she insisted that I remain engaged in the wider world. No sleeping late just because I wasn't working, no keeping my condition a secret, no trying to deal with it on our own. No avoiding other people.

She reached out to her friends, sought and received their help. She recognized that my friends cared too, but were hesitant to call, either because they were uncomfortable and didn't know what to say or because they wanted to respect our privacy. She goosed me to pick up the phone, and I was surprised to find that most of the time people were thrilled to hear from me, had been wondering if they should call, and were anxious to carve out time from their busy schedules to get together. We took walks, sat down for coffee, or met for a beer. But whatever the setting, the subtext was always caring, concern, and love wrapped in stimulating conversations that were more genuine, open, and substantial than before I was sick.

These social engagements were great for me, a little gift, one of the silver linings bestowed by my illness. While working more than full-time and devoting most of the rest to Heidi and the kids, I jealously guarded my limited free time. Now, suddenly I found myself with too much, and being able to see friends more often and to deepen friendships with people I liked but knew only superficially was an unexpected pleasure. And occasionally, these meetings turned out to be more than enjoyable; some were instrumental in my healing.

During a walk early in treatment, my friend asked, "Are you going to go back to work when this is all over? What do you think your next act will be? What are you going to do once you get better?"

I said, "I don't know. I don't really have any plans. It's hard to look too far ahead when I'm living in three-month blocks from scan to scan."

We walked silently for a hundred yards until he said, "I'm just going to say it. That really makes me sad. No one knows how much time is left. Everyone is kind of living day to day. But we all have to live as if there's a future. Otherwise you're just paralyzed. You have to have something to aim for."

He was right. Later that week I enrolled in Introductory Spanish at our local community college, hoping there was enough time to remedy the mistake I made by taking French in High School. His loving concern during what I expected to be an hour of fresh air, exercise, and innocuous chatter shook me out of my funk and led me to reengage with learning and living.

Who has the time or energy to sit down for an hour to schmooze during the workday? Chuck, who retired as administrator of my medical group the same week I was diagnosed, also had free weekdays for the first time in decades. Although we worked closely for years and liked and respected each other, we never hung out because he avoided socializing with his employees and bosses (me). But now we were both somewhat adrift and began to meet for coffee and conversation almost every week. The first time we walked into a crowded Starbucks at 10AM and found the line backed up to the door, he asked, "Don't these people work?" He was incredulous that a parallel world existed alongside the one in which we both had been cloistered. We looked forward to our meetings, and soon other people asked to be invited too. Every few weeks we had a 'guest speaker', and for the price of a cup of coffee were able to stay on top of news and gossip from our working lives.

Heidi also encouraged me to resume participation in a men's group that I had attended for several years. These dozen men, mostly physicians and dentists, both Christians and Jews, with an occasional Hindu or Sikh, meet at one of our homes each month. The idea is that when men get together, we usually talk about news, weather, women, sports and other diverting but inconsequential things. We rarely feel comfortable discussing more significant topics, like ethics, morality, religion, and personal concerns. So, when this group gets together, we drink wine and eat munchies for an hour, then have dinner, all the while talking about news, weather, sports, and women. But when we clear the dishes, we devote the next hour to more serious subjects chosen and announced in advance. We might discuss a selection from scripture, might brainstorm about forgiveness, or talk about assisted suicide, abortion, or guns. We never reach a consensus or conclusion, never change anyone's mind, but in an atmosphere of trust, openness, and respect, have learned from and about each other and have become unique friends. It was salutary, after missing a meeting at the start of my treatment, to walk back into the welcoming arms of the men in this group.

I am convinced that social isolation is detrimental to health and healing. When you are sick, it is essential to become more enmeshed, to burrow deeply into a network of friends, family, and communal organizations, to enlarge your circle and give yourself the best chance of having a good journey through, or with, illness.

While you are grateful for all that your friends do for you when you are ill, it is easy to slip into the habit of taking and to forget your obligation to give. But no one gets a pass for long just because of illness. Sometimes you pitch and sometimes you catch. Even when you don't feel like yourself you still need to be available to your friends and family, still need to do as much as you can of whatever you used to do for them, or the relationship will, at some point, become one-sided, strained, and unsustainable. You have problems, but so does everybody else, and it helps no one if you come to see yourself as uniquely afflicted.

To be worthy of your friends and family, you need to reciprocate, to reach out to them, and to try, under trying conditions, to be as equal a partner as possible. People who depended on you before still do; they miss the old you as much as you do. The new you needs, and needs to be, a friend.

When illness forced me to stop working, I wanted to find another way to remain socially engaged. In Charlotte, the Lions Club runs a remarkable sheltered workshop that employs hundreds of visually impaired people, giving them income, the dignity of meaningful work, and an antidote to their own social isolation. The Club also operates an eye clinic where people without money or insurance can get free eye exams and glasses. While I was working full-time, I devoted an afternoon every few months to see patients at the clinic, many of whom live for years with blurry vision because they cannot afford glasses or an eye exam.

During my radiation and chemotherapy, I stopped working entirely to concentrate on getting better and to avoid close contact with coughing, sneezing patients. I gave up the office and surgical practice I worked so hard to build. But a few weeks after treatment ended I put on my white coat and returned to the Clinic. Now every week I spend an afternoon there. It is good for them, because we have been able to chip away at the long waiting list for appointments. And it is even better for me, allowing me to keep my skills intact and to continue, in a new setting, to use my training to serve my community.

I try to reach out in other ways too. Since the start of my cancer journey, several people I know have embarked on their own. Our experiences are not identical but, without barging in uninvited, I offer to share what I have learned with new members of the cancer club.

One of my friends hadn't been able to exercise for several weeks because of pain in his hip. He found out that he had cancer there and was distraught. We talked about what to expect, and I tried to get him in the right frame of mind to face his treatment. I wrote,

> *Eddie—I just had lunch with Harry, and he brought me up to date. I am so sorry to hear about what you are going through. This stage is one of the hardest, meeting new doctors you don't know if you will like, waiting for test results and then for the treatment plan. Once you have a strategy, it's just a matter of plunging ahead and doing everything you can do to make it easier on yourself and your family and to give yourself the best chance of healing. But for now, you are in limbo. Sometimes life serves up something you didn't order. I too have hard won experience with this sort of thing, so if there is any way I can help, either by interpreting what your doctors tell you, by bringing dinners, by talking to you about how to stay strong and resilient, anything, please just ask. I won't presume or intrude, but please let me know how I can help.*

He needed radiation and was nervous, almost queasy thinking about it.

> *The radiation is easy, no big deal. Doesn't hurt at all, though after a while you can get a sunburn. And if they heavily radi-*

*ate your chest it can hurt to swallow, but I got a tremendous amount and that never happened to me…*

*The facts are whatever they are, but there are always both helpful and damaging ways to honestly interpret the same information. I am trying to help you stay focused on the most healing approach to your situation. Think of it this way: tomorrow will be the first day of killing your cancer.*

He told other people that these notes helped him pivot to a more hopeful mindset, and to focus on doing what he needed to do to get better rather than dwelling on awful things that might never happen.

When another friend's daughter became ill, I offered some hard-won free advice.

*Julie —I am so sorry that your normal life has been put on hold so you can deal with your unexpected and unwelcome illness. I know the feeling. Since I have already been traveling down the same road for a few years, maybe some of the things that have helped me will resonate with you.*

*The support that your friends and family have shown is wonderful and critical. Your Caring Bridge site is a great way to keep everyone informed and to drink from the well of good wishes that are being sent your way. But there are things you can do yourself to optimize your healing and minimize negative thoughts and distractions.*

*People mean well and often don't know what to say, but that doesn't mean you have to indulge their emotional needs. Not that you should become gratuitously cruel toward people who are concerned about you, but for the next few months you have license to put yourself first. You don't have to spend time with people you don't like or who bring you down.*

*During the several months I was receiving treatment, I developed a routine. On chemo day I was knocked out by the Benadryl, so I just went home and took it easy. During the infusion, I tried to drink a lot of water to quickly flush the drug from my body. And I never skipped breakfast. I had lost a lot of weight before being diagnosed, and my oncologists told me to expect to have trouble eating because of the chemo and the effect that radiation would have on my esophagus. So I packed in the calories whenever I could, gained weight during treatment, and luckily never did have any trouble eating. Still don't! You may read that cancer lives off carbs, and that you should minimize your sugars and starches, but I wanted to regain my lost weight and my strength, so I indulged in anything I wanted —donuts, ice cream, all of it. It was very liberating, but soon, when it became apparent that I might not die right away, I got back to eating a more sensible diet.*

*In the outpatient chemo room, I noticed that some people, like me, just liked to read, listen to music, or nap during the infusion, while others enjoyed having lots of people around, surrounding themselves in a distracting, raucous, party atmosphere. Whatever gives you strength and focus is what you should do.*

*I avoided crowds to reduce my risk of getting infections, but on days when I was not getting chemo, I always exercised, usually taking a 60–90 minute walk. The exercise, the sun and fresh air were very helpful. I also tried to do something social most days. It was an unexpected bonus to be able to use my time off work to develop and deepen friendships with people I knew and liked but rarely had a chance to see.*

*I disagree with people who feel that negative emotions cause cancer. And I don't believe that positive thinking cures cancer either. But I have no doubt that it is essential to enlist the mind and spirit to help the body heal, so I did three things every day.*

1. *Relaxation or Meditation: It is important to calm your anxiety so that you can focus on healing. Every day I meditated or did relaxation. I had no experience with either before getting sick, but I have come to enjoy both and try to spend 20–30 minutes doing one or the other each day. The meditation I do is mindfulness meditation. I am sure there are places in your city where you can learn to do this, but even without formal instruction online resources can get you started.*

2. *Visualization: During chemo, I visualized the drugs collapsing and destroying my tumor. During radiation, I imagined the rays causing it to boil off and evaporate. And when I wasn't actually getting treatment, I spent ten minutes each day imagining that I was doing cataract surgery on the tumor to remove it. I know, kind of strange, but the point is that you can find a powerful, reproducible, personally compelling image of the treatment working to remove or destroy your cancer.*

3. *Affirmations: Can saying something make it so? I don't know, but why not try? I developed ten affirmations that I repeat several times a day, including the last thing before I fall asleep at night. You will come up with your own list, but this can be a healing habit, a way to calm your mind and remind yourself of what is important.*

*I am sure you are inundated with advice from well-meaning people, and all of this may be worth only what you paid me for it, but I hope there are one or two things here that you find helpful.*

*Be healthy, Michael*

**FIVE YEARS!!!**                                    *Feb 23, 2018 2:01pm*

When my cancer was discovered back in February of 2013, if someone told me that I would be here enjoying a gorgeous early spring day I would have been incredulous but thrilled beyond words. And I am, because my scan this week was stable. This means that although my X-Rays are not and never will again be normal, they don't look any different than they did soon after I finished treatment more than four years ago. The tumor hasn't disappeared, but neither is it growing, spreading, or changing. I am so grateful, and hope I will be lucky enough to get the same report every six months into the future. Wishing you and yours only good health and happiness, with thanks for all your love and support over the past several years.

Michael

**UPDATE**                          *Sat, Mar 24, 2018 at 6:26 PM*

Remember a month ago when Michael had a good scan that basically meant we were going to be on cruise control for a year?

Well, Thursday Michael had a stress test and echocardiogram to check out some changes in his EKG. Unfortunately, we found out he has another strange health problem—something growing in his heart. He has NO SYMPTOMS, but we both saw it on an ultrasound. We love you and are very sad we have this news to share…

# PART SEVEN

# 20/20

A T THE BEGINNING of my life as a patient, I tried to recall all I learned during my years as a caregiver. I looked back across decades of watching people approach illness both constructively and not, to seek urgent guidance for my own mindset and behavior. And I enlisted my friends to help me identify the characteristics of patients who are more likely flourish during and after the disruption of disease.

No surprise, their lists were all over the place. But as I reviewed their ideas, these stories and the lessons they hold ricocheted between my ears and helped me reconcile my friends' thoughts. And once I combined their insights with my own, I realized that from 40,000 feet, the features of both good doctors and good patients have a lot in common.

Maybe this should not have surprised me; it turns out that what makes someone a good doctor or a good patient is also what tends to make someone a good person. Here are the essentials boiled down to a single list for both patients and doctors:

1. Active and informed participant in own (or patient's) care

2. Understands importance of mind/body/spirit connection

3. Honest, forthright, and realistic

4. Collaborative, does not operate in isolation

5. Kind, good listener, respectful

6. Grateful, hopeful, and humble

I don't know the next chapter of my cancer story, but do I know how this journey will end. Everyone does. Nobody gets out alive. Life is an invariably fatal condition; meanwhile, it goes on. I am still a fully engaged husband, father, and friend. I am still a caregiver and treasure my work and the opportunity it gives me to help people see better. I value the wisdom I have gained by being a patient myself, and gratefully share it with others who need perspective and reassurance when facing their own unknowns.

The main challenge in every life, after securing basics like food and shelter, is figuring out how to strike the right balance between today and tomorrow, between enjoying every day and deferring gratification long enough to get anything done. Life threatening illness just makes this calculus more pressing and the choices more stark. My goal is to feel, at the end of each day, that I did not waste it, that I had a reason to get out of bed, and that I did some good while awake. To feel that, if this turned out to be my last day, I would not regret how I spent my time and energy. As always, I have fun, go out with friends, exercise, and mess around, but now I try not to squander too many hours playing solitaire on my phone or watching meaningless TV. I plan for the future knowing tomorrow may not come. This is true for everyone, every day, at every stage of life, but since dwelling on this fact can be paralyzing, we usually stash awareness of it way in the background, lock it in the shed out back, kidding ourselves that it isn't there. Truth is harder to ignore while chemo drugs flow into your vein.

Although neither caregivers nor the people they help can alter the past, have the benefit of complete information about the present, nor control over the future, we all have the freedom to determine how best to approach every today.

The question for me and you is not how much life do we have left, but what will we do with it? A life focused on fun and diversion is pleasant, but selfish and shallow. A lifelong vacation is vacuous. A life of service, learning, kindness, gratitude, honesty, and resilience can bring deep joy and fulfillment while enriching the lives of those lucky enough to know you.

# APPENDIX

C HARACTERISTICS OF PATIENTS who navigate their ill-nesses well:

1. Active participant in own care

    a. Informed, assertive, self-advocate

    b. Active, motivated to heal

    c. Seeks information, struggles against denial

    d. Unintimidated by doctor's expertise and status, dele-gates wisely

    e. Asks questions, listens to answers

    f. Resilient and organized

2. Understands importance of mind/body/spirit connec-tion

    a. Believes in own capacity to heal

    b. Devotes all energy to healing

c. Self-acceptance

d. Relaxation, meditation, affirmations, prayers

e. Healthy lifestyle

3. Honest, forthright, and realistic

   a. Recognize, accept, and embrace the new normal

   b. Truthful and realistic

4. Collaborative, does not operate in isolation

   a. Seeks social support, avoids being isolated

   b. Goals and values in synch with family and physician

   c. Shares information with others

5. Kind, good listener, respectful

   a. Respect self and others

   b. Avoid blaming self or others for disease

6. Grateful, hopeful and humble

   a. Positive and hopeful, optimistic

   b. Does not waste energy on resentment or hostility

Characteristics of the best doctors:

1. Active and informed participant in patient's care

   a. Knowledgeable and intelligent

   b. Thorough, tenacious, resilient

   c. Service oriented

   d. Lifelong learning

e. Energetic, skilled, confident

2. Understands importance of mind/body/spirit connection

   a. Lifestyle sets an example

   b. Learn about other perspectives

   c. Acknowledge limits of knowledge, enlist spiritual

3. Honest, forthright, and realistic

   a. Factual, not heartless

   b. Communicate without jargon

   c. Know when to change from curing to enhancing quality of life

   d. Integrity and professionalism

4. Collaborative, does not operate in isolation

   a. Creative

   b. Align goals with patient

   c. Seek help freely

   d. Associate with colleagues who are worthy of respect

   e. Trust and train staff

5. Kind, good listener, respectful

   a. Cares about, curious about, interested in, people

   b. Good listener

   c. Appropriate use of humor

   d. Respectful, courteous

    e.  Empathetic and compassionate

    f.  Understand patients' health beliefs, attitudes

6.  Grateful, hopeful and humble

    a.  Positive and hopeful

    b.  Enjoy work

    c.  Remain humble

    d.  Be good steward of patients' trust

# ACKNOWLEDGEMENTS

NOTHING GETS DONE without help from other people, and this book is no exception. First of all, my undying thanks to Steve Plunkett and John Mahoney, without whose belief, skill, creativity, and persistence I would not have been here to write or, for that matter, to breathe. I also appreciate Anthony Bracken, Arun Rajan, and Charles Simone for the healing gift of their tenacity and expertise.

Thanks as well to Emily Cronin, Heidi Rotberg, Dick Blackwell, Paul B. Brown, Lorrie Klemons, Joy Libethe, Joe Parisi, Karen Garloch, and Amy Rogers. Each took the time to read critically and to offer helpful, though sometimes conflicting, advice that allowed me to see the work through fresh eyes. Phillip Gessart's interior design and Shimon Gorkin's cover wrapped my words in a welcoming package. The final version is better because of all their suggestions.

The encouragement I derived from conversations with friends and from the constant support of so many people, in person and online, made writing feel like a community project. My gratitude to Scottie Crenshaw, Carol Davis, Elizabeth

Fisher, and Michele McCormick for making my work life a pleasure and for always doing their best for our patients. And I am indebted to Chuck Hoch for his early, and generous, unrestricted creative grant.

But most of all, and for everything always, I thank my family: Emily and David, Josh, Ella and Max, and especially Heidi. Without them, there would be no point.

# ABOUT THE AUTHOR

M ICHAEL ROTBERG IS an ophthalmologist, eye surgeon, and glaucoma specialist who graduated from Haverford College and Duke Medical School. He was named one of 'America's Best Doctors' for more than a decade, and has written for peer reviewed medical journals and medical textbooks, as well as 'Another Ride On The Cyclone,' a book of family stories. He has two children and two grand-children and lives in Charlotte, NC with his wife, Heidi, a psychologist.

24399407R00209

Made in the USA
Columbia, SC
22 August 2018